Feather
Your
Nest

CERENTHA HARRIS

Feather Your Nest

The complete guide to outfitting, cleaning,
organizing and caring for your home

Marlowe & Company
New York

FEATHER YOUR NEST: *The Complete Guide to Outfitting, Cleaning, Organizing and Caring for Your Home*

Text copyright © Cerentha Harris 2004, 2005
Illustrations copyright © Wai-Heung Hui 2004

Published by
Marlowe & Company
An Imprint of Avalon Publishing Group Incorporated
245 West 17th Street • 11th Floor
New York, NY 10011-5300

AVALON
publishing group incorporated

First published by Penguin Group (Australia), a division of Pearson Australia
Group Pty Ltd, 2004. This is a revised edition, adapted for North America and
published by arrangement.

Library of Congress Cataloging-in-Publication Data is available from the publisher

ISBN 1-56924-355-7

9 8 7 6 5 4 3 2 1

Design by John Canty © Penguin Group (Australia)
Printed in the United States of America

Contents

To Brian and Jack

Introduction

I'm part of that group Canadian novelist Douglas Coupland dubbed Generation X. For most of us, the art of keeping house has been lost. By the time our parents were getting married and starting their families, keeping house had become politically loaded, a ripe battleground for arguments about gender roles and equality. Coming of age under the bright light of feminism in the sixties and seventies, our mothers (and most of the time it was our mothers not our fathers) were often reluctant to pass on the skills they saw as chaining them to the home. The children of baby boomers have now grown up and become doctors and lawyers and journalists who have made their parents proud. They have learned to hire a cleaner to do the work that they don't have time for and often don't know how to do well.

So, why write a book about keeping house if none of us has time to do it? The answer is simple. The cleaner isn't there for the day-to-day chores that turn your house into that much-needed sanctuary. And, contrary to the bad rap housekeeping receives, this kind of work is really rewarding.

Plus, Gen Xers are having babies, a life-changing experience by anyone's measure. With the greater emphasis on careers for my generation, we're now having babies a decade later than our parents did. At thirty-three I was at home full-time for the first time since I left high school – with a baby son, endless piles of laundry, floorboards that were sticky with baby food and a dishwasher that had to be stacked and unstacked daily. And, unlike in my old full-time job, there was no one to delegate to.

Finally I'm teaching myself to keep house – with lots of help from my mother-in-law, grandmother, aunts, family friends, and the many books that guided these women when they were starting out in their first homes with young families. And, of course, from my mother, who is thrilled that I am taking an interest in what she is skilled at, which I once saw as so mundane.

I lived in New York for seven years and during that time worked on *Martha Stewart Living* magazine. It was an interesting place to work, staffed by lots of very smart people who took pressing napkins very seriously. The office physically reflected the magazine's obsession with creating a homey environment. Pristine pale-green linoleum floors were polished to a soft gleam each week. There were always fresh flowers in just the right vases and the whole place was laced with delicious smells from the test kitchen. It was there that my eyes were opened to the possibilities of turning housework into high art. My first job was to research a piece on vacuuming – how to do it properly (slowly and with the grain of the carpet) and what exactly all those attachments are for (everything from cleaning venetians to cornices). I went on to cover other housekeeping duties including ironing, sewing, cooking, gardening, painting, and repairs.

But keeping house is about so much more. It's about turning a one-room studio or a six-bedroom mansion into a home. A place you can't wait to return to after a hard day's work. A place you are happy to spend time in. A place to be on your own, share with your partner, raise children. A place to relax.

Within the pages of this book, you'll find out exactly how to do this – at your own speed and to your own standards, because everyone lives differently.

I wrote this book while I was on maternity leave from the *Sydney Morning Herald*. My home, a two-bedroom flat in Sydney, is where I spent most of my time. It's where I snatched moments to sleep and work, cook, create, listen to music, eat meals with my husband, and play with my baby, Jack. And while Jack slept I wrote and cleaned – caring for this house like I'd never done before. Now I fold hospital corners in sheets. I've learned to keep polished floorboards dust-free. I clean the fridge out once a week instead of once every few months. And I'm surprised how much pleasure I get from doing this work.

1. Setting up House

As the former editor of the *Sydney Morning Herald*'s "Domain" section, I used to see photos of a lot of houses. It was hard not to be envious of that perfect house with just the right furniture/artwork/sunlight/floor plan/backyard. You name it, I wanted it. But in keeping house, in keeping my particular two-bedroom flat, I've learned to love every nook and cranny. Maybe because every nook and cranny looks the way it does through my hard work. And this nest I've made for my family is infinitely more special to me than anything that used to pass across my desk.

Whatever your taste in houses and furnishings may be, the ultimate goal of keeping house is still the same – the transformation of a house into a home. But mastering a particular look takes time and research. An architect I met whose own home was full of impeccable pieces gave me the best advice on this subject: be patient and slowly build up a collection of solid pieces that you

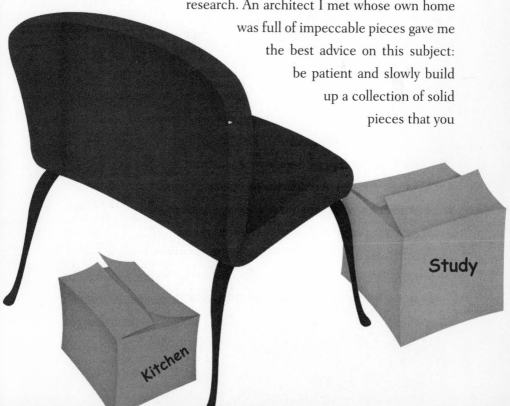

Kitchen

Study

love. Invest in big pieces (like a couch) and if you are swayed by the fashion of the day, change the style of the room with items that won't cost too much to replace (a few cushions, an inexpensive rug, or curtains can change the look of a room without costing you a fortune).

To establish your style, immerse yourself in books and magazines. Flag the pages of houses or rooms or color schemes you are drawn to. Collect photographs, clippings or brochures to start a storyboard. You'll soon see a theme emerge. (I like to mix old pieces with new pieces – I love the surprise of an ornate chandelier in an otherwise minimalist space.) Visit shops that stock that kind of furniture – get to know the owners. You'll be surprised how much information you can glean from a friendly chat. When's the next shipment of furniture arriving? Is there a new line of sofas arriving next month so the current range will be on sale soon?

Of course, you probably won't start from scratch when it comes to furniture. Most of us live with pieces we've inherited in one way or another – from parents, roommates, ex-lovers. It would also be rather expensive to throw everything away and start again. But it is often the hand-me-downs that give our homes their own flavor. That comfy old chair from your grandfather and the chipped teapot from your mother give your place heart and, if you love them, should never be thrown away. Use them as starting points for new pieces. Perhaps the chair has a great shape but worn fabric – have it re-covered. Use the teapot for inspiration for the rest of your dishes.

Most of us live in a house or apartment where there is always something we'd love to redo. So where do you start? Following are just a few ideas that you'll need to think about if you're changing the look or feel of your home.

Color

Color can be transformative. When my husband and I were looking to buy a flat we visited an apartment in a building designed by Harry Seidler and fell in love with its dark-red hallway. When we moved into our own flat we decided to try the same effect. It was a disaster. The walls looked like they'd been painted with blood and every time I walked through the door I felt like I'd stepped into a scene in *The Shining*. We painted over it and have since stuck to a much more calming palette of greens.

Major paint companies offer the services of professional color consultants if you aren't willing to take the leap into color yourself. Of course you can simply stick to white and use your furniture and artwork to add color to the space. Freshly painted walls give the house such a great lift. It is always surprising what a huge difference a coat of paint makes.

A recent trend has seen the return of wallpaper used in the home, just as we've seen the revival of the strongly colored feature wall. Be adventurous with wallpaper. There's no need to cover a whole wall. Think about doing just one panel, following the line of some architectural detail, or perhaps using strips in each corner. Do keep any leftover rolls of wallpaper, which you'll probably need at some stage for patching. A good tip here is not to roll it up to store it. Try pinning it inside a cupboard or closet. That way it will age at the same rate as the rest of the wallpaper and make patching easier.

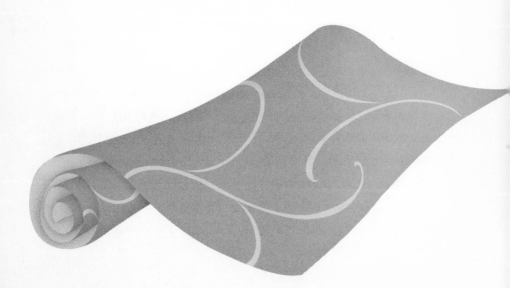

Lighting

There's nothing more inviting than a well-lit room. Often, when you don't realize what it is about a room that makes it feel so comfortable, it's the right lighting. A few carefully placed lamps casting a soft glow can make or break a space. Good lighting can also hide a multitude of flaws. If I haven't had a chance to really clean before a dinner party, I turn on lamps and light candles and the soft glow hides many sins.

If you get the chance to start from scratch in any of the rooms in your house, consider the following alternatives. Around the home you need a good mix of practical task lighting – for working in the kitchen, reading, applying makeup – and mood lighting (otherwise known as ambient).

Ambient lighting

Ambient lighting should be strong enough so that you can do what you need to in a room but not so bright that it strips the room of any mystery. Well-placed overhead lights are essential here. In the kitchen make sure your ceiling lights don't cast your shadow onto the counter. Place them far enough forward so that your shadow falls directly down or slightly behind you. For the bedroom make sure the light is bright enough to get dressed by and lights you from the front when you look in the mirror. Ambient light in the bathroom should be strong enough for kids to bathe safely and any tasks like shaving to be done without accident. Dimmers can work well and increase the flexibility of ambient lighting.

Task lighting

In my kitchen there's excellent task lighting under the cupboards that hang above the countertop. This is essential in a kitchen that flows into your living space. When I'm cooking for friends, the benches where I'm working are very well lit, but I dim the main light in the living/dining area so my guests aren't sitting in a glaringly bright space. It is also advisable not to have too much contrast between brightly lit task areas and the rest of the room as this can cause eyestrain.

If you are lighting a kitchen or dining table with a pendant light, make sure it hangs at least two feet above the tabletop, otherwise it will glare in diners' eyes and guests will not be able to see each other across the table. Task lighting, using any sort of spot light, can also be used to great effect for illuminating artwork or other features of a room.

How to stay: warm or cool

Having lived in New York, I always think of Australia as a warm place, but some of my coldest winters have been spent in Sydney. Australians seems to think the way to keep warm in winter is to put on another sweater and try to remember to switch on the electric blanket before going to bed. For anyone who dislikes the cold, this is far from adequate. The best way to heat the house is, of course, to have it designed properly in the first place. If your home faces the right way, you'll get lots of lovely low winter sun warming the interior. I've never lived in a house that faced the right way, but in my experience gas or oil-filled heaters are both excellent sources of reliable heat. And electric heaters, which are usually the least expensive, also work well if the room is small. Each year there are new models of heaters and they just seem to get better and better. Try to find one with a timer so that you are heating the house only when you need to. I set mine to come on an hour before I get home at night and again an hour before I get up in the morning so that the place is warm. Gas heaters can be drying, but you can try placing a shallow dish of water nearby. See pages 176–9 for information on fireplaces.

Cooling a home is something we're much better at. There's a real push amongst builders and architects to make homes with good ventilation that take advantage of the weather, rather than relying on air conditioners. I've never had an air conditioner and don't believe they are necessary for anyone living in a moderate climate. Fans, especially ceiling fans, move around enough air to cool a room perfectly. My cousins in Darwin both have houses where one room in the house is air-conditioned and the others are cooled by fans. To get a break from the heat they'll retreat to the air-conditioned rooms but the majority of their time is spent in tiled-floored, fan-cooled rooms.

Storage

A tidy house is much easier to clean and the only way to keep a home tidy is to have a place for everything. Often, when a job seems overwhelming, I'll tidy first and tell myself I'll clean later. Somehow splitting the job in two makes it more manageable.

Good storage is the key here. If your shoes have a home, your home is that much easier to maintain. There are excellent storage options for just about everything in your house. Don't limit yourself to the obvious sources of inspiration – local hardware stores offer up a plethora of storage ideas and discount stores often have great storage containers. I got two big plastic, lidded boxes on wheels from a discount store to store all Jack's toys. They've been handy not just for storing his odds and ends but also for packing all his paraphernalia when we've gone on vacation. (For more details on storing children's "stuff," see pages 219–20.)

Flooring

You have various choices when it comes to flooring.

Carpets and rugs

Always buy the best carpets and rugs you can afford. This goes for any major purchase for your home. It's not worth skimping on the things you come into contact with every day. Consider where the carpet or rug is going. Carpet in private areas of the house is often a good option. It absorbs sound and gives rooms a feeling of luxury and softness. Carpets and rugs can also act as excellent insulation and on a cold wintry morning there's nothing nicer than putting your bare feet onto a soft rug. I've got a sheepskin on my side of the bed so the first thing my feet touch every morning is wonderfully soft. In more public parts of the house, a good rug can act as noise insulation on a clattery wooden floor and also as decoration – a highly patterned oriental rug with its rich reds looks great in an otherwise white and minimally decorated room. Remember that any carpet with a high pile, especially a shag pile or a flokati rug, is hard to clean. But they do feel luxurious underfoot.

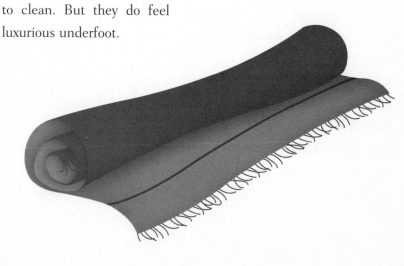

Consider the area where the carpet or rug will be placed. Is there a lot of traffic through that area (doorways, hallways, stairs)? To determine how well the carpet will wear, take a strand of the fiber between your fingers and roll it back and forth. If the strand easily unwinds and/or becomes fuzzy, it will not wear well, especially in high-traffic areas. You should be looking for a tightly rolled thick yarn. Carpets with a multilevel pile will wear more quickly on the higher strands so are not great for high-traffic areas, especially stairs.

The denser the weave of a carpet, the more wear you'll get. To check this, take a sample and bend it in half. If a lot of the backing shows it is not a dense weave.

Check the backing of a looped or tufted carpet. You want a polypropylene backing as it resists mildew, not jute that can rot and get moldy when wet or in humid conditions. You may also find backing made from vinyl, latex, or plastic. Our wool-tufted living-room rug has jute backing. I loved the simple design and color so much that I didn't even think to check the backing. Though even if I had noticed it was jute, I'm pretty sure I still would have bought it. (See pages 38–46 for details on cleaning and caring for carpet, and removing stains.)

To measure a room for carpet, take the length and width and multiply them to get square yards. Add about 10 percent for any odd shapes that may be in the room, spoilage, or matching of patterns. Have this number with you when you shop. Make sure the carpet retailer remeasures your space before the carpet is ordered. Get a quote in writing that includes underlay, labor costs, and removal of old carpet.

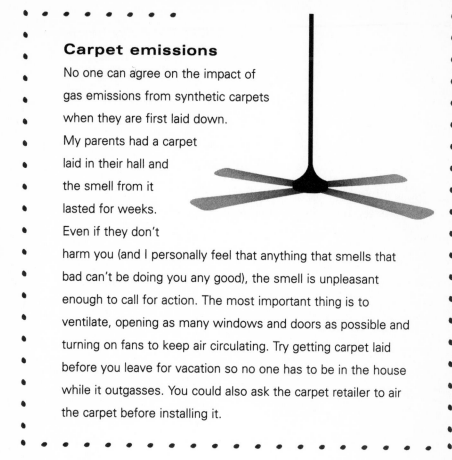

Carpet emissions

No one can agree on the impact of gas emissions from synthetic carpets when they are first laid down. My parents had a carpet laid in their hall and the smell from it lasted for weeks. Even if they don't harm you (and I personally feel that anything that smells that bad can't be doing you any good), the smell is unpleasant enough to call for action. The most important thing is to ventilate, opening as many windows and doors as possible and turning on fans to keep air circulating. Try getting carpet laid before you leave for vacation so no one has to be in the house while it outgasses. You could also ask the carpet retailer to air the carpet before installing it.

Natural vs. synthetics

Carpets made from synthetic materials, such as nylon, polypropylene, polyester, or acrylic, actually make much better floor coverings than natural fibers. They are more stain-, mildew-, and insect-resistant, longer lasting, and usually cheaper than wool or silk. But they don't have that immeasurable tactile quality and the beauty of natural fibers. Wool is also antistatic and dyes better than synthetics.

Wood flooring

A wood floor wears well, is easy to clean, and has enough give to be comfortable to stand on for long periods. Most original polished wood floors were hardwood; softwood was used under floor coverings. If you are buying an old house and intend to rip up the carpet and polish the boards, you are probably looking at a softwood floor, which is fine, but it will mark up more easily than a hardwood floor. Stiletto heels, for example, will make a serious dent on softwood. If the floor was intended to be seen, such as parquetry, you can almost guarantee it's hardwood. The majority of new floorboards now laid are hardwood. The latest trend is suspended flooring, which utilizes the advantages of hardwood. Thin sheets of hardwood are attached to particleboard or plywood and laid over an existing floor. The thicker the hardwood sheet used, the better (and usually more expensive) the floor. (See pages 47–53 for details on cleaning and maintaining floorboards.)

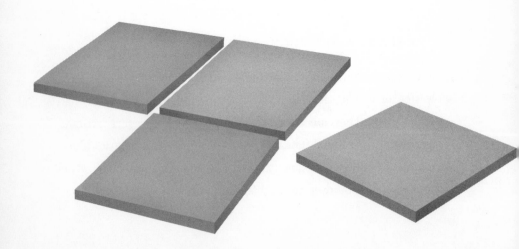

Other flooring

Concrete floors may seem like a good, cheap alternative but they are too hard to stand on for any length of time and really need some kind of rubber matting in high-traffic areas to protect your back. The same goes for stone and tile floors. You need to weigh up the ease and beauty of these products with their effect on your body. Vinyl and linoleum are good alternatives but they are also laid on a hard surface (usually concrete) and can be tough to stand on for long periods.

Since everything seems to come into fashion again, including lino, cork is overdue for a revival. I can remember my parents putting down a cork-tiled floor in our back room. It was a major production that included a pretty smelly seal that we couldn't walk on for what seemed like weeks (and was probably hours). The floor always felt like it had a little extra bounce when you walked on it and no matter what we dropped on that floor I don't remember anything ever breaking. Both cork and linoleum are wonderfully resilient and inexpensive materials for the floor. Linoleum is probably a bit more versatile, as it comes in so many colors, but cork's bounciness makes for a great floor covering in places where you stand a lot (think around kitchen counters). A good friend in Sydney did her whole apartment floor in a lovely pale-green linoleum. The look is very streamlined and clean, and it makes for an easily maintained and inexpensive alternative to a wood floor.

In warmer regions tiles (which can be ceramic like terra-cotta or made from a stone like slate or sandstone) are the perfect choice for living areas. They are cool, easy to clean, and look good.

Laminated floors are a cheap alternative to wood flooring and can be used throughout the house. Here, a photograph of a material (usually wood) is sandwiched between plastic and a wood-based sheet. The plastic coating gives a variety of finishes from matt to high gloss and is normally durable and stain-resistant. Clean as you would a hard-sealed wood floor (see page 47), making sure not to use too much water as it can soak into the base material and cause warping. Remove stains as for linoleum (see pages 54–5), and try rubbing alcohol on any other sorts of stains. You'll probably need turpentine to remove grease or tar.

Stone floors are finished by either polishing or honing, but honed finishes are best as they are less slippery. The finish on stone floors is quickly dulled if you leave dirt and grit on them to be ground in by traffic. Rugs are a must in high-traffic areas – just make sure they have nonslip backing.

Window coverings

Fashion seems to play a big role in window coverings. I think you should choose what works best for the room, not what looks great in the latest *Vogue*. If you've got a small room, think about blinds or shutters that sit flush with the wall. Billowy curtains or anything that is plump will project out into the room and take up precious space. If noise insulation is a consideration, shutters or heavily lined curtains can make a big difference. They also work well in keeping out light. Privacy is another issue when choosing window treatments. Venetian blinds are often a good choice here as the blades can be angled to allow light into the room and still block out nosy neighbours.

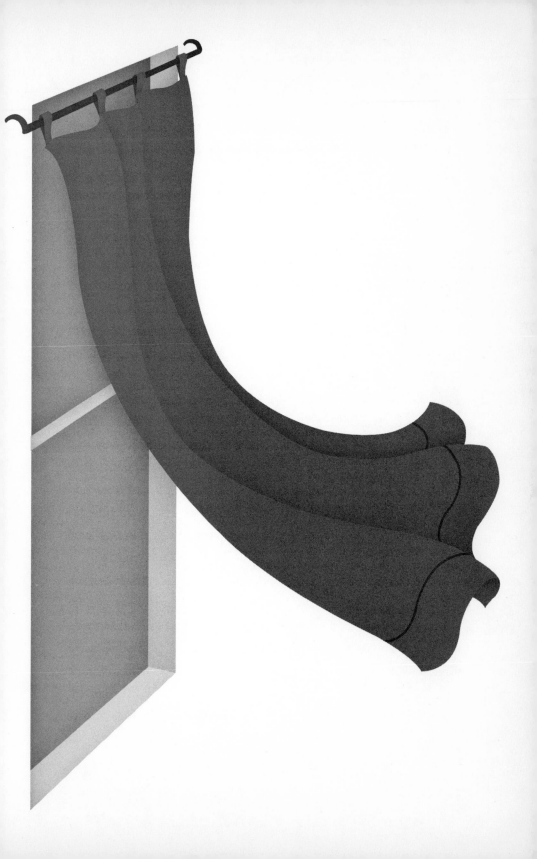

2. How to Clean

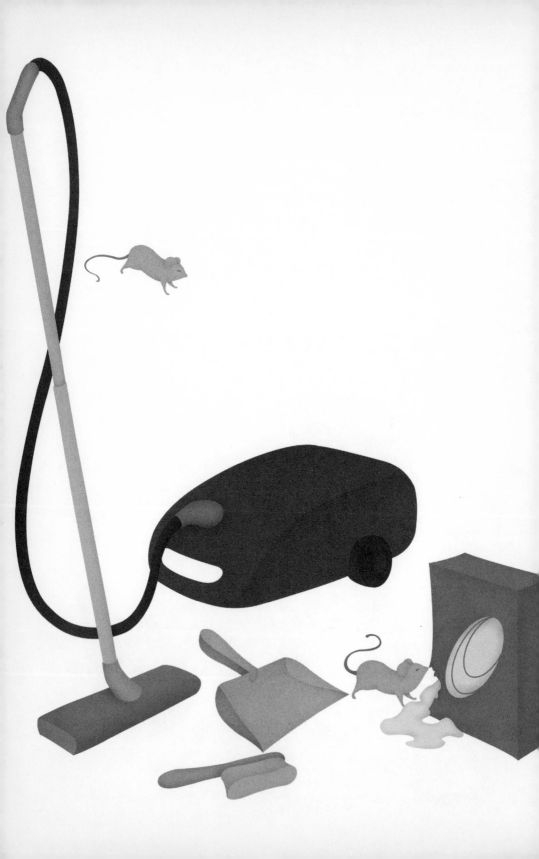

The question of whether to use less toxic chemicals in your home almost seems passé these days. Of course we don't want poisons in our home and of course we don't want to pollute our environment. But we also want a clean house. I've found in most cases a mild cleaner, whether it be vinegar or baking soda or just hot water, works as well as more caustic versions. Often what you need is more elbow grease and perhaps a little more time. But there are also moments when a good splash of bleach, or a scrub or spray with a commercial cleaner, does a thorough and speedy job. Throughout the book I've tried to give you the choice. I usually start with the least toxic option and end with the most.

When is clean too clean?

A recent British study showed that households that are too clean don't allow people to build up their immune systems. Children don't get a chance to build up resistance to things like dust because they don't come into contact with these things often enough. The idea that a little dirt is good for you is an interesting one. For every hardworking parent that hasn't had a chance to mop the floor, it will come as a welcome relief to know you aren't poisoning your children but may be helping them.

For most people, the question isn't whether dirt is good or bad for you, it's at what point you can no longer stand to look at it and live with it. When does dirt bother you? I think for all of us the answer is different. If you are an asthma sufferer it may be a few hours; if you aren't, it could be a day or a week before you get around to vacuuming the carpet in the hall or scrubbing the kitchen floor.

Cleaning products

What we need to do is know how to clean the floor properly, so when we can't stand it anymore – after a day or a week – we can clean it thoroughly. Below are recipes for my usual repertoire of cleaning products. When I mention a baking soda paste (which I do often) I'm not going to give you the fine details on how to make it every time. So here is a basic guide that will help you through the rest of the book.

Hot water

The most overlooked cleaning product. Again and again I've pared back all the chemicals – whether it be bleach or lemon juice – and found that really hot water cleans wonderfully. Try it on mossy bricks or a sticky countertop. The key is the temperature. The hotter the better. So before you head to the cleaning cupboard, try hot water – it just may surprise you. (But do remember not to use hot water on blood, as the heat sets the stain.)

Detergent

Your next port of call is plain old detergent and hot water. Through-out the book I refer to a mixture of detergent and water as soapy water. Use just enough detergent to make a good head of bubbles. Too much detergent can leave a film over whatever you are cleaning and too little won't work at all.

While detergents and soaps contain the same basic cleaning agent, called a surfactant, they are quite different in composition. Detergents contain a synthetic surfactant (and there are many differ-ent kinds of synthetic surfactant) and other chemicals that boost the surfactant's ability to remove dirt. They dissolve more easily in cold water, often penetrate dirty areas better than soap, and can be used in hard water where soap would not dissolve. (Surfactants consist of molecules that attach themselves to dirt particles. The molecules grab the dirt out of the material and hold it in the water until it can be rinsed away.) Soap certainly has its place in the home but detergent wins hands down when it comes to general purpose cleaning.

WARNING – choose a detergent without phosphates (or with a very low phosphate content). When phosphates enter water sys-tems they overfertilize algae, which grows like crazy and uses up the oxygen supply in the water. Fish and other water life die. We use a concentrate (just because the bottle is smaller and takes up less room in our tiny kitchen) and it is phosphate-free. Check the label of your favorite brand. If it is biodegradable it should say so on the label.

Baking soda

While detergent and hot water will get rid of a lot of dirt, you may need something with a bit of grit. Baking Soda is an excellent gentle abrasive that's good for cleaning the kind of hard surfaces you find in kitchens and bathrooms. Two tablespoons of baking soda mixed with ½ tablespoon of water makes an excellent stiff paste. With this small amount I can clean the kitchen sink (stainless steel), the bathroom sink (ceramic), the inside of the oven door (glass) and the electric stovetop (glass). The key to using baking soda is to buff afterward with a dry rag. If you leave the area to dry on its own, it can streak – especially stainless steel and glass.

Baking soda paste will also get rid of stains on the inside of mugs and ceramic vases.

To clean surfaces in the bathroom and kitchen, you can sprinkle dry baking soda straight onto the sponge, but I find you use more baking soda this way than if you make it into a paste.

I have tried the following method for cleaning silver and never had much luck. But it's certainly a gentler and less smelly approach than using a commercial preparation, so please give it a try and see if it works for you. Mix 1 teaspoon of baking soda with 1 teaspoon of salt and 1 cup of warm water in a bowl. Place a half-inch square of aluminum foil in the bowl and the silver piece you intend to polish. Leave it to soak for 10 minutes and buff dry with a soft lint-free cloth.

Sprinkle 2 tablespoons of baking soda on the inside of the dishwasher door before you turn on the machine. This polishes the inside of the machine beautifully and leaves your cutlery looking pretty shiny, too.

If you have hard water, add 2 teaspoons to your laundry or dishwashing water.

White vinegar

An excellent and inexpensive cleanser. This acid does wonders all over the house. To clean a drain, try pouring 2 tablespoons of baking soda down the sink. (It will clump a little around the top, but don't worry. This stuff will bubble away and clean the sink trap). Wash it down with ½ cup of white vinegar. Leave it to bubble for 10 minutes or so and follow with boiling water.

As a window, mirror, and glass cleaner, mix 1 part vinegar to 1 part warm water. Try adding a drop of scented oil to the water if you don't like the smell of vinegar.

I've read that you can leave straight vinegar in the toilet bowl for about 10 minutes and then scrape lime scale off. I don't have lime scale to test this so can't tell you if it works, but it is certainly worth a try.

To make vinegar into a mild abrasive, try mixing 2 tablespoons of salt with 1 teaspoon of vinegar. This makes a stiff paste that's excellent in removing mildew and soap scum in bathrooms. You can also use vinegar straight to wipe down hard surfaces that have a tendency to mildew.

Add 1 cup of vinegar to a bucket half-filled with hot water to scrub bricks, concrete, and hard outdoor surfaces.

To clean a blackened pot, try filling to just above the burned area with 1 part vinegar to 1 part water. Boil for about 30 minutes (often less) until you see the black start to peel back. You should now be able to get it off with a scourer and hot soapy water. You can also leave the vinegar water solution in overnight for a similar result.

Lemon

As good as vinegar might be as a cleanser, lemons win when it comes to smell (although I must admit I find it wasteful using lemons for cleaning and only do it rarely).

Half a cut lemon dipped in salt is a good gentle abrasive. You can also use this to clean copper and brass. Always rinse with clear water and buff dry.

Before you try bleach on fabric, give lemon a try. Lemon juice and salt together may remove mildew on fabric. Rub the juice of 1 lemon and 1 tablespoon of salt onto the mildewed spot and leave in the sun for 30 minutes. Wash as appropriate for the fabric. You may need to do this a few times to get rid of the mildew marks.

You can also add the juice of 1 lemon to a spray bottle of hot water and use to clean counters and other hard surfaces. It will smell better than vinegar.

To clean a blackened pot, cut 1 lemon into rough chunks and simmer for half an hour. Scrub and wash as usual.

Salt

Add salt to vinegar or lemon juice and you have a mild abrasive good for cleaning hard surfaces in the kitchen or bathroom.

You can use salt to soak up stains on fabrics and carpet. Pour as much as needed straight onto the spill as soon as it occurs. I've found that blotting with paper towels or a white cloth gets better results than dumping salt on the spill, but I know a lot of people who swear by salt. The idea is it soaks up the spill and you then wipe up the salt (use a slightly damp cloth). Once the area is dry, give it a vacuum to get up any remnants of the salt.

Borax

This grainy white powder helps dissolve dirt, grease, and sticky substances and clean most delicate fabrics, silver, glass, and china. You can buy it in the supermarket. Be careful using it around pets and children as it is toxic.

A general purpose cleaner can be made with borax. Mix 2 teaspoons of borax, 1 teaspoon of soap flakes, and 1 quart of warm water (soap and borax dissolve better in warm water). Use this mix in a spray bottle, or dampen a sponge with it, and use it to wipe down surfaces. While this cleans my laminate countertop beautifully, I'm not convinced it does a better job than detergent and hot water, and it certainly leaves your hands feeling very dry. But if you want to try it – go ahead! You can buy soap flakes at the supermarket.

You can also mix 2 tablespoons of borax with 3 teaspoons of hot water to make a stiff paste for cleaning walls and floors. But as borax is toxic, it's probably best to try something else here first. Often walls and floors can be cleaned with hot water and vinegar or detergent.

Isopropyl (rubbing) alcohol

A good general purpose cleanser for windows and mirrors. Mix ¼ cup of rubbing alcohol with ½ bucket of hot water. This mixture will also clean moss and mold from paths (see page 338).

Household ammonia

Helps to remove stains and clean dirty fabrics, silver, glass, sinks, and drains. **WARNING** – always use in a well-ventilated space and don't mix with bleach, as toxic fumes occur. I dislike using ammonia because it smells so much like cat pee (animals think so, too, and will sometimes feel free to pee where you've used ammonia). But it is an effective cleaner for really dirty surfaces. For an ammonia-based cleaner, mix 1 pint of hot water with 1 teaspoon of baking soda and 2 tablespoons of ammonia. To make a stronger mix, double all ingredients except the water.

You can also mix 1 part ammonia to 4 parts vinegar and 8 parts warm water to use as a window cleaner. It works very well but then so does warm water and vinegar or sometimes – if the window isn't too dirty – just piping hot water. (See pages 61–3 for windows.)

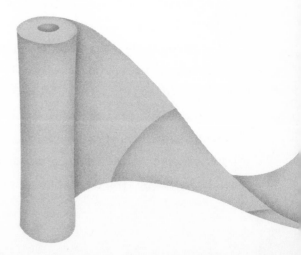

How to clean: painted surfaces

Water-based paints are popular as they are much easier to clean up after the painting is done – brushes won't need to be soaked in turpentine and paint washes off hands with warm water and soap. Once it is on the walls, water-based paint is not as easy to keep clean as oil-based paint, which tends to take tougher treatment. To clean marks, use warm water and a clean sponge. Make sure you wring as much water out as you can. Rub the spot gently. Be careful around electrical outlets, light switches, and phone jacks. It's a good idea to turn the electricity off at the fuse box or circuit breaker when you are cleaning around these points. For spots that don't respond to the treatment above, try making a stiff paste from baking soda and a little water, and rubbing with a sponge. You can also try white vinegar and water. Anything stronger may remove the paint as well as the stain.

For cleaning walls with oil-based paints, try any of the above procedures, but you can also use a detergent solution.

How to clean:
wallpaper and other wall surfaces

Wallpaper can be hard to keep pristine, so best to use it where it won't get too much traffic. Dry wipe only! Try a gum eraser (available from art supply stores) to remove marks. Be gentle. There's also the old trick of using fresh white bread to remove stains. Roll a slice of bread into a ball and gently rub it over the mark.

For **textured** wallpaper – whether it be a velvety flocked wallpaper or one that includes fibers to create a raised pattern – clip any strings or pieces that are dangling to stop further damage. Use the soft-brush attachment on your vacuum cleaner. You can also try the bread trick, or dust a bit of talcum powder or borax onto the stain using a firm paintbrush, leave for 5 minutes then gently brush off.

A **fabric** wall covering where cloth is glued to paper needs special care when it comes to cleaning. The most important thing is to keep it free from dust. Lightly vacuum with the brush attachment. Avoid stains by treating the fabric when it's hung with a protector like Scotchguard. If you must spot-clean, test a small area first to make sure it won't leave an ugly watermark. Use a barely damp cloth that's been dipped in a mild detergent solution or try an upholstery cleaner (check with the retailer or manufacturer for a cleaner suitable for that fabric). Don't forget the white bread trick.

Vinyl walls should be wiped down every few weeks with a cloth dipped in a warm soapy solution and dried with a lint-free cloth (an old T-shirt is perfect for this job).

Dust or vacuum **wood-paneled** walls and dado or hanging rails with the soft-brush attachment. To clean, use a wood soap and make sure the cloth is only slightly damp. Too much water will warp the wood. If the surface is greasy, try adding a dash of white vinegar to warm soapy water and wiping down with a well-wrung cloth. Follow the wood furniture care instructions (page 140).

How to clean: lights

Like cleaning a window – if you've got clean lamps and light fixtures the whole place sparkles. Cleaning ceiling lights is never an easy job. It's so much better if you can take the shades down to clean them. Lay a towel on the kitchen table and do a few at a time. Use warm soapy water on hard-surfaced shades and the vacuum's soft-brush attachment or a paintbrush on cloth shades. If you can't remove them, lay drop cloths or newspaper underneath to catch drips and dust as you clean.

We got our living-room chandelier second hand from a generous family friend. My mother and I cleaned it before it went up, which made the job a lot easier. If you need to clean the chandelier while it's hanging, get a good tall ladder so that you are at eye level to the fixture. And use a drop cloth to catch any dirty drips.

First vacuum up as much dust and grime as you can using the soft-brush attachment and the crevice tool if needed. Some books recommend household ammonia but I found very hot soapy water did the trick just as well. Use a cloth wrung out in the water and a toothbrush to get into the tricky bits (of which there are many!). You'll need to wipe down every single bit of the chandelier with a clean lint-free cloth to remove any soap residue and make each piece shine. Make sure you dry thoroughly as you go along, otherwise the metal bits that join the crystals can rust. Don't be in a hurry. It's not a quick job – it took us 2 hours to clean a medium-size chandelier.

During your weekly cleaning, check to see if a lampshade looks dusty. Vacuum the shade using the soft-brush attachment or, if the fabric is very delicate, use a soft brush (paintbrush or shaving brush) or a dry sponge. You can also try taking the shade outside and turning your hairdryer on it – set it on cool. While dusting the shade, give the bulb a once-over to get up any dust settled there. Never wipe a bulb with a wet cloth unless you remove it from the light fixture.

For a more thorough cleaning, always unplug a lamp or turn the electricity off at the fuse box or circuit breaker if you are working on a ceiling or wall fixture. Remove the shade and bulb. Dust the bulb with a clean damp cloth. If the lampshade is made from a hard material like plastic or glass, simply wipe it down with a cloth dipped in warm soapy water and buff dry. Never immerse a shade as there may be glue used in its construction that will dissolve in water. And any metal may rust. If the shade is silk, have it dry-cleaned professionally. If the stands or shades are metal, wipe with a slightly damp cloth to remove any dust, then clean with a commercial metal-cleaner made specifically for that metal.

To remove stains from a lampshade, try using a gum eraser or a rolled-up ball of fresh white bread. This works best if you press something firm to the back of the spot so you have something to rub against (I've used a deck of cards).

How to clean:
heaters and air conditioners

Dust all types of heaters very well before you use them. If appropriate, disconnect them before you do any dusting. Use the soft-brush attachment on the vacuum cleaner to dust the inside of the heater; pay close attention to removing dust from the bars on the electric heater (if you miss some dust it smells awful once the heater gets going). Wipe down as much of the interior as you can with a barely damp cloth wrung out in hot soapy water. You want to make sure any reflectors are spotless.

Keep ceiling fans dust-free. Vacuum blades with a soft-brush attachment. If they are metal, wipe down with hot soapy water and buff dry. If wood blades have a soft finish, they may need to be oiled or waxed once they've been dusted, and wiped with a damp cloth. If the finish is hard, clean as for metal.

To clean an air-conditioning unit, follow closely the instructions for your unit. Most often this will involve wiping down the exterior of the unit with a damp cloth and then removing a filter that will need to be thoroughly cleaned (usually in hot soapy water) and then dried before replacing. Make sure you do this regularly. A badly maintained air conditioner won't work well for very long.

How to clean: flooring

Whether you have bare floorboards or shag pile carpet, you need to clean it thoroughly and regularly to keep dust and dirt at bay and to prolong the life of the floor. In our apartment we've ripped up the coir matting and had the floorboards polished and bought a big rug for the living room. I find myself sweeping and vacuuming much more than I did when we had carpet. One of the reasons for the extra attention is you can see the dirt and dust more easily. But it is also because the floor is our son's favorite place to be – whether he's crawling around or playing with his toys – and if it's dirty, he's dirty.

How to clean: carpet

The best way to care for your carpet is to try to reduce the amount of dirt that gets onto it in the first place. Dirt quickly becomes embedded deep in the carpet pile and is ground in underfoot, often cutting the fibers. Place mats inside and outside each exterior door. If you can't bear the look of a mat inside, at least make sure you've got one outside – and give it a good beating once a week to keep it dirt-free.

* Dents in natural fibers from furniture can be vacuumed out. Try rubbing an ice cube on synthetics to plump up the dents. Dry with a clean cloth and follow with a thorough vacuuming.
* If the edges of the carpet roll or buckle, you can iron them flat. Use a damp cloth and iron through it on both sides of the carpet.
* To store a rug or carpet, make sure you roll it (don't fold it) with the pile out so that it won't crush. Big rugs benefit from being

stored on a large roll (it saves them from folding in on themselves and wrinkling). Check with your local carpet seller; they will often have large cardboard rolls to give (or sell) you. Store with mothballs and make sure you check the rug regularly to make sure there are no pests making a meal of it in the dark closet.

How to vacuum

Get the carpet ready to be vacuumed by picking up visible debris (bits of paper, buttons, etc.) and shifting easily moved furniture to one side. The trick with vacuuming is to do it slowly and give your vacuum a chance to suck everything up. This means going back and forth over the same area at least five times. Vacuum in overlapping parallel lines so that it's easy to keep track of where you've been.

This is my least favorite job and I tend to be impatient with it – and the results are not always the best!

Make use of the tools that come with your vacuum cleaner – the crevice tool will clean moldings and window frames, creases in carpet on stairs, and behind and underneath bulky furniture. Use the brush for curtains, lampshades, and walls.

Try to vacuum once a week, or twice a week in high-traffic areas. If you can do it more often then do, but once a week should be your minimum. Regular vacuuming will also keep dust mites and any moths or beetles out of your carpet.

New homes sometimes have vacuum systems built in. You plug the hose into an outlet in each room. This is a very effective way to vacuum but it's an expensive alternative to a portable cleaner if you're thinking of putting one in yourself.

How to choose: a vacuum cleaner

Don't be bamboozled here. I tend to get swept away by the design. This has led to some rather dubious purchases. There are a lot of cleaners to choose from and the best way to pick one is to consider the following:

1. What kind of floor do you have? Upright cleaners are best for carpets. Canisters can do both carpets and floorboards but aren't as easy to maneuver as upright cleaners. If you live in a small apartment, consider a stick or broom vacuum – they are a pared-down version of an upright. They don't have as much power but make up for it by being very easy to store.

2. Test-drive the vacuum in the shop. It's the only way to tell if it is well designed for your height and how heavy it is. If the shop isn't set up to do that, go to another one.

3. If you suffer from allergies, make sure the unit is fitted with a HEPA (High Efficiency Particulate Air) filter. This filter claims to collect 99.9 percent of all particles. Filtration systems make the vacuum more expensive.

4. Make sure it has all the attachments you will need. If you have curtains, for example, you'll need a vacuum with a drapery attachment.

5. If noise is an issue, there are models that have extra insulation around the motors.

6. Don't be won over by motor power (measured in amps). It doesn't always mean more sucking power. The key here is airflow, which is measured in cubic inches per minute. The stronger the airflow, the better the vacuum. >

7. The dust collector can be a bag made of thick paper or fabric, or a plastic container. Both systems work well.
8. It's important the cord is long enough to do each room in your house without having to change outlets in that room.
9. If you are cleaning carpets, then a roller with bristles that spin will be more effective.

How to shampoo carpet

After a particularly messy party season, you may want to give your carpet or rugs a good deep-cleaning. Or you may shampoo more often because someone in the house suffers from allergies. Regular vacuuming should keep your carpet clean enough that you won't need to deep-clean too often. Once a year is fine if the carpet or rug looks like it's in good condition.

You can have your carpet deep-cleaned professionally (at home or off-site), you can hire special equipment to do it yourself, or you can use commercial shampoo or your own cleaning solution. As long as the cleaning solution is not too wet, you can use your own vacuum cleaner to vacuum it up. Most store-bought cleaners are foam-based and easily vacuumed. Of course, if the rug is valuable, an antique, or simply has sentimental value, have it cleaned by a professional.

To clean the carpet yourself, try the mildest of approaches with a foam carpet-spray first. Or, you can buy a cleaner that's in the form of a dust. You sprinkle it on and it absorbs stains before it gets vacuumed off. Make your own version of this with plain talcum powder mixed with a little baking soda.

I use a commercial foaming shampoo cleaner that you spray on, leave for a while, then vacuum off. I do it at the beginning of summer and then the beginning of winter. I also spot-clean every now and again (as the red wine spills demand it). Just follow the directions on the bottle for the product you've chosen.

Move all the furniture out of the area you are cleaning. If you can't move it, wrap the feet in plastic wrap or a plastic bag to stop any stains that might result from the legs getting wet. Then vacuum thoroughly. You should always vacuum before you try any type of carpet cleaning.

You don't want to get the carpet too wet from the foam or cleaner, which can cause the carpet or rug to mildew. Don't walk on wet carpet. It ruins the pile. Replace furniture once thoroughly dry.

How to steam-clean

Steam cleaning uses water under great pressure, forced into and then out of the carpet. You can do it yourself, but it can be difficult wheeling this cumbersome equipment around and may be worth investing in a professional. Your local carpet dealer will often be able to recommend reliable professionals.

To hire the equipment can cost up to $60 for the day. Make sure the charges include detergent and a stain remover. Follow the instructions given to you by the hire company. Be careful not to overwet the carpet. Even if you don't overwet it, the carpet can take a long time to dry. Make sure the room is well ventilated. Place a heater in the room with a fan if you want to speed up drying. This kind of a thorough cleaning (water is forced into the fibers of the carpet and then sucked out again) can take its toll on the carpet and really should be done only as necessary. Once a year is fine, but certainly not more often than that.

How to remove: carpet stains

Remember two things when attacking a carpet stain – speed and blotting. The quicker you act, the better. And if you can blot the mess up rather than rub it in, it will clean up without much fuss. Blotting is also kinder on the carpet; rubbing will eventually damage the pile. Some stains simply won't budge, no matter what you try. Consider having the square of carpet replaced (professionals can do this seamlessly). If that isn't an option, maybe you can place a piece of furniture or a rug over the offending patch.

Follow this process to remove a carpet stain:

1. **Contain** – move from the outer edges of the spill to the middle, to help contain it. Blot wet spills with something white and absorbent (a paper towel or clean rag is fine), scrape up solids with a dry clean cloth or blunt knife, and vacuum dry spills.

2. **Dab** – the idea is to lift the stain onto the clean cloth. Use a small amount of cleaning solution (depending on the type of stain – see below) on a cloth or directly onto the carpet and gently blot the stain. Turn the cloth frequently so you are always using a clean bit.

3. **Rinse** – spray a little water on the area to remove any cleaner. Never overwet the carpet as this can damage it.

4. **Blot again** – and leave overnight to dry completely. Vacuum the area to fluff up the pile.

5. **Repeat** – some stains will need a few tries with a cleaning solution before they respond.

If you haven't got to the stain before it dries, try smearing with glycerine and leaving for at least four hours. Then apply a solution of 1 tablespoon of borax mixed with 1 pint of warm water. Make sure you don't get the area too wet. This should work for most dried stains. If the stain is blood, make sure you use cold ingredients. Don't attempt to clean an antique or precious rug; wipe up as much of the spill as you can, wrap the rug in plastic (so the stain doesn't dry) and take it to a rug cleaner ASAP.

Chewing gum and wax – scrape off as much as you can. Harden the gum by rubbing with a sandwich bag filled with ice cubes and chip away at it with a blunt knife or spoon. Vacuum. Blot area with detergent solution or try a commercial spot remover if any marks are left.

Crayon – scrape up as much as you can with a blunt knife. Dip a short-bristled brush (a nailbrush is good) in warm soapy water and gently scrub the spot, moving from the outside to the center. Don't overwet the area. Dab with a clean white cloth to dry. You can also check out www.crayola.com for excellent cleaning tips to do with all kinds of markers on all kinds of surfaces. One suggestion is to spray the area first with WD-40, which is a lubricant, and then to sponge with soapy water. I suggest trying soapy water first and using the WD-40 only as a last resort.

Dirt or mud – remove as much as possible without spreading it, then let the remainder dry, scrape up what you can, and vacuum the rest. Dab the spot with a solution of 1 teaspoon of dishwashing liquid, ¼ teaspoon of white vinegar, and 1 quart of warm water, until just damp. Leave it for 10 minutes and then blot up. Rinse spot in cold water.

You can also try a solution of 1 part white vinegar to 2 parts water (straight from the tap is fine).

Another good tip is to use the foam from dishwashing liquid. Half-fill a sink with hot water and detergent, making sure there's a good lot of foam. Wipe just the foam over the spot, then gently wipe off with a dry cloth. To make sure you've removed all soap, wipe with a 1:1 white vinegar and water solution, blot dry, and then rinse the spot with warm water. Blot that dry also. (Blotting will stop a water-mark forming.)

If you think you've used too much water, use a hairdryer to dry the area thoroughly.

Drinks (including coffee, tea, wine, juice, and soft drinks) – blot, then apply a detergent and vinegar solution (as above) or mix 1 tablespoon of borax to 1 pint of warm water. You may have to apply the solution a few times before the stain disappears. Follow with the vinegar solution (as above). Then rinse the area with plain water and make sure it dries thoroughly. Using salt or baking soda before you blot will soak up the stain but won't get rid of it. And by leaving the stain to be soaked up, you might do more damage. It's best to blot up the liquid immediately with a paper towel or clean white cloth.

Food (including fruit, vegetables, and meat) – apply a detergent solution and vinegar solution (as above) and rinse thoroughly with water.

Grease and oil – dust immediately with baking soda or talcum powder to soak up as much of the mark as possible. Let sit for at least three hours. Vacuum up the baking soda and apply a commercial cleaner, or try wiping on some laundry detergent for woolens mixed with warm water. Rinse with vinegar solution (as above) and then cold water, and blot dry.

Paint – if it's water-based and still wet, try spot-cleaning with a detergent and vinegar solution (as above). Oil-based paints will respond to mineral spirits while they are wet. Don't use too much as it will soak through the carpet and damage the backing. If either kind of paint is dry, scrape off as much as possible with a blunt knife or spoon, vacuum well, and then clean as above.

Pen/ink – sponge with a very small amount of nail-polish remover. (Only do this if the carpet is color-fast; if it isn't, simply use hot water and detergent). Follow the nail-polish remover with the detergent solution (use hot water rather than lukewarm). Blot with cold water.

Rust – if the stain is fresh, treat with 1 part white vinegar to 2 parts water. You can also try a paste of lemon juice and salt (or lemon juice and baking soda). Spread the paste over the area, leave overnight, and vacuum off. If the spot is dry, call in the cleaners!

Shoe polish – colored shoe polish will come off with a little turpentine.

Urine, feces, vomit, or blood – if there's a baby in the house, you'll find yourself scrubbing away at all sorts of spots. Don't panic. Scrape up any lumps first, then follow the steps for drinks above. When you've removed the stain, dab the area with a laundry detergent for woolens before rinsing. This should hide the smell. You'll need lots of clean cloths or white paper towels here.

How to clean: wood flooring

The only way to protect a wood floor is to keep it dust-free. It is everyday dust and dirt that scratches the finish on wood floors.

* Hard-sealed floors will really benefit from a quick daily once-over with a dust mop (if you have the time and inclination). These mops (available from your local supermarket or hardware store) are specifically designed to pick up the dust and dirt that will scratch the finish on a wood floor. You can also attach an old cotton T-shirt to a sponge mop and use it as a dust mop. Dampen the T-shirt to get a deeper clean.

* I've read that you can scatter the floor with damp tea leaves and then sweep them up, to remove all the dust and dirt particles. However, this is rather messy and any gaps in the floorboards would collect way too many tea leaves. But feel free to try it if it appeals to you.

* Vacuum with the floor-brush attachment once a week.

* Mop up wet spills immediately.

* Consider placing mats in high-traffic areas like at the sink. Never allow water to stand on a wood floor.

To wash a wood floor . . .

* Add mild detergent to a bucket of hot water. The idea is to produce as few bubbles as possible. If the floor is sticky after washing, it means you've used too much detergent. Follow up with something that will get rid of the soap – either vinegar or a mild ammonia solution.

* Never pour water on the floor. Dip your mop into the bucket and wring almost dry.

* When cleaning any wood, whether it is furniture or floors, always move with the grain. Wipe the mop over the floor in long parallel loops.

* As soon as the mop becomes dirty, rinse in the water and squeeze as before. I sometimes rinse the dirty mop in the sink rather than back in the bucket to keep the soapy water cleaner longer.

* Change the water as needed and wipe up excess water or spills immediately.

* To make sure you get all the soap off the floor, you can go over it again with the mop (soap-free) and fresh water, but this means you are doing the job twice. I don't do this often. Buffing seems to work just as well (if you haven't got overly soapy water to begin with) to remove any residue.

* Buff the floor to make sure it's completely dry after you've mopped. There are a few ways to do this. Drop a couple of old T-shirts on the floor and push them around the wet/damp spots with your feet (this is my preferred method). Or wrap a lint-free cloth around the head of a dry mop (or get a buffing attachment for the mop) and go over the floor you've just washed. This brings up a shine and ensures that the floor is thoroughly dry.

If the surface of your wood floors is particularly shiny and the finish sits on top of the grain, then it's got a hard seal, probably made from polyurethane. (Polyurethane is a group of thermoplastic polymers used in resins and coatings. They form a strong shiny surface on top of the timber. It's almost like looking at the grain through a sheet of glass.) Without regular cleaning, these surfaces become dull and scratched. To get the glossy finish, they need to be sanded and another coat of polyurethane applied. If you are really keen to maintain a high gloss, you'll find a floor needs to be refinished every two to three years. This process is messy, time-consuming, and expensive so it's best to avoid having to do it too often by keeping the floor clean. (See maintenance on pages 52–3 for more on finishes.)

Soft seals on wood floors are often finished with shellac, lacquer, or oil. They aren't as tough as urethane and will not seal the wood against water damage to the same extent. These finishes often have a coat (or two coats) of wax on top to help strengthen them. Soft finishes can be cleaned as hard finishes – sweeping or vacuuming regularly, mopping once a week, and buffing to a shine. Spot-clean spills with a sponge wrung out in warm soapy water.

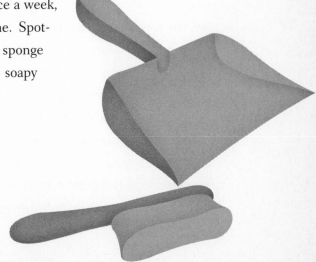

Waxes

Waxes are used to protect floors – not just wood but also concrete, linoleum, and cork. Wax a floor once a year, unless the area receives a lot of traffic – then do just that area as required. You'll know you need to rewax when the floor doesn't shine up after buffing.

Solid or paste wax – this wax in a can is used on unvarnished hardwood floors, true linoleum (not vinyl), unfinished cork, and concrete. It shouldn't be used on vinyl or floors with a urethane finish. (Wax will be too slippery on these surfaces and when they need to be refinished the wax will have to be thoroughly removed – which is a very difficult job.)

Liquid wax – use this on unvarnished wood, linoleum, and unfinished cork. This stuff is easier to apply than wax in a can, but the finish won't last as long. Apply just as you would the solid wax. As the solvents in the polish dry and dissolve, the wax is left behind and, once dry, will need buffing.

To wax a floor. . .

1. Clean floor well using a vacuum to get up all the dust.
2. Remove old wax using a commercial wax remover or a small amount of mineral spirits. Follow the instructions for the commercial remover. For mineral spirits, put about 1 teaspoon onto a clean dry rag and wipe onto the floor. Wipe off with a clean rag.
3. Let the floor dry before applying a new coat of wax. For liquid wax, follow the instructions for that product. For paste, take a walnut-size piece of wax in a clean cloth and work it until it's soft. Apply the wax by hand, as thinly as you can, using an old lint-free cloth. Let the floor dry (this may take several hours)

before buffing with another clean cloth. You may want to do another coat (just repeat the steps). Or you can rent a buffing machine – which would be wise if you are doing a large room. You can also try buffing using a sponge-mop covered with an old towel. Don't wash the towel you used to wax the floor in your washing machine – wax can attach itself to the drum and ruin other loads.

If your floor has been oiled and you want to switch to wax, simply wash the floor down with a barely wet mop, let dry, and wax as above.

How to maintain: wood flooring

Avoid scratches to the finish and the wood by always lifting (never dragging) furniture. Get felt or plastic glides for all furniture, and try to avoid walking on wood floors in high heels. A scratch in your floor will tell you what kind of finish it has. If the scratch or stain sits on the surface of the wood then you probably have a hard finish – most commonly a type of urethane is used that completely seals the wood. Most new floors have a urethane finish. If the scratch or stain penetrates the timber then the seal is soft and probably an oil finish.

Scratches aren't easy to repair in a hard finish – do not try sanding them out as this will compromise the finish. Do not use anything abrasive, like steel wool, on the floor. Your best bet is to go to a wood flooring supplier and see if they have touch-up kits. In the worst-case scenario, get a professional in to refinish the floor for you – pricey, but it will look good. If you've marked a soft-finished floor, it's easier to fix it yourself.

Dark spots – try a bleach or vinegar on the spot. Wipe off after about an hour and rewax using a fine (000) steel wool and floor wax (follow the instructions for that particular wax).

Dreaded high-heel marks – best treated with floor wax and a fine steel wool. It's hard to remove them completely. Best to take your shoes off.

Soil-based stains – treat with detergent to break down the grease and rinse with clean water. Then sand back the spot with fine sandpaper and finish with a soft cloth and floor wax.

Light scratches – can be covered up with floor wax and buffed lightly with a clean cloth. Deep scratches may need to be treated with a stain stick, or stained to match the floor color.

White stains or water marks – clean the spot with 000 steel wool and floor wax. If it is a deep stain you may have to sand back that area of the floor before treating with steel wool and floor wax.

Mops

Dust mops – often impregnated with an agent that attracts dust. The best ones have removable surfaces attached to the head that can be washed. You can make your own dust mop by attaching an old T-shirt to the end of your broom or mop.

Sponge mops – perfect for mopping smooth floors (vinyl, wood, etc.) and small areas like kitchen and bathroom floors. Make sure you squeeze out as much water as possible before mopping. When buying, look for heads that pivot (they get into tight spaces more easily) and are easy to wring out, easy to change, and readily available. To store, wring out all water and hang or lean in a closet with the head elevated and away from the wall so the sponge doesn't lose its shape.

String mops – good for large and uneven areas. Choose one with a removable head for ease of washing, and make sure it wrings out well. To store, wring out and suspend from a peg with the mop strings hanging down.

How to maintain: cork and linoleum floors

Cork is a lightweight, spongy material obtained from the bark of the cork oak tree. It doesn't absorb water easily, which means there's little chance of mold or rot forming. When made into tiles, cork is a resilient, insulating, and long-lasting floor covering. It is most often sealed.

If the cork floor is sealed with urethane, clean and treat it as you would any hard-sealed floor. Sweep or vacuum regularly to remove dirt and grit that can damage the seal. Mop with mild soapy water and rinse well. Clean up spills and excess water immediately. Cork floors will need to be refinished every six to eight years, depending on how high-traffic the area is.

Linoleum is flexible and resilient flooring made from linseed oil, resin, and wood flour on a jute backing. The term linoleum, or lino, is often used incorrectly to describe any sheet flooring, when in fact flooring can be made from other materials such as vinyl (petroleum-based polyvinyl chloride).

To clean and maintain linoleum floors, sweep, mop with a detergent solution, rinse with a clean mop to remove soap residue, and dry. You'll know you need to wax when the floor becomes dull even after a mop. Apply a coat of paste or liquid wax and buff.

To maintain vinyl, wax every six months. If you need to remove wax, use a wax stripper and follow the directions for that product. Then apply a thin coat of liquid wax by pouring it directly onto the floor and spreading with a sponge mop. You can try wrapping the mop in a lint-free cloth for better coverage. Let the floor dry; it should dry to a shine with no need to buff. Clean the floor with a damp mop between waxes. Spot-clean with a sponge wrung out in warm, soapy water.

How to remove: stains on cork or linoleum

Black heel marks – rub off with a gum eraser, or try a dab of toothpaste and buff the mark off with a soft cloth.

Fruit juice, wine – ¼ cup of bleach to 2 quarts of water.

Ink, hair dye, crayon, lipstick – try rubbing alcohol or lighter fluid.

Paint, varnish, nail polish, permanent marker, shoe polish – if dry, try scraping it up with something blunt (try an old credit card). Wipe up what's left with rubbing alcohol.

Rust – rub with ½ lemon dipped in salt. Wipe dry.

How to clean: tiles

Glazed tiles – ceramic tiles are often glazed. Stone tiles can be sealed but will rarely come with a glaze. The glaze means they are impervious to most stains and easy to clean. Sweep daily to stop grit damaging the glaze. Mop with a mild detergent and water once a week (more often in high-traffic areas like the kitchen). To remove scuffs or marks, you can use a commercially prepared floor-tile cleaner, or try a mix of equal parts white vinegar and very hot water. In fact, you might find that the very hot water does the trick all on its own. Commercial cleaners often contain a mild abrasive that is needed to remove stubborn dirt off floors. You can try making a paste of baking soda and water – it should have a similar effect. Don't wax or polish glazed tiles as they become very slippery.

Unglazed tiles – these are very hard to keep clean, so I'd recommend sealing them. You can do it yourself. Try your local hardware or tile store for commercial sealers. There are two kinds of sealants – one that sits on the surface and is usually water-based, and the other that soaks into the tile. Any sealer will need to be redone eventually; it may need to be redone a little earlier if you use a mild soap in the water when you mop these tiles.

To best maintain unglazed tiles, sweep before you mop. Mop using a mild detergent, rinse with clean cold water, and buff with a dry cloth. Don't let water pool on these tiles. Cleaning this way will shorten the life of your finish, but it is impossible to get these tiles really clean by simply using water to wash them.

How to remove: stains on tiles

Blood – bleach or peroxide.

Food and drinks (especially fruit juice, coffee, tea) – detergent in water followed by a little bleach if needed. Make sure you rinse and dry the area to remove any bleach residue.

Grease and fats – detergent and warm water.

Inks and colored dyes – bleach (let it stand on the spot, keeping it wet until stain disappears).

Iodine – scrub with ammonia. Make sure the room is well ventilated.

Lipstick – as for food and drinks.

Mercurochrome – bleach. If you are concerned about the bleach taking color from the tile, dilute it with cold water. You can use straight bleach on glazed tiles. Don't splash it around too much. Best to wet a rag with bleach and apply that to the stain.

Nail polish – nail-polish remover. Follow with bleach if there's still a stain.

Rust and limestone stains – white vinegar and water. Make sure you rinse the spot thoroughly afterward. If the stain is a tough one you may have to purchase a commercial stain remover (follow the product's instructions).

Sticky substances like chewing gum, wax, or tar – scrape away as much as you can with a blunt tool (an ice-cream stick or old credit card is excellent). Use an ice cube to chill the substance to make it easier to scrape. If there is any left, it can be removed with paint stripper (follow the product's instructions).

How to clean: curtains

Heavy curtains or drapes are usually lined and reach the floor. When you open or close them, give them a slight shake and that will lift a lot of the dust. A vacuum once a week with the soft-brush attachment will also help maintain them. Start at the top and, using short strokes, work your way down to the bottom of the drape.

I'd recommend getting heavy drapes professionally cleaned. Most domestic washing machines won't handle the weight of lined drapes.

If you do want to wash your curtains, try doing it by hand. Give them a good shake before you immerse them in the bathtub full of cold water. Let them soak there for a few hours and add a mild laundry detergent (dissolve it first if need be) and gently squeeze it through the fabric. Drain the soapy water and rinse in lots of cold water to remove all the soap. Hang outside to dry. If you can't hang outside, hang in the bathroom with the window open. When they are still slightly damp, rehang at the window or, if they are very wrinkled, iron and then hang.

Lighter, unlined curtains should be machine-washed when you notice they are looking dirty. Make sure the machine is on the gentle cycle and use cold water. Tumble dry on low or hang out to dry. Iron on the back.

If the seams have puckered, try spraying with a little cold water and gently stretching – don't pull too hard as you don't want to break the stitches.

Lace curtains can be put in the tumble-dryer, on low, to remove dust. To wash in the machine, use the gentle cycle and a mild detergent formulated for delicate fabric like wool. Or, as with heavy curtains, give them a good shake and hand-wash. If you hang them while they are still a bit damp then the creases should fall out.

How to clean: blinds

Venetian blinds – to properly clean these you really should take them down and hang them from the shower rod, or take them outside and hang them from the clothes line. First, vacuum to remove as much dust as possible, by running the soft-brush attachment along each slat. Then work your way from top to bottom with a sponge wrung out in warm soapy water. Repeat the process with a clean sponge and fresh water to remove any soap residue from the slats.

Never use ammonia or any kind of abrasive cleaner on aluminum as you can ruin the finish. Make sure the blind is fully dry before you rehang, especially if the cords are made of natural fibers that can stretch when hung wet.

If you can't take the blinds down, put newspaper underneath to catch the drips. Vacuum off as much dust as you can with the soft-brush attachment. Then put on a pair of cotton gloves, dip your fingers in warm soapy water, and run your finger and thumb along each slat. You'll need to follow up with clear water and finally a dry cloth to thoroughly dry the blind. For metal blinds, you can also try wrapping a stick, spatula, or wooden spoon with an absorbent cloth. Sprinkle with rubbing alcohol and rub it between the slats. This will remove dirt and leave a shine.

Pleated blinds – these can either be washed as for venetian blinds or, if they are very fragile, done professionally.

Roll-up blinds – if the blind is made of paper, wash as for wallpaper (see pages 33–4). Bamboo blinds shouldn't come into contact with water. Just vacuum regularly and replace when they get really dirty. But most of the blinds now sold are washable. The easiest way to clean them is to take them down and roll them out on a flat surface like a dining table. Wash each side with warm water and mild detergent, then wipe down with clear water to get rid of any soap residue, and wipe dry.

Roman blinds – roll out flat and wipe as for roll-up blinds. If you can't take them down, you'll have to wipe them hanging. Just make sure they don't get too wet as they'll stretch out of shape.

How to clean: windows

Choose a cloudy day to clean as sunlight will cause the windows to streak. Wash stained glass as you would normal glass, but be very gentle as it will bow easily. If the glass is painted rather than stained, do not use water. Wipe with a dry cloth or try a soft paintbrush.

Necessities

****

* **2 buckets** – 1 for warm soapy water, 1 for plain water
* **1 sponge**
* **1 squeegee**
* **1 cloth**
* **Newspaper**
* **White vinegar and/or household ammonia**

Clean the frames first. These can get very grimy. Vacuum or dust and then wash with mild detergent and warm water. Use a toothbrush to get into particularly dirty corners. Wipe dry when you are done. They may need another minor wipe down when you have finished cleaning the glass, just to catch any drips. If you are cleaning glass on a sliding door, make sure the runners are free of dirt and debris. Aluminum window frames and door frames can be washed with a mild detergent, dried thoroughly, and polished with silicone car polish.

Clean the glass with a solution of 1 part white vinegar to 1 part warm water (add a little household ammonia if you like). Or, if the windows aren't very dirty, just use water. Some people swear by commercial window-cleaners and by all means use one. But if you are looking for a streak-free window, you can get it by using a homemade solution and polishing the glass with newspaper.

Start at the top of the window and work your way down. Spray cleaning solution straight onto glass and wipe off with a lint-free cloth. If the window is very dirty, sponge the solution on and then use a squeegee. Don't get the glass too wet as you'll spread the dirt with drips and runs. Wipe the squeegee with a clean cloth between swipes.

If you are cleaning both sides of the glass (and you should), wipe horizontally on one side and vertically on the other so you can see more easily where you've cleaned and which sides the streaks are on.

Polish off streaks with scrunched-up newspaper. Or you can try using a squeegee. In our 1930s building, the windows and French doors out to the balcony have panes that make squeegee use difficult, so I find a sponge or spray and newspaper a much easier cleaner/polisher.

Screens

Remove them if possible and wipe down with a sponge dipped in warm soapy water. Wipe again with a sponge dipped in hot water and tea-tree oil. Dry thoroughly in the sun and replace. If they don't come down easily, simply brush with a small broom (the dustpan broom is good here) and wipe with a dry cloth.

Glass and mirrors

Use a commercial glass-cleaner or a white vinegar and water solution, or 2 parts white vinegar and 2 parts household ammonia to 4 parts water. Apply with a lint-free cloth and polish off with newspaper.

3. The Kitchen

I grew up in a house where the kitchen and dining room were one. The dining table often
doubled as a kitchen counter. I remember
my father teaching himself how to make bagels. He had hundreds
of loops of dough spread all over the dining table late into the night.
When we got up the next morning there were lovely golden fresh
bagels waiting for us. (But he never made bagels again . . .)

The best kitchens match their uses and the best furniture works
hard and earns its place in the room. It's best not to get swept away
by other people's kitchens. Figure out not just what you need (or
think you need) but what you actually have room for. A family of six
may need a breakfast counter, two ovens and room for an enormous
fridge. Even if you live alone in a tiny apartment where the kitchen
is the size of a cupboard and you eat at a coffee table planted in
front of the couch, you will still want this space to be
fairly practical. Round tables that can double
as work areas and eating spots do well
in smaller spaces. Larger kitchens often benefit

from a wheeled utility cart that holds key items and is pushed around the room to serve whoever needs it. A cleverly designed, well-stocked, and tidy kitchen is the secret to a well-run house. I always find that once the kitchen gets out of hand the rest of the house seems to follow.

There are a few simple rules to organizing a really successful kitchen.

1. **The golden triangle** – the fridge, sink, and oven are the cornerstones of this space and shouldn't be more than a double-arm span apart. The idea is that you don't want to be walking too far to get what you need. (See opposite page for suggested dimensions.)

2. **Lighting** – natural light is a blessing in a kitchen. My kitchen faces west and in the afternoon there's a lovely sweep of sun across the room, which makes working in there a real pleasure. At night a well-lit kitchen is a must. (See also lighting on pages 11–12.)

3. **Ventilation** – above the stove, ventilation is important. There are two types of ventilation systems:

* Ductless – this is easy to install as there's no pipes to join it to. These units sit above the stove and should be the width of the stovetop. Air is sucked in by a fan through a filter and then released back into the room. Grease and moisture are caught in the filter, which needs to be cleaned regularly.

* Ducted – the ventilation system is linked to the outside of the house via a pipe or duct. A fan pulls the air from the stovetop through a filter and it is released outdoors. As with the ductless system these filters need to be cleaned or replaced regularly.

To clean filters, follow the manufacturer's instructions. Charcoal filters, which can't be washed, should be changed once a year.

Dimensions

Use these figures as a guide when you're planning a kitchen:

* About 2 feet around the edge of each object gives people room to move.
* 40 inches is needed in front of a door that is in constant use (could be your back door).
* 32 inches in front of a door that is used less frequently.
* A minimum of 3 feet between counters. Any tighter and you'll be uncomfortable.
* 1 foot between an oven or burners and the corner of the room.
* Between 4 and 6 feet of preparation space.
* Around 18 inches of counter space for loading/unloading next to a fridge, stove, or storage unit.
* 2 feet is a standard depth for kitchen countertops. Then the cabinets underneath are not so deep that things get lost, but deep enough to house even the heftiest kitchen appliance. The standard height for countertops is 3 feet, but you may want to consider adjusting this, depending on your height.

How to stock: your kitchen

Once you've figured out what furniture will go into this room, you'll need all the bits and pieces that go into making the space truly functional.

1. The bare-bones kitchen

To set up a kitchen from scratch you will need:

Appliances – hand-held mixer, toaster, microwave oven, tea kettle.

Stovetop – 1 small saucepan, 1 large saucepan, 1 saucepan that goes from stovetop to oven, 1 frying pan, 1 nonstick frying pan. (See pages 78–80 for help with choosing saucepans.)

Oven – 1 rectangular and 1 round baking dish, 2 baking sheets, 1 loaf pan, 1 round cake pan.

Gadgets – measuring cup for liquid (clear glass ones are the best) and metal measuring cups for dry ingredients, measuring spoons, can opener, bottle opener and corkscrew (an all-in-one saves space), colander, ladle, spatula, pasta server (although I find the best thing here is a trusty pair of metal tongs), plastic chopping board for meat, wooden chopping board for everything else, potato masher, kitchen scale, set of mixing bowls (the metal ones are long-lasting and inexpensive), slotted spoon, vegetable peeler, wire cooling racks, wooden spoon, grater, kitchen scissors, garlic press, pepper and salt grinder.

Knives – a serrated knife for bread, a medium-sized, general-purpose, good quality knife, a small paring knife. Get the very best knives. It's worth spending money on these, as you'll use them every day. (See pages 73–4 for help with choosing knives, and page 76 for a note on knife storage.)

Dish towels – have as many of these as you can fit! As soon as a dish towel becomes dirty or too wet, it should be washed. Two pot holders are also a must.

2. The I-don't-live-on-my-own-anymore kitchen

Take everything from the bare-bones kitchen and add:

Appliances – blender, food processor.

Stovetop – medium-size saucepan, double boiler and a cast-iron frying pan, wok.

Oven – muffin pan, pie pan (may be glass or ceramic), pizza pan, roasting pan with rack.

Gadgets – basting brush, rolling pin, food mill, zester, mandolin, whisk.

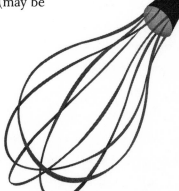

3. The busy-family kitchen

Everything from the two lists above plus:

Appliances – bread machine, four-slice toaster, rice cooker.

Stovetop – cast-iron griddle (so you can make four pancakes at a time).

Oven – large Dutch oven, large baking dish, various-sized casserole dishes, ramekins.

Gadgets – cookie cutters, hand juicer, meat mallet.

How to choose: tableware

I am always so torn when it comes to china and cutlery. I like to mix clean modern pieces like big white dinner plates with delicate linen napkins and silver cutlery. I love those modern Georg Jensen pieces, the cool knives that lie at an odd angle. But I am also drawn to fine old ornate-handled silver cutlery and I must admit to a secret love for anything bone-handled. As a result we have a rather schizo-phrenic collection of tableware. For me, the mix of old and new is a bit more interesting than having everything perfectly matching. But a friend of mine has bought a Wedgwood dinner set and now, when-ever her birthday rolls around, her friends buy pieces to add to it. She loves the floral pattern, the fineness of the china, and the fact that it all matches. She uses the Wedgwood for special occasions and has a plain white set for everyday use.

If you've got room to store two sets of everything, a plain white dinner service for everyday use isn't a bad option. I don't have a lot of storage and I tend to use the very good stuff with the pieces I've picked up at Ikea or discount stores. Think about the way you entertain and the way you use your tableware. If you love your crys-tal glasses, store them somewhere that's easy to get to and use them regularly. Just make sure you don't put them in the dishwasher. (For cleaning cutlery and glassware see pages 91–2.)

How to choose: knives

There's an element of fashion here. For a while Mundial knives with their carbon blade and three-riveted black polypropylene handle were the ones to have. Then it was the high-carbon stainless-steel Global knives. (I was given one as a present and I must admit that I love it. The handle and blade are crafted from the same piece of metal so there are no pesky joins to gather food or break.) However, your choice of knife should be very personal.

A leading Sydney chef says the thing to look out for with a knife is the weight. He recommends using as heavy a knife as you are comfortable with. Feel the weight of the knife and make sure it's right for you – not too heavy, not too light. Think about the way you cook and buy only what you need. Don't buy a set as you'll be paying for knives you never use. Better to spend that money on one or two good knives you'll use all the time. And do be guided by price – generally, the more expensive knives are better.

These are the most common knives:

* Chef's or cook's knife, also known as a French knife – for chopping, dicing, mincing, and cutting; designed to rock as you chop.
* Carving knife – designed to cut thin slices of meat.
* Paring knife – for peeling, trimming, and cutting small things.
* Serrated knife – for bread, cakes, fruit that need to be cut with a sawing action.
* Boning knife – used to cut through meat joints and remove flesh from bone; a strong knife with a thin blade that's flexible and narrow.
* Filleting knife – has a thin flexible blade, used for fish.

The chef also recommends getting your knives sharpened by a professional with a good reputation. Only do it when the knife is dull. In the meantime, maintain your knives with a sharpening steel.

To clean, wipe down with a soapy sponge and rinse in warm water, then wipe dry. Never soak good knives or anything else made from wood, bone, ivory, or cast iron.

What goes where?

My husband and I were lucky enough to be able to rip out the kitchen in our flat and start again. I became obsessed with getting the placement of everything just right. Here was my chance to have exactly the right storage, an accessible pantry, glasses where I could reach them, shallow drawers for utensils so I could easily find everything. I got most of it right.

The fundamental guide to kitchen storage is to place items where they are most often used – glasses above the sink, pots and pans in drawers by the stove, etc. And make sure your pantry shelves aren't too deep. The higher the shelf the shallower it should be. My pantry shelves are eighteen inches deep and the high shelf has a lot of wasted space in the back where no-one can see or easily reach. A pull-out storage unit is a great space-saver but don't scrimp on it. The cheap ones are flimsy and the shelves tend to let items topple and block the sliding mechanism.

When I was planning my new kitchen I spent hours poring over a Häfele catalogue, reading about all the options for spice pullouts, drawer runners, and cutlery dividers. This was my moment to right every wrong kitchen I'd lived in for the past fifteen years. Here's what I learned.

In general . . .

* Make sure you can easily reach all those things you use on a daily basis.
* Keep like with like – baking things should go with other baking things.
* Drawers should vary in depth as their purpose dictates.
* Store heavy things low or at waist height. Lighter things can go on higher shelves.
* Store food away from the stove and any other heat source (the dishwasher, for example, can get hot).
* Have things stored close to where they will be used – glasses above or near the sink, plates near the dishwasher, saucepans near the stove.

Specifically . . .

Glasses and china – store them high up but not too high. Mine are to the right of the sink and directly above the dishwasher. Fine glassware is stored on higher shelves above the ordinary glassware. My fine china is in a low cupboard simply because we've got lots of low cupboards but it could also go on the higher, less accessible shelves. You may want to display your fine china and glass, and a china cabinet – or open shelving – is perfect for this. The advantage of a cabinet is that it keeps dust at bay. Otherwise, you may store these items in a sideboard in the dining room.

Cutlery – keep it in the top drawer next to the dishwasher. I wish I had one more drawer to store good cutlery (which is in a box under the bed and not very convenient.).

Utensils – my major breakthrough here was to design two shallow utensil drawers rather than one deep one where I can never find anything. Sharp knives sit in the first one along with serving spoons, wooden spoons, salad servers, and other things I use regularly like the vegetable peeler, can opener, and bottle opener. Everything else is in the drawer below. A quick note on knife blocks: it's impossible to clean inside the slots and knives left out make for easy access for children. I do think knives belong in drawers.

Baking dishes and serving platters – usually best stored in a low cupboard as they can be heavy.

Dish towels, placemats, napkins – I designed a deep bottom drawer that holds all the kitchen linen (plus a hammer and flashlight and a few other odds and ends).

Pots and pans – low cupboards or deep low drawers near the stove are best for these items. I've got two drawers but I could easily fill four.

Food – best kept in a pantry if you have one. If not, cupboards away from all heat sources are best.

Cleaning products – it does make sense to have these under the sink where you can easily get at them, but this can prove a serious hazard for young children. I moved most cleaning products – except dishwashing detergent – to the laundry; otherwise, make sure the kitchen cabinet containing the products has a good child-proof lock.

How to choose:
saucepans and bakeware

I'm always a little baffled by the sizes of saucepans. Bakeware seems to make much more sense. There's a standard size for a cake pan and loaf pan, but there seems to be no standard for saucepans. The best guide here is to think about what you cook. Lots of pasta? Go for a large saucepan with a lid for cooking pasta and a smaller one for the sauce. You like to cook your food slowly? Try a heavy-bottomed pan that will spread the heat evenly and not burn the food as easily as a thin-bottomed one.

When choosing what type of pan or bakeware to buy, the simple rule is the thicker the metal, the better. Whether it's a cookie sheet or a saucepan, a high-gauge metal will be kinder on the food because it offers more protection between the flame and the food. Nonstick finishes are excellent for baking and cooking fish and chicken on the stovetop. The only drawback is they can easily be scratched with metal utensils. Use only plastic or wood against nonstick surfaces and wash with care.

As I write this, there is a new range of nonstick stoveware available that is much less delicate. I just bought an excellent nonstick pan that the manufacturer says can cope with metal utensils. So far so good.

Aluminum – a set of aluminum saucepans in different sizes is a good basic essential for any kitchen. Aluminum heats quickly and uniformly. It's inexpensive and lightweight, but can react with acidic foods so best to buy lined or anodized. Anodized (the matte black saucepans) won't chip or peel, as the oxidized surface is part of the metal. Stainless steel–lined aluminum will also protect food.

There was talk of aluminum saucepans and cookware contributing to Alzheimer's disease. The National Institute of Environmental Health Sciences has an excellent Web site (www.niehs.nih.gov/external/faq/aluminum/htm) that discounts the effect of aluminum on the disease. And as they point out, cooking in uncoated aluminum pots and pans can increase the amount of aluminum in certain foods such as fruits, which are high in acid,

but the amount is minimal. Most aluminum is coated these days, and cooking foods in coated, nonstick, or hard-anodized aluminum pans adds virtually no aluminum to food. I think the bigger issue with aluminium is that it heats up so quickly, I'm always burning things when I use it. It feels a little light and flimsy, and I prefer to cook with something heavier.

Cast iron – heats slowly and evenly, and is good for stews and casseroles that need time to cook. Le Creuset makes excellent heavy iron pans that are coated in enamel. They are expensive but you'll have them for a lifetime, and I've found everything I cook in them works. They are the most forgiving of pans (but don't scrub them with Brillo).

Copper – can last for generations. It is expensive and requires good care, but copper saucepans are a lovely thing to have in the kitchen. Copper heats quickly and evenly and also cools quickly. Best to buy lined copper as the metal reacts with acid foods. Copper is excellent for cooking things that need to be heated evenly – think omelets and pancakes.

Glass and ceramic – not safe for the stovetop. Use them only in the oven. They heat quickly and evenly.

Stainless steel – heats and cools quickly. If it's a heavy gauge it will cook food well without burning. My set of saucepans (two small ones, one large one, and a big frying pan) were a wedding present and they are all heavy stainless steel with hollow metal handles that stay cool. They are a dream to use and easy to clean. I certainly wouldn't go out of my way to buy anything else now that we have these.

How to clean: the kitchen

You need only one rule in the kitchen – whatever you use, put it away. That goes for everything from the pen used to write a shopping list to the muesli and your cereal bowl. If everyone does their own bit of tidying up, then cleaning will not seem like such a daunting task. The general rule for cleaning this room works for all rooms in your house – start from the top and work your way down. Dust first, then wipe down surfaces, then vacuum or sweep, then mop. High-traffic areas, such as kitchen floors, should be done daily. (See pages 38–57 for further information on cleaning floors.)

When we had the baby, I changed the way I did things in the kitchen. Suddenly germs seemed a big deal and I was madly sterilizing bottles and pacifiers. Now that Jack is on solids I am very conscious of keeping the kitchen as germ-free as possible. I've discarded wooden chopping boards for white plastic ones whose hard surfaces are more germ-resistant. Wood can harbor germs in tiny grooves and cracks. I use one plastic board for meat and fish and the other for fruit and vegetables.

Once a month I sanitize most things in the kitchen, by boiling for five minutes and wiping over with, or soaking in, a bleach and water solution – a few drops of household bleach to 1 quart of water. Don't rinse in water, as this will negate the sterilizing effect of the bleach. (The solution is mild, so you don't need to be concerned about putting food on a chopping board after sterilizing it.) You should do this with any object that might carry hazardous microorganisms – basically anything that comes into contact with things like raw meat, chicken, fish. Of course this won't rid your home of germs but it will certainly reduce them. It all sounds a bit obsessive but once you start doing this it gets folded into your cleaning schedule and really takes very little time.

To wash babies' bottles, first rinse bottles in cold water to remove any old milk and then wash in hot soapy water. Then rinse in clear hot water. To sterilize, you need to boil the bottles in a saucepan full of water for a few minutes or – as we did – buy a sterilizer that kills germs with steam.

How to control: bacteria

The best way to control bacteria that can contaminate your food and make you sick is to create an environment where it doesn't feel welcome. The two bacteria to watch out for are staphylococcus (spread by hand contact) and salmonella (spread by contact with uncooked meat and poultry).

* Make sure you wash your hands thoroughly before and after cooking. Plain soap and hot water kills the majority of bacteria on your hands. Thorough rubbing and scrubbing should get rid of the rest. There's no real need for antibacterial soap. If you want to use it go ahead, but it can be harsh on your hands and the chafing it may cause can leave you more open to infection.

* Keep your fridge set at the correct temperature: 34–38°F is the safety zone for commercial fridges. Your fridge at home should also fall within these measurements.

* Cover food before you put it in the refrigerator to stop any cross-contamination.

* Freeze meat in quantities that you will serve so that you're not defrosting more than you need for that meal.

* Never thaw food at room temperature. Try thawing in the fridge in a plastic container. If you aren't that organized (I'm not), try

thawing in a sink of cold water. Replace the water every half hour or so until the food is defrosted. Or, even easier, defrost it in the microwave.

* Use separate chopping boards – one for meat and another for everything else. Clean boards thoroughly with very hot soapy water and then wipe with a mild bleach solution (a few drops per quart of water). Wipe up meat juices with paper towels, not your regular sponge. You can also soak boards overnight in a sink full of water with a dash of bleach. Dry thoroughly the next morning.

* Keep countertops clean with bleach and water, hot soapy water, or a commercial cleaner.

* Do your grocery shopping right before you return home so nothing sits in the car for long. On hot days take a cooler in the car for cold products like dairy and meat.

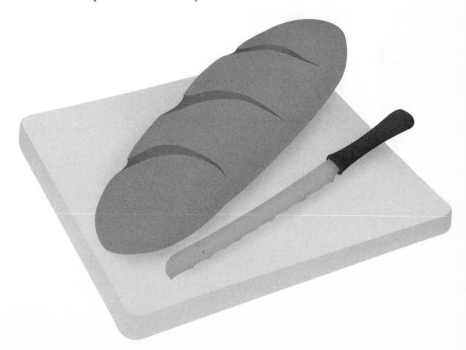

How to wash: the dishes

Washing dishes by hand is really easy. And there will be times when you need to wash by hand. Not everything can go in the dishwasher and not everyone has one. It's important to know how to wash by hand, to keep your dishes looking their best. And best of all, it's very simple.

Necessities

****

* **Good detergent** – a concentrated detergent won't clean dishes any better than normal detergent but it will produce lots of suds so the trick is to use it sparingly.

* **1 sponge** – I like a sponge with a plastic scourer on the back, my mother uses a small square sponge and separate scourer, and a friend swears by those thick velvety sponges that look like a car chamois. It's up to you. The only thing that really matters is that the sponge is clean.

* **1 brush** – excellent for getting into places your hand can't reach. Try brushes designed to clean baby's bottles. They get into all the nooks and crannies.

* **Dish towels** – you'll need more than one. Make sure they are lint-free and very absorbent.

Of course it's best to clean items as you go along when you're cooking, and to do the dishes straight after a meal. But that's just not always possible. You might not want to abandon dinner guests or you just might not want to wash then and there! If you can't get to the dishes right away, at least scrape all the food from them into the trash and rinse all the plates and glasses so you don't attract ants or cockroaches, or start growing bacteria. (See pages 82–3 for information on bacteria in the kitchen.)

1. First, **put away** all the food left over from the meal. If possible, I leave it in the bowls I've served it in (less to wash). Just cover it in plastic wrap (better than aluminum foil because you can see what's in there) and pop it in the fridge.

2. **Collect** everything that needs to be washed. There's nothing worse than finishing a big wash and then finding random cups and glasses scattered around that still need your attention.

3. **Drain** fats into a can or container, not down the sink. I know people who use a small bucket lined with a plastic bag for these food scraps and oily bits. They tie off the bag at the end of the clean-up and throw it in the trash. That seems an excessive use of plastic to me but it does result in cleaner kitchen trash. I like to then wipe out any oil with a paper towel. Now is also the time to put food scraps into the compost bucket if you have one (see page 115 for more on trash).

4. **Rinse** everything in warm water and restack ready to be washed. It really helps to place them in the order they will be washed (least dirty to most dirty): glasses, cutlery, plates, bowls, cups and saucers, serving dishes, mixing dishes and bowls, pots and pans, and cooking utensils. Fill pots and pans that are greasy or sugary with hot soapy water to soak while you tend to the rest of the dishes. Soak in cold water pots and pans that have had eggs or starchy foods (like rice and pasta).

5. Fill the sink about half full. Make the **water** as hot as possible. Rubber gloves will enable you to have hotter water and will

protect your hands, but aren't essential. Change the washing water as soon as the bubbles die back or it begins to look at all gray or oily, or has become cool. Don't overfill the sink – you need just enough water so the items you are cleaning will be fully immersed.

I use a **sponge** with a scourer on the back. My mother swears by a thin sponge that you can feel food lumps through and a separate scourer. It doesn't really matter as you'll be using your hands (not your eyes) to feel for food scraps that need to be removed.

6. Place the clean dishes in the second sink, if you have one. If not, then place the dishes on a towel. When the towel or sink is full, **rinse** the dishes with very hot water. Do this in a bowl or pour water over the dishes. Don't run water to rinse as it uses too much water. Hot water kills bacteria, removes soap residue better than cold water, and aids in drying.

7. To **dry**, place the rinsed dishes in a draining rack or on a towel in such a way that no water pools – for example, bowls should always drain upside down. I don't have a draining rack so I use a towel and a breadboard to stack bowls and glasses against – on a slight tilt so that they drain and air properly. Or (preferably) I dry the items right away.

Use a linen towel for glass, crystal, and fine china, as it is highly absorbent and lint-free. According to food experts, wet towels hold a lot of bacteria, which you are wiping back onto the dishes you've carefully cleaned. So, make sure the towel is clean and dry. This may mean using more than one towel. They are cheap and easy to wash so don't scrimp.

My mother always stands her cast-iron pots and pans over a burner on the stove to dry them properly. This is a great way to rid them of water and stop any rusting.

8. After you've put the dishes away, make sure you don't neglect the **sink** and surrounds. They'll need a good washing. Be sure to clean the drain's strainer basket, if there is one (there should be) and remove any food scraps that have accumulated in the drain. Lastly, wash and rinse your sponges thoroughly in very hot water and clean any food scraps from the brush. Hang them to dry. If the sponges get a bit smelly, half-fill the sink with very hot water and a splash of bleach. Soak the sponges for a few hours. Rinse in warm water to remove bleach.

How to clean:
burnt saucepans and stubborn stains

Burned- or baked-on food can be hard to remove. Scrape off as much as you can with a wooden spoon or rubber spatula. (I often find myself using my fingernails – not great for the nails but it can be a pretty effective method.) Never use metal to scrape as it may damage the dish or pot. Then try one of the following:

*   Sprinkle baking soda liberally on the baked-on food and scrub well, but don't use a metal scrubber as it's too harsh on most pans. (Do not use baking soda on aluminum; try cream of tartar instead.)

*   Simmer water in the offending pan with 1 tablespoon of bicarb or vinegar and then wash as normal. One of the benefits of an electric stove is that you can turn off the burner, fill the pot with hot water, and leave it to simmer away as the burner cools.

* Soak pan in very hot water with a little dishwashing liquid or powder, or dishwasher detergent (which is stronger than normal detergent).

* Finally, if you are still staring at stubborn marks, try soaking in 1 quart water in which 1 tablespoon of automatic dishwashing detergent has been dissolved. Use it with a plastic scourer, a little hot water, and a lot of elbow grease. I find this gets the majority of pots and pans perfectly clean.

Nonstick pans will discolor over time. To remedy, try pouring boiling water into the pan, adding 2 tablespoons of baking soda and letting it stand in the pan for about half an hour. Wash as usual.

How to wash: fine china

I thought fine china was terribly passé. Why have different china for different occasions? It seemed crazy to have a whole set of something you rarely used taking up room in the cupboard. Then my mother-in-law gave us a beautiful, delicate white fine-bone china dinner set when we got married. It's the first time I've ever owned anything so grown-up and I absolutely love it. My good friend Wenona has a similar set – hers is white with a black-and-silver art deco pattern and she brings it out for dinner parties. It always makes the occasion feel a bit more special.

If you've bought it recently, most fine china will be all right in the dishwasher – although even on the gentlest cycle you risk chipping, scratching, or cracking, especially if you haven't stacked properly. And the piece will age more quickly than if it were hand-washed, regardless of whether the manufacturer says it is dishwasher-safe. But if the piece is old, has any metal detailing (such as gold trim) or handpainting, or if you are concerned about it simply because it seems fragile, then wash it by hand. Don't let food stand for long in good china as the acid can stain it.

There are various sorts of china. Porcelain or fine china is fired at very high temperatures (2462–2610⁰F). It has a blue-grey cast. It is strong, glasslike, and opaque. Bone china is another form of fine china but has bone ash added to the clay to make a bright white ceramic. Like porcelain, it is glass-like and strong, but bone china is translucent. Vitreous china is twice-fired to give it a strong glass-like finish. The finish on vitreous china is not a glaze, so if you see a crack in the surface it means the actual vessel is cracked.

For a very gentle washing, fill a plastic tub or towel-lined sink with hot soapy water. Wash the pieces individually and don't let them soak for too long in the water as it can seep in through cracks and damage the china. Remove stains from cups with a paste of salt and lemon juice or vinegar. Wipe it on with your fingers and work it over the stain until it disappears. Wipe it off with a soft sponge. Don't use abrasive detergents or scouring pads, as they will dull the glaze. And try to avoid scraping china with a knife or fork; a rubber spatula will be much kinder as will a soft cloth. Rinse with warm water. Wipe dry with a clean lint-free towel. As with crystal you can try drying hard-to-reach bits with a hairdryer set on cool.

Everyday china can be washed in the dishwasher. Although don't expect cheap china to hold up well to the rigors of the dishwasher. If you want it to last longer you'll have to wash by hand.

How to fix: china

If you do crack a piece of china (and you will), it can be repaired at home if the break is a clean one. However, once you've fixed the piece, you can really only use it for decorative purposes as the repair should not be exposed to water. If the break is complicated and the piece is precious, take it to a professional. Use a strong, transparent glue like Duco Cement; a tiny amount is all you will need. Make sure you clean any excess glue while it is still liquid; once it sets, it's near impossible to remove.

How to wash: glassware

Everyday glasses can go in the dishwasher. I used to get annoying build-up on my glasses after they'd been through the dishwasher. The trick to avoiding that is to keep your filter very clean, use a rinse agent and make sure you stack the glasses so no water can pool in them during the drying process. (For more on the dishwasher see pages 93–4.) The problems with dishwasher soap etching glassware seem to have passed and new products are much gentler. This is because they include less phosphate, which is the culprit when it comes to etching. Phosphate-free dishwasher detergent is much gentler on your dishes and the environment.

Fragile glass pieces, such as champagne flutes that may have long stems or be particularly fine, should really be washed by hand. Of course you can put them in the dishwasher and they may be okay, but you risk breaking the glass and you'll then be faced with the awful task of removing glass from your dishwasher – not to mention the loss of the glass in the first place. Wash the glass as you would precious china. You can use a plastic tub or line the sink with a towel. Make sure the soapy water is very hot. Use a soft sponge and try a brush designed for baby's bottles for hard-to-reach spots. Rinse in hot water and dry with a lint-free cloth.

How to wash: crystal

Best not to put this in the dishwasher although I know a lot of people who do. Crystal contains lead, which makes the surface softer and therefore easier to scratch. It also makes it less likely to shatter than normal glass. If you do use the dishwasher, do so knowing you may lose the piece. Make sure that you don't overload it and that each piece of crystal has no chance of banging up against anything else. It is very easy to chip the delicate edges of glasses in a dishwasher. A much better way to clean crystal is to wash by hand. Soak the glasses in warm soapy water (water that's too hot may crack the crystal). A small amount of household ammonia added to the water will help give crystal that extra sparkle. You can also wash crystal in 3 parts water and 1 part vinegar to give it a shine.

Try a soft nylon brush for hard-to-reach places, especially in decanters and vases. Another trick here is to add crushed-up egg-shells or uncooked rice to the decanter, with a little vinegar or a mild detergent solution, and shake well. The eggshell or rice will help dislodge any stains (a good tip for all glass vessels). Also try to wash one piece at a time so there's less chance of breakage. Rinse with warm water and set out on a towel on the countertop. Wipe dry with a soft lint-free cloth to prevent streaks. To dry the inside of decanters and vases, you could use a hairdryer set on cool, or roll some paper towel into a cylinder and slide it down the neck of the vessel. Leave it overnight and it should absorb any remaining moisture.

To get rid of water lines in crystal vases, fill with water and white vinegar or a few drops of ammonia. You may have to leave for over a week before you can wipe the mark off. The idea here is to avoid using abrasives. You can also try dissolving denture tablets in the vase and leaving it overnight.

The dishwasher

I initially thought rinse agents were a bit of a plot to get me to spend more money. But I am now a complete convert. They help prevent watermarks on crockery and utensils, and seem to make the glasses extra sparkly. There should be a special dispenser for this, with a setting. If you find you are getting streaking on dishes and the dispenser is full, try turning the setting down. If you're getting watermarks, try it on a higher number. Or just use less or more rinse agent.

Never use dishwashing liquid in a dishwasher as it creates too many suds and will flood the machine. If the dishes aren't really that dirty, use less detergent than recommended.

Most detergents will contain either phosphates or chlorine. Without phosphates there may be white marks left on glasses. You can avoid this by adding a little extra detergent.

No chlorine means there's a reduced bleaching effect that can leave, for example, tea stains on mugs. To remedy this, set the machine on a higher temperature or increase the amount of detergent. Don't put the following in the dishwasher: anything made from wood or with wood on it; anything delicate (glass, china, ceramics); plastic objects that aren't resistant to heat; copper; pewter; silver; anything with a painted decorative pattern; ashtrays or anything else with tobacco ash in it (tobacco ash is fine and can leave a residue on things in the dishwasher); wax or paint.

For the best wash . . .

* Do rinse. Even if the manual says you don't have to, it's important to remove food particles that will clog your dishwasher's filter. Eventually food builds up and that's what makes your dishwasher smell.

* Don't cram. Take note of where the jets are and stack dishes so that water can get to all of them.

* Place anything that may hold water upside down. Anything with a recess or crevice should be placed on a slant to stop water pooling.

* Place plastic containers on the upper rack away from the hottest part of the dishwasher.

* Bowls and plates can be stacked on the bottom or top rack depending on their size. The key here is not to cram too many in. Make sure water can get between everything.

* Don't place glasses too close together as they can smash. Wash any delicate glass or china, or any silver, by hand.

* Use the basket for cutlery. It's easier to place like with like for unloading. The manual for my dishwasher says always put cutlery in random order with handles facing down. That way the water jets can get to the dirtiest part of the cutlery easily. I don't always do that and everything still gets clean. Always wash sharp knives by hand.

* Pots and pans should go on the lower rack and be well spaced to allow water to get at them.

* Platters, cooking sheets, and large serving plates should be placed on the outside edge of the bottom rack to avoid preventing the spray arm from turning. Often, the top rack of the dishwasher can be adjusted to allow for more room below. Check your manual.

How to clean: kitchenware

Look after your kitchenware in the right way and each item will last much longer.

Plastics – these suffer in the dishwasher. Extreme heat and abrasives can permanently pit them, discolor them, and shorten their life. With that in mind, it's not such a good idea to put things like food-processor parts in the dishwasher, even though manufacturers say you can. The exception here is plastic chopping boards – you can put them in the dishwasher.

Plastic containers do seem to hold the smell of whatever has been stored in them. Wash them in very hot soapy water and soak if necessary. You can also try putting in a few teaspoons of cream of tartar or baking soda and leaving for a few days. If they still smell, try putting them in the freezer overnight. Store empty containers without the lid on.

Cast iron – the best thing about a lovely jet black cast-iron pan is that it improves with age. Cast iron is a rather indestructible mix of iron, carbon, and silicon, and it will be the least precious addition to your kitchen in terms of cleaning. My parents still use a pan they bought when they moved into their first house together. My cast-iron pan is looking set to last us just as long.

The care for these treasured pans is peppered with old wives' tales, but one thing is sure – they do benefit from being seasoned when you first buy them. Wash in hot sudsy water, dry with a clean cloth and wipe with oil. Then place in a 300°F oven for 1 hour. My uncle is a chef and, in his commercial kitchen, all cast iron is washed in hot soapy water, then dried thoroughly. He says there's no need to oil a cast-iron pan (after the initial seasoning) because it's not going to rust if it's dry. But my mother swears by washing the pan in hot water (no soap, which she says removes the seasoning) and drying by placing the pan back on the stove over a low flame. She then wipes it down with olive oil before putting it away. Her cast-iron pans, which are in constant use, have a lovely deep black velvety finish. The problem is this does leave oil in the pan that may go rancid if it's not used often, so best not to oil your cast iron unless it's used regularly. And it won't damage the cast iron to be washed in soapy water (I've found it does remove more of the grease). If you find the pan rusts, you can remove the rust with a scourer and simply reseason.

Aluminum – the best way to clean aluminum is with a mild detergent and hot water. Use a metal scourer for hard-to-remove stains and baked-on food. Don't put it in the dishwasher, as it will discolor. If the pan is lined with a nonstick surface, do not wash with anything abrasive and don't use any metal on it. To brighten a dull pot, try 1 tablespoon of cream of tartar in the pot full of water, boil for 5 minutes, empty, and wash as usual.

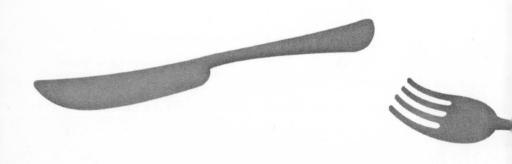

Stainless steel – this is a very kitchen-friendly material. Countertops, your favorite chopping knife, and your cutlery can all be stainless steel. As its name implies, it's a great material for coming into contact with food, as it doesn't stain easily. It can be washed in detergent and hot water using a scouring pad or nylon brush. Strong abrasives can scratch the surface, but don't be put off by these marks. Scratches won't make the pot or pan work less well, they simply make it look liked it's been used. Salt can pit the surface of a stainless-steel pot and leave white marks. The pits are there for good but the marks can be removed with a metal scouring pad. To avoid these marks, add salt once the water is already boiling and stir in well.

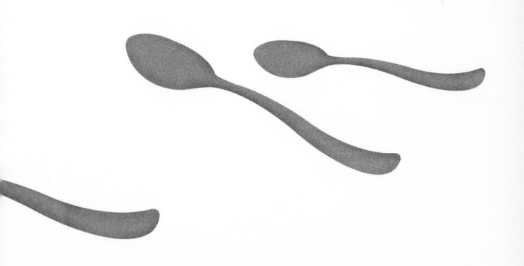

Clean food off utensils and cookware as soon as possible, as acids can etch steel. Stainless is best washed by hand. It can become dull in the dishwasher – the abrasives in dishwashing detergent scratch the surface and, if the detergent contains lemon, the acid can darken the steel. I've found a paste of vinegar and baking soda works well on stainless to get rid of baked-on food.

Silver and silver plate – silver is actually a mix of silver and copper, as pure silver is too soft to use for implements. Silver plate (a thin layer of silver electroplated to a base of copper or brass) and sterling silver (silver mixed with copper) should be cleaned in the same way. You will need to handwash these items in a plastic basin or in a sink lined with a dish towel and then filled with water. Soak the items in hot soapy water for a few minutes and wash with a soft sponge. Rinse in hot water and, while still warm, dry with a soft clean cloth to give the silver a shine. Do not use any kind of abrasive pad on silver, as it will scratch. If you find food is caked on, try removing it with a soft toothbrush.

For shining silvery pieces, I use an old white T-shirt and a polish formulated for silver. Go for a soft lint-free cloth; paper towels can scratch the surface. Wash the piece in warm soapy water before you polish to remove any grit or dust that may scratch the surface. If you are really serious about this job, wear cotton gloves to stop acid from your skin tarnishing the silver. You can also try putting your hand in an old cotton sock and using that as a polishing rag. Follow the instructions given for the polish. Make sure you don't leave any polish in crevices. Use a soft toothbrush or cotton swab to remove any leftover polish.

I must admit I've tried the following and have never had much luck, but some people promise it works. For bulk cleaning of silver cutlery, line a bucket or the sink with a sheet of aluminum foil, sprinkle on some baking soda, add the cutlery, and cover with hot water. Once the bubbles have died back, remove the cutlery and rinse. Buff dry with a soft cloth.

Chrome – you may find chrome as the trim on dining tables and chairs from the 1940s and '50s. It also appears in older style kitchens as the trim along Formica countertops and on old stoves. Don't panic too much if you're not sure if something is chrome. The cleaning of it is gentle and simple and won't damage other surfaces. Simply wipe with warm soapy water and follow with a cloth dipped in clear water to remove soap residue. Buff dry with a clean soft cloth. To protect chrome from moisture, you can rub on a small amount of silicone-based car wax.

Copper – my uncle has an enviable collection of beautiful copper pots and pans. They are a dream to cook in as they heat slowly and evenly. It seems impossible to prepare anything badly in them. But before you invest in one (they are expensive) consider the work in maintaining them.

Cookware made from copper will tarnish easily and should be cleaned following the manufacturer's instructions. If you don't have the instructions, try cleaning by hand in hot soapy water. Don't scour as it will scratch the lining, and never put copper in the dishwasher. Rinse well to remove any soap and buff dry with a clean cloth. Either polish with a commercial product or try rubbing half a lemon dipped in salt over the surface. Rinse well and buff with a soft cloth. You can also use vinegar and salt or a paste of lemon juice and baking soda. Rub it on in small sections but don't leave on too long or it can tarnish. Make sure you dry the pot well after any of these methods and buff with a soft lint-free cloth for a deep shine.

Ceramic – I had a terra-cotta (Dutch) oven that was perfect for cooking chicken. You popped the bird in, tossed in veggies, herbs, and a lemon or two, and fitted on a deep lid. An hour or so later you had a complete meal. The terra-cotta was unglazed and easy to clean as long as I wiped it out immediately after removing the chicken. Make sure you season it the first time you use it. To do this, soak it in water for an hour, dry it, wipe it down with a little oil, and bake at 300°F for an hour. I've read you're not supposed to use detergent on these items but, as with the cast-iron pan, I have used hot soapy water and there's been no problems.

If the piece is glazed, simply wash in hot soapy water. Leave it to soak for half an hour if there are stubborn stains. Then scrub with a plastic scourer.

Glass – bakeware made from glass is best washed by hand as it can become dull when cleaned in the dishwasher. To clean baked-on food, remove as much as you can with a plastic scourer, then soak in dishwashing liquid and hot water. If there's still grime, try a paste of baking soda and water. You can also try adding a few drops of household ammonia to the water. It will help to remove stubborn stains.

Bone – I have a collection of bone-handled butter knives. They are completely useless for anything except putting butter on bread, but I love them. There's something so elegant about the creamy yellow handles and the long thin knife blade. They also take a certain amount of care when cleaning. Water will yellow bone, which will yellow slowly with age anyway. If you want to whiten bone handles on knives, try polishing with a paste made from baking soda and lemon juice. Wipe the paste off with a damp cloth. It's not worth putting these knives in the dishwasher – the hot water can play havoc with the handles and the detergent is too harsh for the silver, causing it to go dull and gray.

Enamelware – enamel is used to coat everything from cast iron (think those lovely covetable Le Creuset pots) to aluminum (those blue-rimmed white mugs that seem to accompany every camping trip). If it's cookware, it's a good idea to season it first. Follow the same instructions as for seasoning cast iron (see pages 95–6). If an enamel pan becomes stained, fill the bottom with bleach and then fill to the brim with cold water. Leave overnight and wash out with hot soapy water. Don't use anything abrasive as you can scratch the finish. For general cleaning, wash in hot soapy water.

Tin – browsing through aisles at the local thrift shop, for some strange reason I'm always drawn to muffin pans. I already own three and don't use them all that often so I really don't need more. But I love the burnished silver of tin bakeware and I think that's why these pans always catch my eye. Tin isn't actually all that useful in bakeware and has been nudged off the shelves by newfangled, dark-colored nonstick bakeware. But you may have tin cookie sheets or loaf pans tucked away in your cupboards and you'll need to know how to clean them. Tin needs special care to prevent rusting, which simply means it has to be dried properly. Wash with hot water and detergent, then put the item back in the oven as the oven cools. This should dry off any water.

Zinc – this is a very soft metal and won't appear all that often in the kitchen. If you have a very old countertop it may be made of zinc. Wash in warm soapy water and buff dry with a soft cloth. For counters or large pieces, wipe down with a few drops of household kerosene. Buff dry with a clean cloth.

Lead – as with zinc, this metal won't appear often in the kitchen (thank goodness, because we'd all be as mad as hatters). But you may find you need to clean decorative items or vases made with lead. Wash in a solution of 1 part vinegar and 1 part baking soda to 9 parts water. Leave in the solution for 10 minutes then rinse in just-boiled water and stand to dry. Big items can be wiped down with turpentine.

Chopping boards – wash these in very hot soapy water and dry thoroughly. If the board is wooden and needs to be oiled, edible oil – olive oil for example – can be used on chopping boards and other wood that comes into contact with food.

How to clean:
kettles, teapots, and electric tea kettles

Check the inside of the pot every few weeks to see if there is any buildup. As soon as you see any, you know it's time to clean.

Purchase a baby's bottle scrubbing brush to clean spouts. They have a narrow brush that is perfect for getting into hard-to-reach spots. Or you can try pipe cleaners – the larger, more hairy ones are best.

Stainless steel, silver – denture tablets are the secret here. Drop them in, fill the pot with water, and leave overnight. Another method for silver teapots is to drop in small shreds of aluminum foil, sprinkle in a few teaspoons of baking soda and fill the teapot with boiling water. Let the water cool and rinse with very hot water. Dry with a soft cloth.

Aluminum – try boiling 2 or 3 apple cores, allowing the water to cool, then washing out the kettle or teapot with hot soapy water. Or, sprinkle a few teaspoons of cream of tartar into hot water in the kettle or teapot, allow to cool, rinse thoroughly, and then wash in hot soapy water.

Ceramic and enamel – 1 part salt to 2 parts warm water. Let soak overnight and rinse thoroughly. Wash with hot soapy water.

Plastic – a plastic electric tea kettle can be filled with ½ cup of vinegar and then filled up with water. Bring to boil and leave over-night. In the morning, bring it to boil again and let stand for a few minutes, then empty. You may need to repeat the boiling step a few times until the sides are clean. Once they are, boil clean water in the machine until the smell of vinegar goes. Some books recommend bleach but I find this leaves a terrible taste in the machine. If you don't like the idea of putting vinegar in the electric tea kettle, try filling it with water and leaving it in the fridge overnight. The next morning, boil the water and the stains inside the machine should dissolve.

French Press coffeemakers – need to be washed thoroughly in hot soapy water after each use to remove any trace of coffee residue, which will make the next batch bitter. Try removing hard-to-budge stains by soaking overnight with 1 part baking soda to 2 parts boiling water. Rinse thoroughly and dry with a soft cloth.

How to clean: the stove

For vitreous enamel and stainless-steel surfaces (that covers most gas stoves) simply wipe down after each use with a sponge wrung out in very hot soapy water. Remove the burners and grates and soak them in hot soapy water in the sink while you clean the stove surface. Most stoves will scratch if you use an abrasive cleanser. Cream cleansers often aren't abrasive and these products are usually fine. But hot soapy water works just as well. Hard-to-remove spots will usually respond if you lay a hot soapy cloth over them and leave to soak. The burners and grates can be scrubbed, dried, and returned to the stove or put in the dishwasher (just check the instructions to make sure they are dishwasher-proof – they should be).

For electric stoves that have ceramic surfaces, the best way to keep them clean is to wipe them down as soon as they have cooled after each use. Use a cloth dipped in hot soapy water. For stubborn marks, try leaving the cloth on them to soak until softened and then scrub off with a soft brush. For a deeper cleaning, use a special ceramic stovetop cleaner, which you should be able to find at the supermarket. If you buy a new stove, often the recommended cleaner is included (mine also came with a very handy little scraper for removing baked-on stains).

Fake coals are now built into some stovetops. They should burn off any food deposits and not require cleaning. Use a stiff brush on the hotplate that sits on top of the coals to dislodge any food. You can also wipe the hotplate with vegetable oil to help retard rust.

If you've used the broiler, the pan will need to be cleaned. This is never a pleasant job but fat left on the pan can be a serious fire hazard, not to mention imparting a nasty smell. Let the broiler pan cool and remove as much fat as you can with a spatula and paper towels. Then sit it in a sink of hot soapy water and let it soak for a few minutes. Give it a good scrubbing with a scourer and rinse well in hot water. Dry with a clean cloth and replace into the broiler (that you've wiped down with hot soapy water).

The outside of the extractor fan and the range hood should also be wiped off after each use. Make sure no moisture is left there and no grease. Once a month, take the filter out of the fan and clean in hot soapy water.

Smells in the kitchen

I never minded cooking smells until we bought this flat where the kitchen shares elbow space with the dining and living rooms. If we cook sausages and forget to turn the fan on, the whole room smells like sausages for hours. Let's just say we don't forget to turn the fan on! The best way to stop smells is to get them before they get you. Make sure the cooking area is well ventilated. A fan over the stovetop is essential. Open windows when you cook. If you don't have a fan and opening windows isn't an option, consider baking rather than frying. At least most of the smell is then contained in the oven.

Once the smell has escaped, ventilate the room well. There's nothing worse than trying to hide a smell by spraying the room with a deodorizer. You then get layers of scent – a touch of lavender with your sausage fat. The only way to really rid a room of cooking smells is with fresh air – and lots of it.

How to clean: the oven

The front of the stove should be wiped down after each use, especially if anything has spilled. Don't use anything abrasive. A small amount of detergent and hot water should remove any problem spots that don't wipe off with a damp cloth. On our Bosch stove you can remove the gaskets and wash them in soapy water. Check your manual to see if this is possible. For the interior, the wire racks are best cleaned as soon as they get dirty so that nothing gets baked on. Wash them in the sink with hot soapy water. Wipe the interior down after each use to make sure bits don't get baked on. If you do this while the oven is still warm, it will be easier to wipe down.

Follow the instructions on your stove's manual for cleaning the interior. If it's a self-cleaning oven (they have a catalytic coating) do not attempt to clean it any other way as you'll ruin the oven's surface. If it isn't self-cleaning, try a commercial oven cleaner and follow the instructions carefully. I must admit I dread this job because the cleaner seems so toxic. Make sure the room is well ventilated and use rubber gloves. Don't let the stuff get on your skin. Spread some newspaper on the floor around the oven as well, to avoid the cleaner splashing on the floor. Apply the cleaner as per the instructions – they usually advise wiping it on (use paper towels that you can then throw out), leaving for a period (two hours to overnight), and then wiping it off. Make sure you then rinse the oven thoroughly with clear warm water to remove any cleaner residue. If you wipe the oven down after you use it, you won't have to do a big cleaning of the oven very often – once or twice a year should suffice.

To clean the inside of an oven, you can also try using household ammonia. First heat the oven to 400°F. Turn it off and put a bowl of cloudy ammonia in the middle shelf (about half a cup of liquid is fine) and a bowl of water on the bottom shelf. Leave overnight. Sponge the interior the next morning with hot soapy water and then again with clear hot water.

Alternatively, cover the entire inside of the oven with a runny paste made of bicarb and water. Leave overnight and wash off with hot soapy water. This is certainly the least toxic option.

Avoid getting the oven dirty in the first place by always placing pans under items that may drip and cleaning spills as they happen, before they get a chance to get baked on.

How to clean: the microwave

Clean as you go. Every time you use the microwave, check for food spills and wipe them up. A good wash with hot soapy water once a week will keep the interior sparkling. Make sure you rinse with clear water and wipe dry. Never use abrasives on a microwave. Try a nylon mesh pad (in fact, anything that you use on non-stick pans will work here). Take out the removable plate from inside the microwave and clean in hot sudsy water. Cleaning instructions with my microwave suggest removing odours by mixing a cup of water with the juice and skin of one lemon in a deep microwaveable bowl. Microwave for 5 minutes. Wipe the inside thoroughly and dry with a clean cloth. Be careful not to get the control panel too wet when wiping down the exterior.

How to clean: kitchen appliances

Kitchen appliances need to be wiped down regularly, especially if they live on a benchtop where they can get dirty from food preparation going on in the area. The following general cleaning method applies to all plastics in the home, including your television and stereo (although do follow the instructions for cleaning the particular appliance whenever possible). Dust well. I use a slightly damp cloth to dust – it captures the dust rather than spreading it around. Wipe down with a cloth dipped in warm soapy water and squeezed almost dry. Use a mild detergent just to be safe. Most plastics can take a slightly acidic cleaner (a vinegar and water solution, for example), but some will react badly and a mild detergent/warm water solution will work just as well. Get into nooks and crannies using an old toothbrush – the bristles are perfect for removing bits from the thread of plastic bottles and crevices in electric beaters.

Rinse with clear water – you don't want any soapy residue left to attract dust. You can try commercial polishes for plastic if you like, but they aren't necessary.

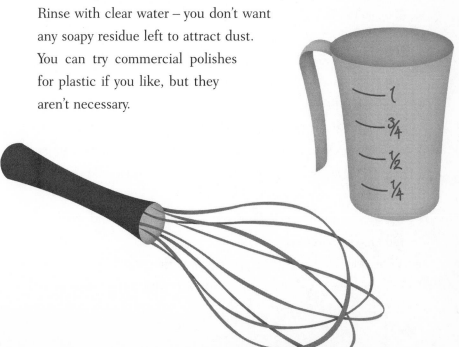

How to clean: the fridge

It's a big job but someone has to do it and do it often. Think of this as a weekly job rather than a monthly (or yearly) one. And if you do it before your weekly shopping, you'll have a nice clean fridge to come home to.

1. Where to start? Begin by emptying. Throw out those containers of leftover takeout you thought you'd take to work, those old bowls of pasta (the lesson here is to learn to cook the right amount). Check use-by dates on jars. In my fridge, capers seem to hang around forever.

2. Pull out shelves (from the door also) and drawers. These can't be properly wiped down in situ. Wash them in a sink full of hot soapy water and leave to dry while you clean the rest of the fridge. Make sure you don't wipe glass shelves with a hot cloth as the heat may crack the cold glass.

3. You can use baking soda and water to clean the inside of the fridge, but a little mild detergent that's not too scented really does a better job. Wipe dry. To make the fridge smell good, finish by wiping it down with a few drops of vanilla on a clean damp cloth.

4. Don't forget the gaskets. You won't have to do these every week, just check them regularly to make sure they are clean. They are a magnet for food crumbs and mold. Use a toothbrush to get into the folds and wipe down with white vinegar to discourage mold.

5. Make sure the shelves are dry, and replace them and whatever food has survived the chuck-out.

6. Wipe down the outside of the fridge with a cloth dipped in hot soapy water. If you like, you can polish with a car polish, but I

don't think that is necessary as fridges have such a high shine finish.

7. If you need to clean the back of the fridge, switch off the machine and vacuum it with the brush attachment.
8. You can deodorize your fridge with a small amount of baking soda. Try placing it in something that gives a good amount of surface area – the more you can get, the better the result.

Keep the freezer working at optimal pace by completely defrosting as soon as you see any ice build-up. If you wait for a big build-up, the job will take twice as long. This is probably a job for once every few months. The easiest way to rid the freezer of ice is to switch off the fridge and empty it completely. Set a pan of warm water in the freezer and wait for the ice to soften enough to be pulled out with your hands. Never use anything but your hands to remove ice. It's easy to pierce the lining of the freezer and seriously damage it. Wash the racks in hot soapy water. Wipe down the inside with warm soapy water and make sure you dry it thoroughly before putting the food back and switching it on.

How to clean: the pantry

Once every so often you should empty out the contents of your pantry and discard anything past its use-by date. Check canisters to make sure they are bug-free (look for cobwebs or eggs, which can be attached to the underside of lids, or little wriggling grubs, moths, or flies). Wipe shelves down with a cloth dipped in hot soapy water, rinse in clear water, and wipe dry. My cousin puts paper towel down on half a shelf in her pantry for oils to sit on. The towel soaks up the inevitable spills and she changes it regularly. I've adopted this easy measure and no longer have sticky rings to contend with when I wipe down my shelves. Restack the shelves, placing cans with cans, baking goods together, cereals together, etc.

How to clean: the sink

To clean a stainless-steel sink, use a small amount of dishwashing detergent and very hot water, rinse, and then dry. Drying will remove any water streaks and buff up the metal. Try using an old towel for this job. You can also try a general-purpose kitchen cleaner on stainless-steel sinks. Spray on and wipe off with a clean dry cloth or paper towel. Never use anything abrasive on stainless as it will scratch. An enamel sink can be cleaned in the same way with hot water and detergent. Don't use abrasives or bleach that will scratch and yellow the enamel. Try removing stains by rubbing with half a lemon dipped in a little powdered borax, or make a paste of baking soda and hydrogen peroxide. Smear it over the area and leave it to dry, then rinse off. Acrylic sinks can also be cleaned with hot water and detergent, but stains should be removed with white vinegar, which is gentler than other removers. The surface scratches easily so don't use abrasives, although scratches can be buffed out with metal polish. Make sure you rinse well after polishing. Corian (see page 117) is a tougher finish so you can use a gentle scourer and detergent to clean. A good way to do a thorough clean and disinfect is to fill the sink with hot water and add a dash of bleach (about 4 parts water to 1 part bleach). Leave for half an hour and rinse well, then dry with a clean soft cloth.

How to clean: taps

If they are brass or copper with a lacquered finish, just wipe with a damp cloth. If they aren't lacquered, you can use a metal polish. Unlacquered metal is also prone to stubborn stains from coming into constant contact with water. To remove, make a paste of salt and lemon juice and rub it onto the spot until it comes off. If this doesn't work, you can try household ammonia. Follow the ammonia with a good rinse with hot water and then polish.

Chrome taps can be cleaned with white vinegar. They'll also respond to a wipe with a cloth dipped in hot water with a dash of household ammonia. Gold-plated taps are easy to clean with hot water and detergent. Make sure you buff dry with a soft cloth. If there are stains, as with chrome, try using household ammonia, rinsing and then buffing. For stainless-steel taps, wash as for gold with detergent and hot water. Polish with a dry cloth or a cloth dipped in a small amount of rubbing alcohol. I've also found that most general-purpose kitchen cleaners clean and shine my stainless taps perfectly well.

How to clean: the drain

There are a lot of ways to clean a drain (which you should do once a week, to ensure it never gets smelly). The thing to remember is that whatever you pour down there will end up in your local water-way. Best to start with the mildest cleaner and slowly step up to the strongest only if needed. So, first try pouring in a good dose of baking soda (up to 1 cup), then slowly follow that with up to a cup of white vinegar. Put in the plug and let it bubble for at least half an hour.

You can leave it overnight. Rinse with boiling water (use hot water, not boiling, if you have plastic pipes). You can also use a solution of 1 part household bleach to 8 parts warm water. Simply pour it slowly down the drain before you go to bed. If the drain needs more than a cleaning, as it is actually clogged, first try using a plumber's plunger. Only if that doesn't work should you resort to enzyme or chemical uncloggers. You'll find them on health food store, supermarket, and hardware store shelves – follow the instructions carefully.

How to maintain: the dishwasher

If grease or white scale appears on the inside of the dishwasher, clean with detergent and a sponge. You can also clean the inside of the dishwasher by pouring 2 cups of white vinegar into the bottom and running the machine on its shortest cycle. Filters should be checked regularly – my manual says after every load.

I probably take a peek inside my dishwasher once a week and inevitably I find an olive pit or a stray bit of lettuce. Remove any food and clean the filter with hot soapy water before you replace. Remnants of food can block the nozzles in the spray arms, as can lime build-up. The arms should be quite easy to remove and clean (check your dishwasher manual). Mine simply pull off. Inspect them once a month for deposits and clean thoroughly in hot soapy water before replacing.

The pump may get blocked by large bits of food that the filter hasn't caught. You will know this has happened if the filter is covered by water. Follow instructions in your manual for cleaning a pump.

How to clean: the trash bin

In an ideal world, you will have a receptacle for the compost, one for recyclables, and another for general trash. Compost and general trash should really be changed daily, but you'll probably do it as soon as the bin is full or begins to smell. My aunt always empties the kitchen bin before guests arrive. It's a good idea as it leaves the bin empty and ready for food scraps, and helps remove any odors lingering in the kitchen from food preparation. Each time you empty a bin, wash it with very hot water and a dash of household ammonia, dry it with paper towels that can then be thrown away, and replace the bin liner. You can rub a little eucalyptus oil over the inside of the bin before you replace the liner, to control smells.

How to clean: countertops

Our countertop runs the length of the kitchen and wraps around into the living room. If it's messy or dirty the whole room feels chaotic. As a result I've become quite a fanatic about keeping it clean. As a general rule, one of the best ways to keep a kitchen clean is to wipe surfaces with a sponge dipped in hot soapy water and then follow with a dry clean cloth. The wet sponge gets up the dirt and the dry cloth buffs the surface. If I don't use the cloth, watermarks are left on the surface and it doesn't look clean. Our bench is laminate but this method will work just as well on stone, metal, or wood surfaces.

Laminate – a thin sheet of plastic attached to a thicker board of wood (usually chipboard). Choose a laminate that has the same color all the way through the plastic layer so scratches will show up less. Laminate is not a very tough surface – you will have to use a chopping board. Heat can melt the plastic so keep a board or trivet handy for hot pots. Put down protective mats for flowerpots or anything that may slide and scratch the plastic. Don't let water sit on the laminate, as it can get into the seams and soak into the chipboard, causing swelling.

To clean laminated counters, do not use anything that is abrasive. Even mild abrasive cleaners can scratch these surfaces. Clean with a mild detergent and buff dry with a clean cloth. Once a week, before you buff, wipe down with a sponge dipped in clear water. (Soap residue can eventually dull and etch the surface.) Add a few drops of eucalyptus oil to the water to act as a disinfectant. I also have friends who swear by window cleaner for a smear-free cleaning, but it's not really necessary.

For hard-to-remove spots, try laying a hot damp cloth over them. This will stop too much liquid sitting on the laminate but will help soften the spot to be removed. Scrub the spot off with a soft nylon brush dipped in white vinegar, or you may just be able to wipe it off with a soft cloth. I find an old toothbrush handy for stubborn spots.

Removing stains from laminate is risky as it is easily damaged, so do a test patch in an inconspicuous place first. Try lightening the stains with a paste made from baking soda and water. Spread it on and let it stand for a few minutes before gently wiping it up, rinsing with water, and drying. If it seems to be working, repeat the process until the stain disappears. Some stains, like ink or beets, may be permanent. In this case, call the manufacturer for help. You could try using bleach on the spot, but I don't recommend it. It can easily ruin the laminate by stripping the color or making the surface permanently dull. You may need to replace it if the spot is really bad.

Laminate does scratch quite easily. You can polish with a non-oily furniture polish or plastic polish once or twice a year. It won't get rid of the scratches but it will help conceal them. Car polishes also seem to hide scratches and shine the surface well.

Corian – a stone substitute which comes in three finishes: matte, semigloss, and gloss (all Corian sinks are matte). This surface is tougher than laminate but still needs to be cleaned gently. It won't take kindly to heat so make sure you use a trivet. Also, use a chopping board when cutting. Clean with a plastic scourer and hot soapy water. Try tackling stains with an ammonia-based cleaner. Your Corian dealer will also recommend commercial cleaners. They all work well but are not essential for cleaning.

Minor surface damage, like a scratch or cut from a knife or stains caused by chemicals or food, and scorches or burns, can be removed by using a light abrasive cleaner (like Brillo). If the mark doesn't respond to this, you may need to sand back the spot. Wet the surface first to help minimise dust and then use a fine sandpaper (400 grit) over the stain. If this isn't successful, you'll need to have the whole piece repaired.

Tiles – clean as for laminate, and do not use abrasive cleaners as they may scratch the tiles' glaze. Tiles will lose their gloss if soap isn't rinsed off, so try using a splash of vinegar in the warm water to rinse after wiping down countertops with warm soapy water. Grout can be scrubbed clean with a toothbrush dipped in a solution of 1 part household ammonia to 10 parts water. Make sure you rinse the ammonia off and wipe dry with a clean cloth. For stains on the tile surface, try the hot damp cloth method as for laminate (see page 116) or rub with half a lemon dipped in salt.

Wood – if sealed, you can treat wood in much the same way as tiles and laminate (clean by simply washing down with warm soapy water, making sure you rinse well). Stains and some burns can be sanded out of this surface. You will then need to reseal. Make sure you don't use the surface as a chopping board, and don't place hot items directly on the wood as it may burn. If the wood isn't sealed, treat it with a mineral oil (food oils like vegetable oil can become rancid). You'll need to wipe regularly with oil to stop the wood from cracking. To clean, wipe with a cloth wrung out in hot soapy water.

Stone (marble, granite, slate, reconstituted stone) – these materials are porous and need to be sealed properly if they are to be used for a copuntertop. When the counters are installed, sealing them should be part of the process.

Marble – clean by wiping the surface with warm soapy water. The surface is porous so you don't want to get it too wet. As with tiles, make sure you rinse with clear water.

To remove stains, try mixing baking soda (or talc) with water and a small amount of ammonia, bleach, or hydrogen peroxide (never mix bleach and ammonia as it produces toxic fumes). Scrub the spot with a soft toothbrush and make sure you rinse well. You may have to repeat this process a few times to get rid of the stain. One supplier also recommends cleaning stains with a mixture of chloride of lime (a white powder used in bleaching and disinfecting) and water. Make a paste, apply to the stain, then wipe off and polish. You can also try cleaning with a little toothpaste. Wipe a little over the spot with your fingers and rub until the stain disappears.

Rinse and buff. Marble can be polished using a good beeswax and a soft cloth.

Granite – clean with a cloth dipped in hot soapy water. Wring the cloth out well. You don't want water to sit on the surface as, like marble, this stone has a porous surface. It will also absorb fats and oils so look out when you are cooking. Try cleaning stains as with marble or use a few drops of household ammonia to clean greasy spots. Don't use abrasives to clean as they scratch the polish.

Slate – clean with hot soapy water. Try wiping with lemon oil and buffing with a soft cloth to give a nice shine and minimize scratches.

Reconstituted stone – clean as for laminate, using hot soapy water. This is a mix of aggregate, pigments, and polymers with up to 97 percent quartz. It doesn't absorb water, and is resistant to acid and scratching. It comes in an array of colors, some very similar to granite. It doesn't require sealing.

Stainless steel – you can buy special cleaners for this surface or clean with hot soapy water or vinegar diluted in water, and buff with a dry cloth. Window cleaners also work wonders. Don't use anything abrasive as it will leave scratches on the surface (steel wool can also leave behind fine particles that will rust). It's easy to remove stubborn dirt by dabbing on a bit of straight detergent – leave it on for a few minutes and then wash off with hot water. You can polish the surface with rubbing alcohol. Don't cut directly on this surface as it will scratch and also dull your knife; always use chopping boards. Foods containing acid can bleach out the metal if left on the stainless-steel surface for a long time. Try removing the white area using a fine scouring pad, making sure you scrub with the grain.

How to clean: splashbacks

These take a good beating – especially if you like to cook a lot at home. Glass, metal, and tiled splashbacks can be treated in the same way. Always wipe them down after each meal. Fats and oils can be wiped down with a sponge wrung out in hot soapy water. If there's a lot of fat, wipe up as much as you can with a paper towel before you use the sponge. Buff with a dry cloth and the splashback should look as good as new. You can use commercial sprays for this job but, as in most cases, hot soapy water is just as good. The grout in tiled splashbacks may get stained. Try scrubbing with a toothbrush dipped in 1 part chlorine bleach to 5 parts water or 1 part household ammonia to 10 parts water. Wipe down with a clean damp rag and then buff with a dry one.

How to clean: cabinets and drawers

In a busy kitchen you will need to wipe down most cabinets and drawers daily, especially around handles. For my cupboards, I used a polyurethane finish on medium density fibreboard (MDF), which leaves a lovely clean shiny surface, and white laminate for the insides of all storage areas. It's cheap, easy to keep clean, and looks crisp.

Laminate cupboards – wipe with a commercial surface spray or try a vinegar and water solution. Dry with a clean rag. Try a paste of baking soda and water on stains.

Painted cupboards – oil-based paint takes wiping better than water-based paint. Try cleaning with warm water and vinegar, or an all-purpose cleaner. Follow with a clean damp cloth. As with all wood surfaces, make sure you don't use too much water. To remove grease, use ammonia and water. Don't use abrasive cleaners or scouring pads, as they will scratch the paint surface.

Wood cabinets – use a sponge wrung out in hot soapy water for everyday cleaning. It depends on the finish as to what you do next. (See wood floors on pages 47–53 for general wood care.)

Tidying cabinets is an easy job. Simply empty out the cupboards one by one, wipe down the shelves with a hot soapy sponge (add a few drops of household ammonia to the water to get rid of grease), rinse in clear water, and wipe dry. Replace pots and pans in each cabinet.

Empty cabinets once a month and give a thorough cleaning. Wipe down all surfaces with an all-purpose cleaner or white vinegar and water. Wipe with a clean dry cloth. Make sure the surface is completely dry before you replace the items.

Drawers – will benefit from a weekly tidying. You may not want to do all the drawers – I find the top cutlery drawer and the drawer below the oven that holds bakeware collect the most dirt and food bits during the week, so I just do those. Empty them, wipe them out with a damp cloth dipped in warm soapy water, let them dry, and then replace everything. Do a thorough tidying, and clean-up once a month or so, to prevent things from getting out of control.

The top of your cupboards will need a good cleaning. It's not the most exciting job, as the dust up there is often mixed with cooking fat and can get thick and sticky. A good wiping-down with a sponge dipped in hot soapy water will do the trick. If it's really dirty, add a few drops of household ammonia to the water. Dry with a clean cloth. Do it as often as you can bear it (at least once a year during your spring cleaning).

How to clean: kitchen walls

Ideally, this is a monthly job. In the real world, you'll probably get to it once or twice a year. Don't fret. Even once a year will make for a much better-looking wall. It is amazing how grimy walls and ceilings get, especially in the kitchen. The cleaning methods here apply to walls anywhere in the home. High-traffic areas really benefit from a monthly cleaning.

Necessities

****

* **2 buckets** – 1 with water and cleaning solution, the other with plain water
* **Rags**
* **Broom**
* **Vacuum**
* **Ladder**
* **Drop cloth**

First get rid of any cobwebs with a broom covered in a rag. Then vacuum to remove as much dust as possible. You'll need a long-handled brush attachment on your vacuum cleaner.

Fill one of the buckets with warm water and a few drops of a mild dishwashing detergent or all-purpose detergent. Try not to make too many suds as they just make the job harder. You can also try mixing 1/2 cup of vinegar with 2 teaspoons of borax and 5 quarts of water. Wring out the cloth or sponge until it is barely wet to stop any drips that will streak. There is a debate as to whether you should start at the top or bottom. I always thought it best to start at the top and work your way down so you can catch drips as you go. But there's also an argument for starting at the bottom and working up – because dirty water running down a dirty wall can be harder to remove than dirty water running down a clean wall. Whichever method you are following, try breaking the wall down into a grid in your mind. Start at the top left, for example, and work your way across in squares that span your reach.

As you complete one square, rinse the area with a clean rag dipped in clear water. Change both lots of water regularly so you aren't wiping dirt back onto the wall. Wipe and dry the patch of wall with a third cloth – it helps here to have another person working with you.

For general maintenance, a vacuuming and spot-cleaning are all you will need. If the walls are shiny (and therefore probably an enamel paint), take a damp cloth and wipe down any marks, then rinse with a clean cloth. Stubborn marks sometimes respond well to a gum eraser. For matte walls, you can try washing a small area with a barely damp cloth to see what the results are. More often these kinds of walls will need to be repainted if they get really dirty. With that in mind, and if you have the choice, it's best to use a slightly glossy paint in the kitchen and high-traffic areas, as those walls will need to be more thoroughly washed.

4. The Dining Room

My parents are great ones for dinner parties. I can remember lying in bed as a child and falling asleep to the ebb and flow of dinner-party conversation. My husband and I have carried on the tradition and I love a good dinner party. The key for me is to make it as relaxed as possible. After a week of work, the last thing you want is to stress over the right table napkins and serving dishes. These days, a great dinner party calls for a few basic ingredients – good friends, delicious food and wine and, most importantly, a comfortable spot to dine.

With the recent trend to open up houses and have multipurpose spaces, the single room devoted just to dining is not so common anymore. More often, dining rooms are defined by a rug and some pieces of furniture. This makes arranging these spaces very important. If you do have a separate dining room, you'll need a table, chairs, a sideboard to hold plates of food and store china, silver, and

linen, and perhaps a china cabinet if you like that sort of thing. If the room is small, consider built-in cupboards or shelves that can be tailored to fit your needs exactly. For a more formal dining room, think about heavier curtains; they will add sumptuousness to the room without overpowering it. For less formal rooms, especially when it's a dining area that merges with another room, perhaps a simple blind might be more appropriate. Unlike the bedroom, you don't really have the same privacy issues with a dining room, so another option is to leave the window bare and enjoy the view.

When you're setting this room up, think about the style of the rest of the house and how you like to entertain. If you are the cook and you don't want to be separated from your guests, an open-plan kitchen that includes the dining room is a great option. Our kitchen and dining room open onto the living room. We've marked it off visually by placing a large rug in the living room and leaving the area under the dining table rug-free. My cousin, who is an interior designer, has done the opposite to great effect. Her kitchen, dining room, and living room are one huge space at the back of the house. She has a rug under the dining table and another under the coffee

table where the couches are placed. The rugs give each space a very clear definition. But rugs and carpets in dining rooms seem like a bad idea to me – a bit like carpet in bathrooms. Wherever there's the chance of carpet getting wet, it's best to avoid it altogether. If you do have a rug or carpet under the dining table, be prepared to tackle stains swiftly (see pages 43–6 for stain removal in carpets). The quicker you get to stains, the better.

I find the hardest thing about my set-up is that I'm cooking right under people's noses. There's no escaping, no counter to hide behind, so any disaster (and I have had my fair share, including discovering a whole baking dish of potatoes cooked to a blackened mass) is very public. It also calls for a level of tidiness, which is not my first inclination when cooking – like my father, I tend to use every pot in the kitchen. But I have got used to it, and I do love having people to chat to while I cook. The ideal design would be to have a chest-high counter that I could work behind. You also need a quiet dishwasher and plenty of sink space for dirty dishes. A good vent above the stove is essential for controlling cooking smells, and an open window is a nice addition.

The dining table

Buying furniture for the dining room can be a bit of a challenge. The French provincial dining table you've been lusting after may be right out of your price range. Stores like Pottery Barn and Ikea have lots of choices here, but I do wonder whether our houses – especially our dining rooms – are all beginning to look rather alike! Who wants to live in a house that looks like a furniture catalog? Check out your local Salvation Army store for cheap finds that will add character to your home. Friends of mine nabbed an excellent dining set (a table, eight chairs, and a sideboard) for $400 at the local junk shop. They had the chair seats reupholstered and the whole thing cost them less than $1,000.

Or, better still, find a local carpenter who can build you exactly what you want. Have photographs of pieces you like and make sure you have a good idea of what color you'd like the table to be. They'll want to know if you'd like solid wood or veneer. Veneer is cheaper and probably fine if you use the table only occasionally. Solid wood is more expensive but it will last a lot longer and really is best for a table that is going to be used often. Also consider what kind of finish you'd like. My parents have a polyurethane finish on their dining table that gives a lovely silky shine and is easy to clean. But you don't get much sense of the wood underneath. The grain is completely covered by the glasslike finish. A wax finish is softer and gives you a better feel for the wood but will take more time and effort to maintain (see wood floors on pages 47–53 for general information on finishes and how to maintain them).

Perhaps your budget may stretch to antiques or collectibles – early Australian kauri pieces or a great Danish-designed piece from the mid-twentieth century. You know you'll get something with a bit of life and history if you buy an older piece. A good friend recently moved house, and she and her husband bought a dark wood sideboard and dining table with matching chairs from their local antique dealer. They'd bought pieces from him before, so they could be confident that the furniture they bought was good quality. I think quality is the key to antiques. To me, it's not whether the table and sideboard are Georgian and match perfectly but whether they are sturdily built and lovingly cared for. The best way to find that out is to buy from someone you trust.

We've used everything for a dining table except an actual dining table. For a while we had a door we converted by screwing legs to each corner (it was rather wobbly) and now we have an old desk that my father built. It's much more stable but a bit too narrow for an ideal dining table. You will need a table large enough for your needs and for comfortable chairs. Expanding tables are handy. One thing to look out for – don't get carried away by fancy leg design. Make sure that the table legs aren't in the way when you put in the maximum number of chairs. The best place for leg decoration is flush with the corners or as a pedestal.

A good guide for dining table dimensions are:

* Table surface height – 30 inches.
* Elbow room – 24 inches is enough room for an adult to use a knife and fork comfortably.
* Leg room – 24 inches between the underneath of the table and the floor.
* A rectangular six-seater table – allow a minimum measurement of 60 × 40 inches.
* A circular dining table – 42 inches in diameter will seat four people, for six people it should be 48 inches, and for eight the table will need to be 60 inches in diameter.

Regardless of the size, you'll need 30 inches behind each chair to make it easy to get up and down. Also consider sturdiness. When buying a table, lean on all sides of it to make sure it is stable and doesn't wobble.

Table finishes

Bleached wood appears almost white and is often finished in a lacquer to protect the surface. Painted wood (gloss or semigloss) is another choice of finish that is easy to clean. Wooden tables can be finished in linseed or tung oil. The surface will scratch easily but a very light sanding and reoiling will fix the problem. It could also be sealed with a hard finish (usually polyurethane), which is much more durable, although it can still scratch. If the finish does get badly scratched, you will need to remove it completely with a thorough sanding and then refinish it, usually with a few coats of polyurethane. Wax provides a protective coat either on its own or over the top of other finishes. The level of sheen depends on the amount of buffing you do. To protect a precious table, use a pad (often made from felt) between the cloth and the table.

Wash a wooden table down with a cloth wrung out in warm water. Don't use soap on soft finishes as this will dissolve the finish. For hard finishes, you can use soapy water. Wooden tables with a soft finish will need to be rewaxed (see pages 140–5 for details on how to care for your dining table).

If you have a glass-topped table, wash it with white vinegar in hot water and polish with newspaper. For granite- or marble-topped tables, you'll need to be careful because these stones are porous. Clean up spills immediately. To clean marble that has been polished, wipe down with a cloth wrung out in a little hot soapy water, and then buff dry with a clean cloth. You can use beeswax to give the marble a polish after cleaning. Wash unpolished marble in the same way.

Dining chairs

These are notoriously expensive. I had rather cheap and nasty dining chairs for a while and you couldn't spend much time at the table without the circulation to your legs being cut off. I've now invested in some very comfy chairs and wish I'd done it years ago. Good chairs will last a lifetime (or two) so are worth the investment. If your budget is tight, try shopping for secondhand chairs, scouring the sales (don't forget local garage sales) and checking the local classifieds.

No matter where you are buying from, always sit in a chair first. Like a mattress, there's no way of telling if the chair is right if you haven't sat in it. My husband is six feet tall and I am five foot four, so our chair needs are a little different. It took us a while – and a lot of testing – to find the right chairs. (The ideal seat width is anywhere from 16–18 inches.)

Upholstered chairs are a popular item for dining because of the comfort factor. The important thing is to get fabric that is easy to clean. It's essential, no matter what the fabric, to get it treated for spills before you spill anything. You can try Scotchguarding it yourself (follow the instructions on the can). However, having attempted this smelly job myself on one occasion, I'll leave it up to the experts from now on.

How to set: the table

To make entertaining as stress-free as possible, try to be organized. I get out all the tableware and glasses well ahead of time so I'm not fishing around in cupboards when the guests are here. It makes sense to have things like water pitchers filled and wine opened before people arrive. As far as food goes, I try to prepare something that won't keep me in the kitchen all night. If you are doing more than one course, make sure at least a few things can be prepared beforehand. I'll often put a salad together and leave it in the fridge to be dressed just before serving. A good friend of mine, who doesn't really like dessert, either serves cheeses and fruit (which are trouble-free) or places a big bowl on the table, full of storebought ice-cream pops. It's always fun to end an informal dinner with a Popsicle, and it saves on the dishwashing.

One of my jobs as a child was to set the table. My mother was taught how to set the table by her mother and she in turn taught me. It's so important to get this right. The thing to remember is that once you know the rules, it's fine to break them. But you must know them first. It's very simple really. The fork goes to the left of the plate, with the tines pointing to the ceiling, and the knife (blade pointing to the plate) and any spoons (soup or dessert with the bowls of the spoon facing up) to the right. Jeffrey Steingarten, the food critic for American *Vogue*, says that the base of knives must line up, while the tines of forks must align – although I'm not sure many of us really go in for such detail. For family dinners we always had the napkin folded under the fork but, if you are setting the table for a formal dinner, you might have the napkin neatly folded on the side plate (which is to the left of the fork). Glasses sit above the knife. When setting cutlery, think about how the food will be served. Whatever you need first should be placed on the outside, so that you work your way toward the plate. If you are serving bread, place the butter knife on the right. Once the napkin from the side plate is on your lap, the butter knife can perch on that plate when not in use.

Our dining table is quite small, so I might place dessert cutlery (spoon or small knife) above the plate rather than beside it. I also know people who place the knife and fork together on the napkin,

on the left side of the plate. I really don't think it matters too much as long as everyone can find everything!

Once you've mastered the rules, have a bit of fun with your table setting. Perhaps replace flowers with some beautiful pebbles. Or write people's names on the pebbles and they become place cards. Use food as a centerpiece – whatever is in season and looks good. Have your kids decorate placemats made from cardboard for an informal family gathering – the grandparents will love it! None of these things takes much time – just a little thought.

How to set: the atmosphere

For my mother's last birthday we had a dinner party and lit the whole room with candles. I must admit it was a little too dark to eat by and we did end up turning on a lamp or two, but that initial impact of the candles instantly made the evening feel special.

If you include candles on the table, make sure they aren't too close to wineglasses. I've had the unpleasant experience of picking up a very hot glass that was too close to a candle. And don't forget the rest of the room. Tea lights on a windowsill or a sideboard will give a soft warm glow and make the room seem more inviting.

For lighting over the dining table, a pendant light controlled by a dimmer works best. Just make sure the shade doesn't hang too low. Our neighbors have a very cool globe that dangles over their glass dining table, but once you sit down you can't see the person opposite! (See pages 11–12 for more on lighting.)

The tablecloth

I don't usually use a tablecloth. I like to see the wood of the table so I use mats, and I like the idea of a runner although I've never seen one I liked enough to buy. If you want to use a cloth, make sure it's well chosen for the occasion. For a dinner party you can't go wrong with a heavy white damask cloth. But for lunch that might seem too formal so try a lighter cotton fabric. I would always choose white as the color for the tablecloth regardless of the fabric. I think food and tableware add enough color and I don't like the look of a busy cloth. If you do introduce color, make it neutral or soft so that the food and table setting aren't competing with the cloth for attention. One of the things I learned when I was working on *Martha Stewart Living* magazine was how to mix colors and tones to great effect – either playing with the same tones or using contrasting colors. Shades of blue or green mixed with crisp white or a sandy stone look beautiful. Or shots of color – a deep red napkin at Christmas on an all-white table – can also work well.

Store tablecloths and all table linen in a deep drawer in the kitchen, if you can. Or perhaps there's space in a sideboard. You'll find you use these pieces more often if they are easily accessible. If there is not enough room, devote a shelf in your linen closet to kitchen linen. In my old apartment, I was very tight for space and kitchen linen was stored in a large plastic tub that slid under the bed. Launder as you would any cotton fabric. (For removing stains from fabric, see pages 279–81.)

How to clean: the dining room

For this room, as for every room in the house, the same basic clean-ing principle applies – start at the top and work your way down. If you don't use the dining room often, make sure you visit it at least once a week to make sure it doesn't get musty. The biggest task will probably be dusting. (Read pages 158–69 for dusting techniques.) Clean this room as often as you feel it needs it. Make sure you air the room regularly.

Care for your dining table and chairs, and any other wooden pieces in the dining room, to ensure that you will have them for a long time. If you do nothing else, make sure you dust all wooden pieces regularly – either with a cloth or vacuum. Dust on wood is like sandpaper and will grind into the surface, ruining a finish (no matter what the finish is). To remove dust from intricately carved wood, use a soft brush – try a soft paintbrush or a baby's hairbrush. Keep water away from all types of wood, regardless of the finish. Once water soaks into the wood, it expands, causing warping and sometimes staining. (It's fine to wipe a table down with a damp cloth, just don't let water sit on the surface for any length of time. See page 144 for information about watermarks.)

To polish or not to polish . . .

You don't have to polish finished pieces. The finish is enough to pro-tect the wood and when it dulls the piece will actually need to be refinished. But you can prolong the life of the finish (and avoid hav-ing to refinish as often) by waxing or oiling the surface to make it too slippery for dust to cling to. But don't overdo it – too much wax or oil can attract dust and dull the surface. If the piece was finished with a wax, it will need to be rewaxed regularly. For some pieces, twice a year will be enough. For others, like a dining table that is in constant use, once a week might be needed. When the piece becomes dull, buff well with a soft cloth. If it doesn't shine then it needs a wax or oil. (See page 145 for different types of wax and polish.)

Urethane-finishes – distinguished by a hard, almost plasticlike surface. Clean weekly, or as often as needed, with a cloth dipped in mild detergent and warm water. Make sure you dry the piece thoroughly once it's clean. You won't need to polish after cleaning.

Lacquer, varnish, or shellac finishes – often used on antiques. These finishes are more delicate than urethane and need to be carefully cleaned with warm water only, as solvents may dissolve them.

Matte finishes – usually wax or oil (you can feel the grain of the wood). These finishes are less hard than urethane and should only be wiped down with a damp cloth dipped in warm soapy water. If a matte finish is particularly dirty, try wiping down with a cloth dipped in mineral turps. This will remove the grime and also any waxy build-up. The piece will need to be waxed or oiled again. See page 142 for polishing. You'll know you need to rewax when buffing can't bring up a sheen. Don't use aerosol or liquid furniture polishes as they can dissolve a wax finish. Maintain the sheen by buffing after you've dusted with a lamb's-wool duster or lint-free cloth.

To polish wooden furniture, wipe off old wax using a clean cloth splashed with a small amount of linseed oil. Take a scoop of wax (a good walnut size should be sufficient to cover a dining table, dresser, or chair, although of course it depends on the size of the furniture and how dry it is) and wrap it in the middle of a square of clean, lint-free cloth. Knead until the wax is soft, then spread over the furniture. The trick is to cover the furniture with a very thin coat of wax – as thin as you can get it. You are done when the entire piece is covered. Once the wax has dried, which takes 5 to 30 minutes (test it with your finger), give the piece a good buffing with a clean cloth. Apply more coats of wax in the same way for a deeper shine and more protection.

Scratches and marks

Tables with oil or wax finishes will scratch easily but are also easily fixed. Harder finishes like urethane won't scratch as easily but are much harder to fix once they do scratch.

Urethane-finished pieces – check your local hardware store for the vast array of scratch cover-up products and follow their instructions to the letter. You'll find wax sticks, liquids, and even felt-tip pens. If the piece is valuable, it's always best to ask a professional to look at it.

Waxed or oiled pieces – simply clean and polish (see pages 140–2). A scratch in a lacquered or varnished piece may be fixed by laying a rag soaked in linseed oil over the scratch and leaving it there for a few minutes, then polishing and buffing. Check a small patch first to make sure the oil doesn't turn the piece dark.

Painted wooden pieces – can easily be wiped down with a very mild warm water and vinegar solution. Rinse with a clean cloth and dry well. If the mark is particularly stubborn, try a paste of baking soda and water. Rub the paste on with a soft rag. (See also how to clean painted surfaces on page 33).

Laminated wood pieces – a plastic laminate may be used to finish wooden furniture (or metal pieces for that matter). Think of a classic 1950s dining table – metal legs, chrome trim, and a laminate top. To clean, use warm soapy water and then rinse with clear water and dry thoroughly. To help remove greasy stains, you can add white vinegar to hot water and wipe well. Don't use abrasives as they will scratch the surface.

Heat or burn marks – may be polished out of a soft finish using a mild abrasive like toothpaste. Protect your dining table by using tablemats for hot dishes and plates.

Watermarks – appear as white rings on varnished furniture because moisture has been trapped under the finish – from a glass of water, anything hot, or even a vase of flowers. This is why your grandmother always whisked coasters under your glass when you put it down on her antique coffee table. The marks often disappear if you use a hairdryer on a warm setting.

Waxes and polishes

A solid wax is more durable than a spray or oil polish. And the harder the wax, the better the protection.

Carnauba (from the Brazilian wax palm) is a good hard wax. **Beeswax** is not as hard and is often mixed with carnauba (but it does have that lovely smell). You can buy colored and clear wax. Use only clear wax on unfinished wood. Choose a colored wax for finished furniture that is slightly scratched and often the scratches will disappear. **Liquid wax** is applied with a brush and takes two or three coats to build up a protective finish. **Paste wax** is applied with a pad of fine steel wool or a lint-free cloth, and buffed with a dry duster for a finish with depth. When you buy a dining table and chairs, check whether you need to do anything to the surface before you use it. In most instances, the shop will have taken care of everything and will be able to tell you how to best care for your furniture.

Furniture polishes containing oil (usually silicone oil) protect wood by making it slippery so that dust cannot stick (although too much oil can attract dust). Always follow the directions for each product carefully; not following the instructions can lead to a sticky mess. **Linseed oil** is good for small objects only, as it takes a few days to dry and doesn't form a hard surface. Boiled linseed oil is only marginally better. **Tung oil** is most durable, although it takes 24 hours to dry. You'll need five or six coats, with light fine sanding between coats to get a good finish.

Dining room disasters

✱ Candle wax can be removed from crystal candlesticks by standing them in a cool place to harden the wax. Remove as much as you can with a fingernail or ice-cream stick. Be careful, as both implements can scratch crystal. There will be a small amount of wax remaining and it can be cleaned off with rubbing alcohol or eucalyptus oil.

✱ To remove wax from silver candlesticks, follow the same directions as for crystal but remove any remaining wax by washing the candlestick in very hot soapy water. Then rinse in clear hot water and dry with a soft cloth. Use the cloth to buff off any remaining wax.

✱ To remove wax from a tablecloth, you need to first harden the wax. Freeze it with an ice cube and then chip away at it with a dull knife or spoon. When you've removed as much as possible, lay a paper towel on your ironing board, place the wax stain on top, and lay another paper towel on top of the stain. Press with a warm iron until the wax is removed. You will need to replace the paper often to absorb the wax properly. Then wash the tablecloth. Use a prewash spot-remover on the wax stain and launder as for that fabric. If the spot remains after the first wash, try washing it again with a small amount of bleach or enzyme detergent.

✱ Remove lipstick from napkins by placing the stain face down on a paper towel and sponging firmly with a prewash spot-remover. As the towel becomes soaked, replace (you'll use quite a few paper towels). Rinse the napkin and then rub detergent around the edges of the stain until the outline has gone. Wash as you would for that fabric. If the spot remains, try repeating the process. My mother looks after her damask napkins by soaking them overnight in a bucket of water with enzyme detergent (follow the directions for that brand to get the proportions right). Then she simply puts them in the machine on a hot setting.

5. The Living Room

My husband and I seem to spend a lot of time in the living room, whether we're playing with Jack or watching television or reading – if we're home, one of us is in this room. After the kitchen, this is usually the most public space in your home. Our living room says a lot about the way we relax. The main concern in a living room is to get comfortable furniture that is versatile enough to cope with all the different functions of the room. The formal living room is a place to sit with guests, sharing a drink before dinner. It's a room for entertaining, not a place for children, whereas the family living room has a whole other life and seems to be a magnet for life's clutter. You will need at least one sofa, the size of which depends on your household. A coffee table and bookshelves are sensible additions, too. If you have children, it's a good idea to have a dedicated spot for toys. A basket or cupboard where they can be stored away is very handy.

We have a long, low built-in unit that houses the television, stereo, CDs and an amazing amount of other stuff (including china). It means that I can close the doors and all those bits and pieces are instantly hidden away. I think this is important in a small space – you don't want the room to be overwhelmed by equipment, especially as televisions just seem to get bigger and bigger!

Light in this room should be soft. It doesn't have to be brightly lit – you can have standing lamps or table lamps positioned in spots where you read. We have a lamp at the end of the couch where I like to curl up with a book, and also a table lamp. If you've got a lamp with a shade for reading, make sure the shade is just at eye-level to stop light shining in your eyes. The lamp should be positioned slightly behind you so the light doesn't cast shadows on your book. When we have guests, both the lamps are turned on and cast a lovely soft light in the room.

How to choose: carpets and rugs

Looped carpet – something most of us will buy at some point in our lives. For example, ubiquitous wool 'sisal' carpets (which seem to pop up in every interiors magazine) are looped. It's easy to maintain (see pages 38–46 for details) and looks great no matter what style of house you have. In a looped carpet, fibres are pushed through backing material and another backing material is then applied to hold the loops in place. There's a huge range of styles. The loops may be left whole for a berber (leaving a loop of wool that looks a bit like a tiny pebble), cut short to create a velvet pile, cut at different heights for a textured rug or left extra-long for a flokati-like finish. (Flokati rugs remind me of Afghan dogs – very long and hairy, super-high maintenance and very '70s! Flokati rugs recently made a comeback, but include one in your home at your own risk. They are notorious dust- and dirt-catchers and, as they are usually white, the long wispy pile shows marks easily.) A multi-level loop has a variety of loop heights giving a textured surface. Cut and loop pile is a mixture of both cut and loop styles.

Woven carpet – usually more expensive than looped. It can be more fragile than looped as it does not have extra backing material. Woven rugs are often made on a loom, where the threads are woven through yarn held taut in a frame. For handwoven rugs, yarn is knotted or tied to a background yarn, or a hook may be used to pull yarn through in a similar process to that used for tufted carpet. Natural fibres used in woven rugs include grasses and sisal (from the leaf of the sisal plant found in Indonesia and Africa), coir (from coconuts) and cotton. Cleaning these means a thorough vacuum. As these materials are prone to mildew and rotting, you should not shampoo or wet them. Spot-clean where necessary and hang outside to dry thoroughly. If you can't hang them, use a hairdryer to dry the affected area.

Oriental rugs – made using one of two knots – a Ghiordes or Turkish knot, or a Senna or Persian knot. The Turkish knot is a twist while the Persian knot is a proper knot. Wool or silk is tied to a warp yarn with the ends pointing up to form the pile. The more knots you have per square centimetre, the better quality the rug. A real oriental rug will have fringing at each end that is the leftover warp yarn – the fringe won't be sewn on (as it is on fake rugs!). In an authentic rug, you should be able to see the design on the back of the rug.

Oriental rugs are often hand-knotted and so can be quite deli-cate. If it's a new rug, it's fine to vacuum it as you would your carpet. You can also spot-clean as usual, but check a small area for color-fastness. If it's an antique or a particularly delicate rug, lay a mesh screen over it, weight the corners with books, and then vacuum. Dirt will come up through the screen but the carpet is protected. You can also try covering the nozzle of the vacuum cleaner with nylon mesh.

Braided rugs – made from fabric rolled and then braided into ropes and sewn together, often in a large coil. If they are small, they can be washed in the machine (place inside a pillowcase) on a gen-tle cold cycle. Try putting vinegar in the final rinse to help get out all the soap. Dry in the dryer on low/cool or drape over a drying rack (this is best if you are worried about shrinkage). You can try washing large rugs in the bathtub, but wringing out the water can be a dif-ficult job. Take large rugs to the dry cleaner or do it yourself with a commercial rug cleaner. Follow the directions on the product.

Kilim and dhurrie – flat, woven-wool rugs. They are reversible and often a lot cheaper than oriental rugs. They are long-wearing and should be vacuumed regularly, as you would carpet. The main prob-lem with cleaning these rugs is colorfastness. Check to see if there are any care instructions and wash as per carpet.

Sheepskin, fur, hides – can be washed in the machine, with a small amount of wool detergent and on a cool delicate setting, whenever they look grubby (probably two or three times a year). Dry flat in the shade. I fluff my sheepskin rug with a brush as it dries. Cowhide rugs and fur floor coverings all benefit from regular vacu-uming. If anything is spilled on them, blot it up immediately and clean as for carpet (you can try a laundry detergent prepared for wool rather than ordinary detergent), but send it to the dry cleaner to be professionally cleaned if the mark is hard to lift.

How to choose: upholstered furniture

When I think of upholstered furniture, I always come back to the couch my parents bought when they first married. It was a thrift shop find, a solid wood construction covered in black- and white-striped nubbly wool with big soft round arms and a gently arched back. Over the years, it has been re-covered in salmon-colored cotton and then a slate-blue linen. It is now retired to their bedroom where it sits gracefully in a bay window and provides a lovely spot for an afternoon snooze.

When buying upholstered furniture, there are a few things to look out for . . .

* A frame made of kiln-dried wood is better than softwood like pine. Particle board is used in cheaper pieces and, although it is strong, it can chip or split.

* Wood joints should be strong. Look for dovetail or mortise and tenon (a reliable indication of quality furniture). Joints that butt up to one another and are screwed together are not as strong.

* You want the piece to feel heavy. If it's light or flimsy, it won't last.

* Check that there is no sagging in the middle of larger upholstered pieces. If there is, it means that the piece is not properly supported.

* Check the coils. Steel coil springs are what you want.

Cushions are a matter of preference. You get what you pay for. If you want a firm cushion that will keep its shape, go for one filled with latex or foam. If you like the softness of feathers, try a feather and foam mix as it won't go flat as easily.

How to choose: fabric for furniture

Different fabrics are good for different pieces; choose appropriately and you'll make your life much easier. The best fabric for furniture is a cotton-linen mix. If it can be removed, you can clean this fabric yourself in the washing machine. If it can't be removed, it can easily be spot-cleaned.

Although I've seen some very beautiful patterned fabric for furniture, my *Martha Stewart* days taught me that it is probably best to go plain – at least when you're starting out. Choose a simple fabric in a classic color and, if you want to follow fashions, you can accessorize with cushions or throws. This is certainly more economical than changing the fabric on the whole couch (which can sometimes cost as much as a new couch when you factor in the price of the fabric and the labor involved in reupholstering). If you do choose patterned fabric, don't be afraid to mix different patterns – one trick I learned as editor of "Domain" is that as long as the colors match, you'll have no problems mixing stripes with florals or other graphic patterns.

Choose from the following fabric types:

Acetate – developed to look and feel like silk. It can wrinkle and fade, so it's not good for large pieces of often-used furniture. It does resist fire, mold, pilling, and shrinking.

Acrylic – developed as a wool substitute. It does pill so isn't good for high-use pieces, but it has a good resistance to fire, wear, soiling, fading, and wrinkling. The higher the quality, the less the pilling.

Cotton – resists wear, fading, and pilling well, but doesn't resist fire, wrinkling and dirt. Can be treated or blended with other fibers to fix those problems.

Linen – doesn't pill. As with cotton, it has a poor resistance to fire, wrinkling, and dirt. But, also like cotton, it can overcome its less desirable qualities when mixed with other materials.

Nylon – like acetate, developed as a silk substitute. Will fade and pill but does resist fire, wrinkling, and fading. It's one of the strongest fibres and is rarely used on its own. In a blend, it lends its good qualities to natural fibers like cotton and linen.

Polyester – bad resistance to pilling, but good resistance to fire, fading, mold, and wrinkling. Not often used on its own as upholstery fabric – usually blended or used for lining.

Rayon – made to imitate silk, linen, and cotton. Good resistance to wear but not to fire and wrinkling.

Wool – good choice for upholstery as it is resistant to wrinkling, fire, pilling, and soil.

How to clean: fabric and upholstery

The best way to keep upholstery looking good is to protect it before it gets dirty. Often, furniture is sprayed in the factory – check with the retailer to find out if that has happened. If it's been sprayed with fluorocarbons, it will be oil- and water-resistant. If it's been sprayed with silicone, it will only be water-resistant. If it hasn't been sprayed, you can do it yourself. The supermarket sells treatments for protecting furniture. Silicon and fluorocarbons both work best on cotton, rayon, linen, and nylon fabrics.

For general care and maintenance, vacuuming is the best way to clean fabric. Dirt, dust, and grime build up and eventually wear the fabric down, so regular vacuuming is a must. Some people use the soft-brush attachment but I find the normal vacuum-cleaner head (on a carpet setting) works best on large pieces because the head is wider and catches more dirt. The soft-brush attachment is good for smaller pieces and getting into crevices. Make sure you vacuum with the nap (run your hand over the fabric – with the nap is smooth, against is rough).

Every year, treat the furniture to a professional cleaning. If you get a few pieces done, it averages out to around $30 a piece and is definitely worth doing to prolong the life of couches and chairs.

To clean nonremovable fabric, you should really rent a steam-cleaner or get a professional in. If you want to do it yourself, follow the directions for that steam-cleaner and use only the cleaning fluid recommended by the manufacturer. These machines use force to get the fluid into the fabric and then suck it out. They are very strong and may damage delicate fabric. If you want to wash by hand, use the foam from a bucket of hot water mixed with upholstery-cleaning

detergent. Apply foam with a soft scrubbing brush and remove with a damp cloth rinsed in warm water. Do a section at a time. Make sure you don't saturate the fabric. Dry fabric thoroughly – if it's a small patch, try using a hairdryer.

Cleaning furniture with slipcovers is a little more straightforward. Even if the slipcovers have been preshrunk, wash in cold water and line-dry. Iron using a starch spray. Put back on furniture while still very slightly damp; they will finish drying and take the shape of the piece. Make sure the room is well ventilated and don't use the furniture until completely dry.

To remove stains, the general rule is to get rid of as much of the offending material as possible: scoop up what you can with a spoon, blot up any liquid, and scrape off anything that is sticky using a blunt knife. Make sure you blot with a white towel or paper towels – you don't want to make the stain worse by adding color from the thing you are blotting with. Once you've removed as much of the spot as possible, a sponge or cloth wrung out in warm soapy water works wonders with most marks. The trick is to get to them straight away. If you are worried about spot-cleaning the fabric, try using just the foam from a bucket of soapy water and a very soft brush.

Leather

I know exactly which leather couch I want, from a store in Sydney. It's broad-limbed and covered in the most perfect dark brown leather. The problem is, it's so broad it won't fit in the apartment – not to mention the fact that we don't have a spare $5,000 to spend on a couch. But if we had the room and the money, that is exactly the piece I'd get!

The most common sort of leather used in furniture is protected or pigment-dyed leather. It is an excellent covering for high-use pieces and is easy to maintain. My father has a lovely leather wing chair made from pigment-dyed leather. He's had it for years and its caramel brown color has gone dark and wrinkly with age. It's the little scratches and marks that are making it age so gracefully. It is easily cleaned by simply wiping with a barely damp cloth and polishing occasionally (see page 162).

Pigment-dyed leather is made to give you a more stain-resistant surface. It is processed to even out markings and grain patterns, and additional color is added to the surface with pigments. The degree of softness is determined by the amount of work done on the leather and the pigmentation used. Pigment-dyed leather is also more consistently colored than natural leather and won't fade.

You can tell if a piece is pigment-dyed if you lightly scratch the surface and the mark left is not lighter than the rest of the leather. Another way to test is to apply a leather cleaner to a small patch. If it's pigment-dyed, the cleaner will sit on top of the finish on the leather and will not darken it.

Occasionally you'll find natural leathers used in furniture upholstery. These leathers are tanned using chromium salts, then

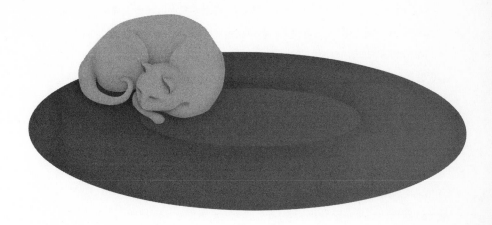

aniline-dyed with transparent colors. There is no mechanical cor-
recting of the hide's natural surface. That is why you can see a wide
variety of natural grain patterns and color. Aniline leather is soft
because the leather is left in a natural state. This also makes it more
likely to absorb stains and to fade over time. You can tell it's aniline
leather if you lightly scratch the surface (in an inconspicuous spot!)
and the scratch leaves a lighter color. This will also happen if the
leather is nubuck (a velvety soft, combed leather very like suede
that's tanned and treated in a similar way to aniline). The other
test is to wet your finger and lightly rub it onto the leather. Aniline
leather should darken slightly but dry invisibly. Nubuck will dry a
little darker.

How to clean: leather

While leather is the toughest of all upholstery materials, it does need some care. As well as any food or drink spills and general wear and tear, perspiration, grime, and body oils can damage leather if not removed frequently. A wipe-over with a warm damp cloth once a week is generally enough to keep leather in excellent condition. You can spot-clean leather using plain water. Just make sure the leather doesn't get soaked through, and never leave water standing on leather. Most spills on leather won't penetrate, they will pool on the surface, and are easy to simply wipe off. Warm water and a small amount of saddle soap or glycerine soap are also safe to use on leather (although always check on an inconspicuous spot first). Make sure you rinse with clear water and towel dry. Do not use ordinary general-purpose cleaning agents as they can cause cracking and make leather sticky. Wax also leads to a grimy buildup.

For a more thorough cleaning, dust the piece first using a soft clean cloth. Then polish using a product designed specifically for leather. Follow the instructions on the bottle. Never use a product made for wood or upholstery as they can contain solvents that will damage the leather. If you notice cracking in the surface, follow the polish with a conditioner (using the instructions for that product). Make sure the piece is perfectly dry before you sit on it again.

For general maintenance, rub the leather with a small amount of leather conditioner and buff dry with a clean cloth once every two months. Leather will absorb the conditioner best if it is warm – so warm the room with a heater or, if the piece is small, try warming it with a hairdryer.

How to remove: stains on leather

To remove greasy marks like butter or oil, wipe up any excess and then just leave it. Normally the grease will soak into the leather and disappear. If this doesn't happen, you will have to call in a professional. For tough stains like ink, you can try using regular toothpaste (not gel) or hairspray. Use a tiny amount, apply toothpaste with a clean cloth or spray hairspray directly onto the stain, and gently rub off. You may need to repeat the steps a few times and finish by wiping down with a cloth wrung out in warm water to remove any residue. Be sure to test on an inconspicuous spot first.

The coffee table

Use an old chest, an upturned wooden fruit crate, or a stack of leather suitcases, or splurge on a classic – the Isamu Noguchi coffee table is my favorite. Just make sure your coffee table is sturdy and not somewhere people will trip over it. Glass coffee tables make cleaning very easy: wipe with 1 part vinegar to 4 parts water. Use paper towels or a lint-free cloth to dip in the solution and wipe down the surface. Wipe with a dry cloth to buff. Most sticky spots will come off if you lay a rag soaked in water and vinegar over them. For other stains, like paint, try carefully scraping off with a razor blade. Older-style wooden sideboards often have a glass surface, which should be cleaned the same way.

How to clean: metal finishes

To clean metal finishes – such as the base of a lamp, coffee-table legs, or a wrought-iron wine rack – wipe with a damp cloth wrung out in hot soapy water. Wipe metals with a slightly damp cloth to catch dust. Wipe with a mild vinegar and water solution to remove tacky dirt. Rust can be a problem for metal pieces. Always make sure you dry them thoroughly after you wash them. Some rusty pieces of furniture may continue to rust no matter how clean and dry they seem. Scrub flaky spots with a wire brush and consider sealing the piece with a matte polyurethane.

Aluminum – wipe with 1 part metho to 5 parts water (straight from the tap). Consider polishing with a silicone-based car wax, although this isn't really necessary.

Chrome – use a few drops of ammonia in warm water to clean chrome. Polish as for aluminium.

Stainless steel – wash with hot soapy water, rinse, and dry thoroughly. You an also try a little rubbing alcohol to give it a shine.

Wrought iron – wash as for stainless steel, making sure you dry well as it can rust. If it does rust, sand off the spot with a fine grade steel wool dipped in a little turpentine. Polish with liquid wax.

Wicker furniture

I think porch furniture when I think wicker – creaky, comfy, relaxed pieces that you sink into for a read on a sunny summer afternoon. I'm also reminded of a bedroom set a friend had in primary school that I deeply coveted. It was a white-painted wicker bed with a matching side table and I thought it was the most beautiful thing I'd ever seen.

Wicker, bamboo, cane, and rattan all belong to the same family of furniture. Branches from woody plants are bent and woven to shape furniture. The furniture is usually lightweight and often used outdoors, although a recent trend for natural shapes and textures has seen wicker pieces making a comeback for interiors.

If it is to be used outdoors, the best finish is a painted one. Either enamel or polyurethane will protect the furniture from the elements and can be touched up when it weathers. Cleaning consists of keeping the piece well dusted. Use the soft-brush attachment on your vacuum for best results. If the piece gets really dirty, you can spot-clean using mild detergent in warm water. Apply with a soft cloth that's wrung almost dry, scrub with a toothbrush if needed, then follow with another cloth dipped in clear water to remove any soap residue. Dry thoroughly with a cloth. Leave in the sun, if you can, to dry completely. Don't use the piece until it is perfectly dry as wet wicker is weak. If it is unsealed, follow the same cleaning instructions but, once thoroughly dry, wipe down with a little bit of lemon oil to help prevent cracking.

How to clean: art and collectibles

It's these pieces that make a house yours. They reflect you, your likes and dislikes, your whims and wishes. Minimalism is soothing in this cluttered busy world, but hiding everything away can be very clinical and, at the end of the day, a rather uninspiring way to live. Don't be led by others – surround yourself with the things you love.

All art and collectibles will benefit from regular dusting, but some materials need special attention when it comes to cleaning.

Brass – to bring the shine back to brass knick-knacks, front-door knockers, or old door handles, use a polish formulated for this metal that contains a wax. This seals it from the elements and stops any kind of a patina forming. If you want a patina, use a polish without wax. To remove tarnish on unlacquered brass, try mixing a paste of lemon juice or vinegar and equal parts salt and flour. Rub the paste onto the spot with a dry cloth, leave for a few minutes, and rub off. Then wash thoroughly with hot soapy water to remove any residue. Dry and buff to polish with a clean cloth. Or just soak a cloth in vinegar, dip in salt, and rub over the piece until the tarnish has gone. Rinse and buff well. Once a year, polish with a brass cleaner, following the product's instructions. To maintain lacquered brass, simply wipe with a dry cloth. To clean, wipe with a lint-free cloth wrung out in warm soapy water.

Bronze – this is an alloy of copper and tin and is a very hard metal. Figurines, sculptures and, to a lesser extent, fittings and fixtures can incorporate bronze. Dust regularly and clean by polishing with a cloth dipped in boiled linseed oil, then buff with a chamois. Don't wash with water.

Ceramics – if these are unglazed, it's important not to immerse them in water when cleaning. Just wipe them down with a slightly damp cloth. If fully glazed, you can immerse in hot soapy water and dry with a lint-free cloth.

Clocks – treat these as you would artwork. Clean the outside as you would for whatever material the clock is made from, and have the inside looked at by a professional if need be.

Cloisonné – this enamel-work should be treated as you do fine china. Wash in warm soapy water, rinse and dry with a soft cloth.

Gold – picture and mirror frames can be gilded in fine paper-thin sheets of gold but you can also find gold turning up in antique furniture, vases, bookends . . . all manner of places! Dust with a soft paintbrush or feather duster. A good way to clean frames is with a can of air (available at camera shops). Professionals use these to clean delicate lenses and they're perfect for ornate frames. My aunt and cousin are gilders and see a lot of frames badly damaged by overzealous cleaners. The only way to clean a gilded frame is to brush off the dust. Never use anything that's wet or even damp, as this will remove the gold. If it needs more than that to clean it, check with a professional. Water gilding can be particularly fragile and even wiping with a damp cloth can damage it. If the piece is solid gold, you can clean it as for silver: wash in warm soapy water, rinse in warm clear water, and polish dry with a soft cloth.

Ivory, horn, or bone – don't let water near these items – it causes ivory to yellow. Wipe with a dry cloth. Don't use solvent or chemicals. If the piece is covered in a tacky dust, wipe very gently with a just-damp cloth (wring it out in warm clear water). Make sure you dry it thoroughly (use a hairdryer on cool if needed).

Lacquerware – these objects are usually made of wood and covered with layers of shiny lacquer. Essentially it's a painted finish and should be treated carefully. Dust well and wipe with a barely damp lint-free cloth.

Nickel – old toys, figurines, vases, cups – all can be made from nickel, or nickel-plated. This is a hard silvery-white metal that resists corrosion well – hence its use in batteries. Wash in warm soapy water and buff dry with a clean cloth.

Pewter – this alloy of tin and lead is a lovely deep silver-gray in color. Vases and other vessels may be made from pewter. You might also find figurines or decorative pieces that include pewter. Wash in warm soapy water. Buff dry with a soft cloth. If the pewter is tarnished, make a paste of vinegar, salt, and flour, and rub onto the spot. Leave to dry and rub off with a clean cloth. Rinse in warm water.

Shells – boil in fresh water with a little household bleach to clean. Dry thoroughly. If shells get dirty, wash them in warm soapy water.

Tortoiseshell – wipe with rubbing alcohol to clean, and buff with a soft cloth to get a shine.

How to hang: paintings

I'm not too particular about this. I know there are certain rules – for example, if the ceilings are low, you should hang the artwork high up to give the illusion of height. It's also recommended that you hang paintings just slightly above eye level, and avoid – if you can – covering art in glass as it reflects badly so that you can't see what's behind it.

Most of our paintings hang on a large windowless wall along one side of the living room. When we first moved in, I laid the art out on the floor – several medium- to smallish-sized works – and arranged them so they made some kind of sense. With the help of my brother, I then hung them in the same arrangement on the wall. I would always recommend placing paintings on the floor in position first, because then you can juggle and rearrange them.

Make sure the wall can take the weight of the paintings. Talk to the hardware-store owners – I'm sure they'll be able to give you advice on what sort of nails you'll need (there are screw systems especially designed for softer walls). There are also excellent hanging systems available where a track runs along the top of the wall by the ceiling and adjustable metal strings hang down to hold the painting. They are available at hardware stores and are a modern version of the old picture rails, which still feature in many houses.

If you're having to store paintings for a time, consider hanging them at the back of closets or cabinets rather than stacking them against a wall. This way the frames are kept from holding any weight and air is able to circulate around the painting. If you do have to stack them, wrap each painting in acid-free tissue first and think about bubble-wrapping the corners of the frames for protection. Paintings, prints, and photographs require regular dusting with a dry cloth or soft paintbrush. Always hang or store them away from sunlight.

How to store: photographs

I am truly terrible at putting photographs in albums. My friend Clare not only religiously puts hers in albums, she also labels everything. Taking inspiration from her, I once asked for photo albums for Christmas but have yet to put a single picture in . . .

When you display photos, keep them away from direct light as this will fade them. Color photos fade more quickly than black and white. Keep the surrounding area free of humidity as this encourages mold. With that in mind it's best not to hang photographs in the bathroom or too close to the kitchen work areas where steam is produced.

How to clean: home-theater systems

It's no good just having a television anymore. Our living rooms have to incorporate a whole theatre of equipment that includes a television (the choices are enormous), a DVD and CD player, and speakers for surround sound (they usually include a bass speaker as well as smaller speakers to spot around the room). It is best to get a professional to install this as the speakers need to be carefully placed to get the full effect of the surround sound. Your retailer will be able to recommend someone to install it. Keep TV and music paraphernalia dust-free by wiping down with a lint-free cloth. You can remove fingerprints with a clean damp cloth and, for particularly grimy equipment, use a cloth dampened with a small amount of rubbing alcohol. To clean the inside of the equipment, follow the manufacturer's instructions. A small soft paintbrush often comes in handy here. The television screen can be cleaned with a soft cloth dipped in warm soapy water and wrung out until it is just damp.

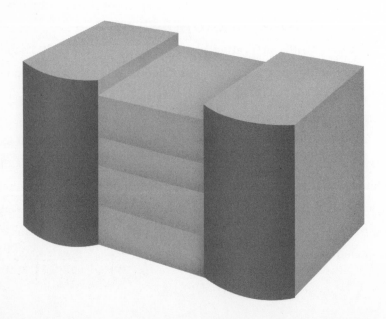

Don't try to clean the inside of a video tape. The best you can do here is to wipe the outside down with a cloth to remove dust. Dust stereos and DVD players with a soft brush or use the brush attachment on your vacuum. Greasy marks can be wiped off with a cloth dampened with a little rubbing alcohol.

CDs and DVDs – use a barely wet cloth dipped in mild detergent to wipe a disc. Make sure you wipe in straight lines from the inside out, not in circles, and be very gentle. Wipe dry. Only clean a disc in this way if it is very grimy with fingerprints. Keep dust-free with a clean dry cloth or a soft brush.

Records – use a record-cleaning solution available from retailers. Dust with a soft brush. We had a black velvet duster that came with our turntable which was perfect for cleaning records. My husband had a huge collection of records that were collecting dust on the bookshelves. When I got pregnant, he packaged up all but a dozen precious ones and sold them. (We bought a very nice baby carriage with the money he made!) We realized we were lugging the records around from apartment to apartment and never listening to them. I think the same rule goes for records as it does the clothes in your closet – if you haven't used them in twelve months, they need to be pretty special to retain a place in your home.

How to clean: the piano

I have to confess to being completely and utterly bereft of any musical talent. But that hasn't stopped me loving music and having a great and deep respect (tinged with a little jealousy) for all those who can play an instrument and sing in tune. The most common instrument to be found in a living room is a piano. Because of its size, it functions as a piece of furniture and should be cleaned accordingly. Other instruments (cellos and violins come to mind) need specialist care best given by an expert.

Dust is the enemy of the piano. Keep the lid down and the keys covered when not in use. Direct sunlight can also adversely affect the piano, bleaching its finish. Try to place the piano away from windows. A good friend insists on placing a piano by an internal wall so that it won't go out of tune as quickly – he says external walls vibrate too much and the heat and cold is more inconsistent near an exterior wall. This makes sense when you consider that the instrument is mostly made of wood and felt (wool) – both of which are sensitive to moisture. If there's not enough moisture in the air, the instrument will go flat more quickly; too much moisture will make it sharper and may cause rusting. A humidity level of 45–50 percent is best.

Dust carefully and polish the wood with a wood polish (see page 142 for how to polish wood). Protect the piano by placing a cloth over it during parties. Inevitably, someone will put a drink or plate of food down on it, and a cloth will help prevent damage.

Older keys are made from ivory that will yellow over time. You can't clean this yellow off so please don't try! Newer piano keys are made from plastic and won't yellow. Dust the keys often and, if there are marks, wipe with a clean white cloth that is just damp. Follow straightaway with a dry cloth. I don't recommend tackling a difficult stain yourself. If a damp cloth doesn't remove it, you could repeat the same method using a very mild detergent and water solution, but it's best to call in a professional. You don't want even a small amount of water getting into the piano.

Every two or so years, the felt on the hammers hardens and will need softening. Call in your piano tuner at this point. (The manufacturer could probably recommend a technician, or try your local piano store, music school, or even church. It's always best to get a recommendation.)

Moths are attracted to the felt that covers the hammers. If you use the piano often, you won't have a problem with these pests. If you don't, try putting a moth repellent inside the piano – get advice from the tuner or retailer as to which one to use. It may be best to do this only when you are storing it, otherwise you'll have a repellent-scented piano in the middle of your living room!

The fireplace

They are not the most efficient way of heating our homes (they produce the kind of heat that warms whatever is close by but not the air) but there are still a lot of fireplaces in houses and apartments, and there is something lovely about an open fire in a living room. Before you begin lighting fires, it's a good idea to get to know your fireplace – in particular, check that the flue is not blocked.

Hearth – the fireplace floor. It extends out into the room to protect flooring from sparks.

Grate – sits in the fireplace and holds the wood off the fireplace floor. Allows ash to fall through and air to circulate up through the wood, helping the fire to burn.

Damper – the flap at the top of the fireplace that opens into the flue. It controls how much air gets into the fireplace.

Flue – the area above the damper that should be lined with fireproof material.

Cap – at the top of the chimney to prevent rain coming down it.

To maintain a fireplace, you'll need the essential tool-kit: a brush and broom designed especially, a poker, tongs, a shovel, fuel (newspaper, kindling, and logs) and matches. A fire screen is also a good safety measure.

How to light: a fire

Open the damper and place five or six sheets of balled-up newspaper in a heap on the grate. On top of this, place a small stack of kindling. On top of the kindling, place a few small logs. These will hold the kindling in place and ignite as the kindling burns down. My father taught me to stuff paper into the flue and light it before you start the fire, to warm the chimney up. This way a draft is created and when you light the fire under the kindling, it is drawn upward more easily.

Light the paper on the grate, starting at the outside edges. Before the fire gets hot, adjust the damper so that it is half open. This way the fire can still draw but the heat is encouraged to go into the room rather than up the chimney. Once the small logs have taken, add a few larger pieces.

Make sure you burn only dry, well-seasoned logs. Young sappy wood (like pine) will leave the chimney coated in creosote, which is a serious fire danger. You also want to choose a hard wood as it burns longer and hotter than softer wood. Check with local fireplace dealers regarding the availability of firewood. Or, better still, if you have a sawmill nearby, see if you can collect their hardwood off-cuts. Around our neighborhood you can also buy logs at most of the gas stations. In place of logs, you can choose to use briquettes made especially for fireplaces – these should be easy to find in your supermarket or hardware store.

How to clean: the fireplace

Clean the outside first. Use a vacuum to suck up soot and dust around the fireplace. Gently rub off any remaining soot with a soft brush. It's important to remove any loose soot as it will mix with water and cause black smears. You can try removing smoke stains from bricks with a mix of 1 part bleach to 4 parts water. Use a strong brush to scrub at the stains and rinse with warm water, and a mild detergent to remove any lingering bleach.

Brick – wipe down with 1 part vinegar to 1 part warm water. Follow by wiping down with clear water. A solution of household ammonia mixed with warm water will remove stubborn stains.

Ceramic tiles – wipe with a milder vinegar and water solution (1 to 4). And, if needed, polish with a liquid wax.

Glass – glass doors can be cleaned with a commercial glass-cleaner, or try a solution of 1 part vinegar to 1 part water. Scrub with hot soapy water if needed. Add a dash of household ammonia if really dirty.

Marble – wipe with a cloth wrung out in warm soapy water. For stains, rub with a paste of baking soda and water. Rinse with clear water. Buff to dry and polish. Pale marble surrounds will take a weak bleach solution. Rinse well and polish with a liquid wax.

Metal – wipe down with a cloth wrung out in mild soapy water. You can wipe cast iron down with a small amount of vegetable oil to prevent rust. Polish other metal with the appropriate metal polish. (See page 165 for more on cleaning metal.)

Stone – sponge with warm soapy water. To remove stains, mix powdered pumice (from supermarkets or hardware stores) with a little household ammonia to make a paste. Then treat as for marble stains.

Then clean the inside of the fireplace. Scoop out the ash left over from the last fire (once you are sure it's not hot). Leave a bed of ash about 2 inches deep to help you with the next fire (it will hold hot ash, let the next fire burn longer, and protect the fireplace floor). Sweep out the top of the fireplace, the damper, and the flue. Dust slowly and carefully so you don't get great clouds of ash billowing up in the room. Give the outside of the fireplace a final wipe with a damp cloth to catch any dust that might have emerged during cleaning. Best to use a metal bucket to carry the ash outside in case any ash is still hot. At the end of winter, brush out all the ash thoroughly so it won't be blown around by any breezes.

6. The Bedroom

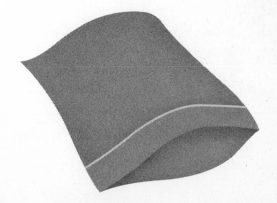

I really

think of our bedroom as my room. Not that it's particularly feminine; it's just very inviting. It's a large room with a high ceiling and very pale-blue walls. There's an enormous deep-set window that frames a eucalyptus tree. From bed, I look out through the leaves to patches of sky. I could be anywhere. It's the perfect room for dreaming and that's what a bedroom should be: a place to relax, sleep, dream, read; a place to be lazy and quiet. I don't think this is the place for crazy-colored walls, busy wallpaper, or too much art. Surround yourself here with things that you love to look at – it might be photographs of family or a painting of a landscape or a beautiful silk kimono suspended on the wall.

You may share your bedroom with a partner and sometimes your kids, but by and large this is a very private space. That means two things – you want this place to be a haven, but also somewhere you can do things you might not do in the rest of the house. If you've always lusted after a really ornate chandelier, why not put it in the bedroom. Hopefully your partner will agree.

You don't need much furniture in a bedroom. A bed, bedside tables, storage, a full-length mirror, and perhaps a comfortable chair is about it. An overhead light is essential. You need to see well as

you dress. We've got my desk and a desk chair because I work in the bedroom. I know experts say that's not a good thing, but when you live in a two-bedroom flat there's not much choice!

There's a debate about whether carpets, which certainly harbor more dust than wood floors, are healthy in bedrooms. My parents have carpet in their bedroom and it feels comfortable and luxurious, and has made that bedroom a lovely haven. We have floorboards and I have a sheepskin rug on my side of the bed. The whole room doesn't have the same luxurious feel as my parents' bedroom, but I know there's a lot less dust in here and I like the smooth glossiness of the boards -- not to mention the fact that they are easier and quicker to vacuum than carpet.

Sleeping soundly

Some people cope with noise at night, some need silence. After living in New York, I can tolerate street noise – luckily, because we live on a very noisy street.

If you have a choice when selecting your bedroom, you might think about choosing the quieter side of the house if noise is an issue. There are other measures you can take – hanging thick curtains, double-glazing the windows, or covering the wall with bookshelves (books are excellent insulators against noise). You could purchase a machine that makes white noise, or install a ceiling fan or air conditioner that will also make noise to mask outside noises. I find, though, that you eventually get used to the noise and stop "hearing" it. It probably sinks in at some level but it doesn't stop you from sleeping.

How to choose: a bed

The recent trend in beds has seen their legs shortened until some are really just glorified mattresses on the ground. One thing to remember when purchasing a bed is that the closer you are to the ground, the more you will notice (and breathe in) any dust in the room. The most important thing is that you are comfortable, so make sure the bed frame is sturdy – there's nothing worse than a bed that creaks every time you roll over.

There's an enormous amount of information around on mattresses – number of springs, best types of filling (latex, wool, cotton, etc.), padded tops, unpadded tops . . . The only way you can tell if a mattress is right for you is to test it. There is no objective measurement of "firm" and "soft" – you must decide for yourself what is best for you. In this instance, it's often the case that the more you spend, the better the mattress. Scrimp elsewhere.

You want two things in a mattress – softness so that your bones don't poke into a hard surface and make sleep elusive, and enough firmness to stop your body sagging and keep your spine smoothly aligned. Without good back support, your spine will be held in an awkward position that usually results in a sore neck and headaches.

The most common type of mattress is an innerspring. Coils of steel are covered with soft padding. The more coils, the longer the bed will last. Look for 300 coils for a double bed, 375 for a queen, and 450–600 for a king. Educate yourself to a certain extent but don't panic if you can't tell the difference between 12 springs per 4 square inches and 15.

When shopping for a mattress, wear shoes you can easily slip off and comfortable clothes, and make sure whoever sleeps in the bed with you is willing to also test the mattress. A good test of whether it's right for you is to lie flat on your back. Your spine naturally curves, so place your hand under the small of your back. If it is hard to get your hand in there then the mattress is probably too soft. If there's room for another hand it is probably too hard. If it slides in easily, the mattress should be just right.

Pillows

I always find choosing a pillow a daunting task because they are so hard to test. How do you know if a particular pillow is right for you? Generally, if you sleep on your side (and you should as it's better for your back), you'll need a firm pillow to support your head so that your spine makes a pretty straight line (parallel with the mattress). Once I realized that, I had a much easier time buying pillows and abandoned my love affair with feather-filled pillows for a sensible Denton foam pillow that's wrapped in cotton padding. However, if you sleep on your stomach, this kind of pillow will give you a sore neck, as it holds your head too high. If you are a dedicated stomach sleeper, then feather pillows are probably best because they won't raise your head in an awkward position. There's a huge choice of pillows at most department stores. The number of pillows you have is a matter of individual choice. My husband and I have two each. We sleep on one, but need the other to prop ourselves up to read.

For help choosing a pillow, check out the Web site www.tenthring .com/pillow.html. For tips on washing pillows, see page 278.

Bed linen

Each bed in your house should have three sets of linen (top and bottom sheets and pillowcases to match): one for the bed, one in the wash, and one spare – just in case. You'll need two mattress protectors. Other pieces include pillow protectors (a slip that zips and sits between the pillowcase and pillow). Don't overstock on bed linen. You can't use it all and it will just age ungracefully in your linen closet. A mattress pad is essential. This can be cotton or wool, and it will stop the sheets slipping over the synthetic material that commonly covers a mattress (it usually feels nicer than sleeping directly on a sheet over a mattress).

When buying sheets, make sure you like the feel of the material, that it will wear well, and that you can wash it easily. Always check the care instructions when you buy bedding – anything that must be dry-cleaned is not very practical.

As for material, sheets can be **linen** (the finest and most expensive thread), **silk,** or **cotton**, which is often blended with linen, silk, or polyester. You can also buy sheets of mixed fibers (cotton/polyester is a popular one). Linen sheets are ideal for hotter climates because of the fabric's natural tendency to cool. Fine linen sheets can also last for decades. Cotton sheets are perfect for any season and have the highest wear of all fibers; in fact, they become softer with repeated washings and use. Cotton fibers are classed according to their staple, or length (extra-long staple is the finest), grade, and color or brightness. When cotton comes from the loom, it has to be finished – through a process called mercerizing, after the English calico printer who invented it – to give the fabric strength and lustre, and to make it receptive to dyes. It may also be mechanically preshrunk to ensure that the finished article doesn't go from king-size to single when laundered.

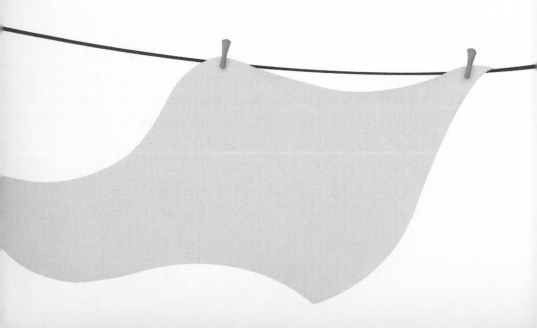

How to read: labels on fabric

The weight, wear, and feel of a sheet depend on the fiber the fabric is made from and the number of threads woven per inch. In most cases, the higher the thread count, the softer and more durable the sheet. I say in most cases because if an inferior yarn has been used, it doesn't matter if the thread count is very high – it won't wear as well as a sheet with a lower thread count woven with a better yarn. A visit to a local store convinced me that there's no real control over the labeling used on bed linen. Percale in the United States means 100 percent cotton. One major Australian manufacturer labels 50 percent cotton/50 percent polyester sheets as percale. Percale is a label that can be used for any smooth, closely woven plain-weave fabric that may be made of cotton, and usually has a thread count of 200 threads per 4 square inches . Go to the label and look for "composition." This should tell you exactly what the sheet is made from (although unfortunately there's often a lack of detail provided). The shop assistant should be of help; if not, you may need to go to another shop.

So the place to start when choosing a sheet is the cotton. There are four main varieties of cotton – the longest fiber (or staple) is the finest.

Egyptian cotton – a fine, lustrous, extra-long staple measuring $1\frac{1}{2}$–$1\frac{3}{4}$ inches. It's usually brownish in color.

Pima cotton – a fine but strong, medium to long staple ($1\frac{3}{8}$–$1\frac{5}{8}$ inches) that is brownish in color. It's thought to be a combination of Sea Island and Egyptian cottons and was developed in the United States in the early 1900s. Check www.supimacotton.org for more information on this type of cotton.

Sea Island cotton – considered the finest of all cottons. It's a silky, white, extra-long staple grown exclusively in the West Indies.

Upland cotton – staple measures $\frac{13}{16}$–$1\frac{1}{4}$ inches. It is thought that the name came from early American colonists who referred to the crop of cotton that grew upland from the Atlantic coast. It's the most widely used cotton, making up 90 percent of the world's cotton crop.

It is rare to find Sea Island cotton in sheets. Egyptian cotton sheets are popular now and the merits of Egyptian cotton are used as a marketing tool. Don't be fooled into buying these sheets just because of the Egyptian cotton label. It is not always the highest quality and can be less uniform than Pima cotton. It's also important to check what percentage of long-staple cotton has been used. Often an Egyptian cotton sheet will only contain a small amount of long-staple. I have a pair of Egyptian cotton sheets and they are lovely but the cost is prohibitive and my other sheets – high count Upland cotton – are just as soft and smooth, and a lot cheaper.

Cotton is then woven into different sorts of fabric.

Flannel – originated in Wales, where it was called *gwlamen* ("allied with wool"). It is loosely woven, heavy cotton noted for its softness, with a napped (raised) finish and considerable variation in weight and texture. Flannel sheets are perfect for winter nights but a bit too warm for summer.

Muslin – named for Mosul, a textile center in ancient Mesopotamia (modern Iraq). It is now a generic term for a simple-weave fabric ranging from sheer to heavy sheetings. Fine muslin is smooth, with a 180–200 thread count.

Oxford – first produced in Scotland in the nineteenth century. It is soft, porous, and rather heavy. Launders well.

Percale – named for pargalal, a centuries-old cloth from Persia. It is a finely combed, closely woven fabric noted for its fine texture and finish. As mentioned, in Australia percale can be used to refer to a polyester and cotton mix. Always check the label for an explanation if sheets are marked "percale."

Sateen – made in a satin weave, in which warp (lengthwise) threads interlace with filling threads, resulting in a lustrous, smooth-faced, durable fabric.

Comforters and quilts

Call them what you will, these are feather-, down-, synthetic- or wool-filled covers for your bed. **Feather-** and **down-filled** comforters are often sold by weight, comparing them to a number of blankets. A down-filled comforter will be lighter and warmer than a feather-filled one, and usually more expensive. The trick is to buy a comforter with a strong cotton shell (a thread count over 200 is good) and "walls" sewn into it to stop the feather or down bunching up in one area. In cooler regions, a feather-filled comforter is a blessing. Warmer parts would probably do better with thin quilts or cotton blankets.

Feather- and down-filled comforters can be washed as for feather pillows (see page 278). You can also try washing them in cold water in the bath – just make sure you dissolve the laundry detergent first and that you rinse well (it will take several rinses to get all the soap out). Hang the comforter out to dry, spreading it over two lines, or drape it over a drying rack. If the insides seem to be clumping, give the comforter a few shakes while it's drying to stop the feathers or down from balling up. If you dry it in the dryer, make sure you use a cool setting. If you like, try including a few tennis balls to help fluff it.

Wool-filled comforters are more common now. I have one and it's perfect for Sydney winters, but too warm for summer when I just use a cotton blanket. The wool is quilted between a cotton cover. And it can be washed in a machine with wool detergent on a gentle cycle. Dry as flat as possible, outside. Don't put in the dryer.

Synthetic comforters are usually filled with polyester or a polyester mix. They offer warmth but little breathability, so you may find yourself getting a bit sweaty under such a cover. They are machine-washable, but always read the care instructions for specifics.

Bed etiquette

I can't abide shoes on the bed, or bags, or anything that has come into contact with the street. I think of the bag sitting on the ground at the train station or the bus stop, where hundreds of people have tracked dirt and who knows what else, and it makes my stomach turn. Unfortunately my husband doesn't share this vision and one of our ongoing "discussions" revolves around him throwing his workbag on the bed when he gets home.

Blankets

Like comforters, you want the right weight blanket for your climate. For colder areas a wool blanket is perfect, or you could go for a synthetic one if you don't like the heaviness of wool. In warmer climes a cotton blanket – waffle-weave ones are good – may be all you need. As with sheets, make sure you can wash the blanket yourself rather than having to get it dry-cleaned. Because the blanket touches your skin a lot less than sheets, it will only need to be washed a few times a year.

Woolen blankets are fine in the machine on a gentle cycle or in cold water, or try washing by hand in the bathtub. Use a detergent formulated for wool. You can also try adding a cup of vinegar to the final rinse water to ensure all soap is removed. If you do wash by hand, consider spinning the blanket in the washing machine to get rid of as much water as possible before you hang it out to dry. To help the blanket keep its shape, drape it over two lines or over a drying rack. It will also dry more quickly this way. Cotton blankets can usually go into the machine. Wash on a gentle cycle as you don't want the threads pulled loose. Check the care instructions. Wash acrylic blankets in a machine in warm water or by hand. With a large item like this, the machine is probably an easier option. Dry as you would for wool or cotton.

How to wash: mattress protectors and pads

Cotton protectors should be washed often and can go in the machine as for cotton sheets. For wool or sheepskin pads, check the label. You can usually put them in the washing machine and wash with a wool detergent.

How to wash: an electric blanket

First read the label on the blanket to make sure it can be machine-washed. You will need a top-loader, as it's difficult to soak in a front-loader. Fill the machine with warm water, add detergent, and stir to dissolve. Place the blanket in the water as evenly as possible and soak for half an hour. Turn the washer on for two minutes on gentle agitation and let the cycle run its course. Place four bath towels in the dryer and run it on high for a few minutes. Place the blanket in the dryer with the towels and dry on a warm setting until just damp. (If you completely dry in the dryer, you can damage the electrics.) It will probably be ready after about 10 minutes. Finish drying draped over a drying rack or on a clothesline.

The bedside table

Our bedside tables – cute little stools from Ikea – might look good, but they really do a poor job holding all my books plus a reading lamp . . . and you can forget about a glass of water. The best ones service all your needs. Do you have items, such as medication, you'd like to keep out of sight? Choose a table with at least one drawer. Make sure the surface area is large enough for your lamp, a book, an alarm clock, a glass of water, and perhaps a phone.

The right bedside lamp is essential. The best ones are on arms so that the light can easily be adjusted to your eye level. If you prefer a lamp with a shade, make sure the shade is low enough to cut the glare from the bulb but still shed light on your book. If space is tight, consider getting an electrician to install wall lights. They are a great space saver and allow you to direct light exactly where you need it.

The closet

Whether you have a lovely old antique armoire or a snappy custom-built walk-in closet, the rules are the same: you want the space to be cool, dark, and roomy.

*   Long dresses and coats need 54–62 inches hanging space.
*   Jackets and shirts need 33 inches and the space needs to be 24 inches deep to accommodate clothes hung on a rail.
*   Warm closets can encourage mildew, which can ruin clothes, and sunlight can fade clothes. Make sure your storage area is dark and cool.
*   Try not to overstuff – good air circulation means less chance of mustiness. If the space does smell musty and you've cleaned it out, try putting a saucer of baking soda on the floor at the back of the closet to absorb smells.
*   To keep moths at bay (and other bugs that might leave holes in your favorite coat) make sure you only put spotlessly clean clothes in the closet. Although moth larvae will eat fibers, moths themselves only eat food bits left on clothes, not the clothes themselves. See pages 381–2 for more information on moths.
*   Always hang clothes with zippers closed, buttons done up, and pockets empty – this keeps the garment in the right shape and leaves less chance for snags from other hangers or clothes.
*   Make sure anything that can lose its shape when hung is treated to a wide padded hanger (or, better still, folded and put away in a drawer).
*   Shelves in your closet shouldn't be higher than 6 feet if you are going to use them regularly.

* If you don't have sufficient hanging space, hang only clothes for that season. We store our out-of-season clothes in suitcases under the bed. The main thing is to make sure all your clothes are spotlessly clean before you store them. In the past, I've added lavender bags and other fragrant pieces, but they do very little to anything except the clothes they are right next to.

* Try to keep shoes off the floor of your closet – my husband is more successful at this than I am. My shoes tend to lie in a heap while his are neatly laid out on a board, with wheels and a handle, which slides under the bed. The only disadvantage to his storage method is that they can get dusty. Shoe trees (those wooden blocks on sticks) are good for helping your shoes keep their shape.

* Storing your shoes in their boxes is a great idea. They won't gather dust, they'll keep their shape, and the boxes are easily stacked. You could also try those inexpensive canvas pockets that hang in the closet (or the ones that go behind the closet door). Anything to get them up off the ground will help. I've always thought a big shallow drawer for my shoes would be a great organizer, but I am yet to put that into practice.

Handbags

Storing handbags is a problem. I can't bear to throw them away and so I have more than a few (you never know when you might want them again – although to date I have rarely resurrected an old handbag). Before you store them, give them a thorough cleaning. Do this by emptying every nook and cranny, vacuuming out the inevitable debris that gathers at the bottom of the bag, and giving the exterior a good wiping with a barely damp cloth. If the bag is leather, use a leather conditioner (follow the instructions for that particular product) and make sure the bag is completely dry before you store it. Then stuff the inside with acid-free tissue so it keeps its shape. To really protect it, put it in a cloth bag. Some handbags come with such a bag. Otherwise, slide it into an old pillowcase or even an old T-shirt.

Now the real dilemma hits – where to put this carefully prepared parcel. I've got mine on the top shelf of my wardrobe. It's not really very convenient and I can't remember exactly what's there. I had a friend in New York who stored her bags in an enormous walk-in closet and had Polaroids of each bag pinned to the protective packaging so she could remember what they looked like. She also stored her shoes in their boxes this way!

The chest of drawers

There's nothing more annoying than not being able to find a pair of socks or a particular bra when you need it. Drawers that aren't too deep will help. Try to purchase (or better still, have made) a chest of drawers with shallow drawers at the top for your "smalls," as my grandmother likes to call them. Bigger items go in the deeper drawers lower down. My husband and I have a chest of drawers each. My underwear and socks go in the top drawer, T-shirts and lightweight things go in the second drawer, and the third holds heavier items like jeans and sweaters.

A guide to buying a chest of drawers:

1. It is essential that the inside of the drawers is smooth, otherwise your clothes will catch. Check that any screws or nails are well concealed and no loose bits of wood appear. Make sure the drawer handles are comfortable to pull and well attached, and that the screw or bolt holding them in doesn't protrude into the drawer, as it will catch clothes.

2. Check the sliding mechanism for the drawer. You don't want a drawer that sticks. The best drawers have rails underneath or on the side, and their rolling mechanisms are smooth. You want the rails to be strong enough to hold the weight of a full drawer easily. Make sure there is a stop so you don't pull the drawer right out every time you open it.

3. The construction is better if the drawer is joined by dovetailed joints at the corners rather than glued and nailed. Also check that the rest of the unit is sturdily made. As with drawers, dovetail joints are stronger and longer lasting than glue and nails.

Once you've bought your chest of drawers, do use it. I know after a long day of work and childwrangling I'm not always inclined to put my clothes neatly away (many of them find their way onto the top of the chest of drawers where they wait patiently for me to fold and put them away). We had a chair in the bedroom, but it became a storehouse for clothes that didn't need to be washed and which we were too lazy to put away. We got rid of the chair in the vain hope we'd be better about putting clothes away. We've improved a bit, but not a lot. There really shouldn't be a pit stop for your clothes between the closet or drawer and the dirty-clothes' basket. If an item is clean, it should be returned to its home. If it's dirty, it should go in the dirty-clothes' basket. Or if it's smelly (think of your coat after a night at a bar), then hang it outside to air, if possible. (I sometimes drape clothes over the clothes line on the balcony or, if the weather is bad, I hang them over the shower-curtain rail in the bathroom and make sure the window is open a crack.) You should only have to air an item overnight. If it still smells, you may need to wash it or have it dry-cleaned.

Jewelry

If the pieces are really precious, consider keeping them in a safe or even at a bank. This always seemed rather odd to me – that you'd own something beautiful and the only way you could really enjoy it was to lock it up – but if it's very valuable, you may have no choice. I have a lilac silk box that's lined in black satin for all my jewelry – there's not too much of it, so this smallish box is perfect. It has compartments for earrings, rings, and larger pieces so everything stays neat and tidy. It makes sense to have a single spot for your jewelry. When you go on holidays, don't hide the jewelry box in one of your drawers. I'm sure it's the first place thieves check. Try to think of an unlikely spot and consider taking pieces that are very precious with you.

My aunt had all her jewelry stolen and she had a very hard time collecting insurance because she didn't have records of all the pieces. She had to wade through years of photo albums to prove what she had. Digital cameras make recording precious items easy. Lay everything out on a dark background so it is easy to see and make sure it is well lit. Record any identifying marks and numbers, and keep the record and photos with your important papers.

To clean jewelry . . .

Try dipping the piece in water with a dash of household ammonia added. Use a soft toothbrush to get into crevices. Rinse in clear water and dry thoroughly (try using a hairdryer). You can also clean diamonds with a mild liquid detergent and a soft **>**

brush. You can wash your pearls in mild soap and water to remove perfume, hair spray, cosmetics, etc. Dry them well and wrap in acid-free tissue paper when storing, or keep them in the box they were purchased in.

Once a year, have a jeweler check your jewellery for wear and tear. This is also a good time to have your pieces cleaned and polished. The jeweler may recommend that this be done more frequently for certain pieces – especially if they are antiques. And it's a good idea to check with your jeweler to see if pearls need to be restrung, especially if you wear them a lot. The string can stretch and also be weakened by chemicals that are in perfume and hair spray.

How to clean: the bedroom

Your bedroom should be spotless. I find the more ordered this room, the more peaceful my sleep is. Don't rush every morning to make the bed as soon as you get out. It does a bed good to breathe a little without any bodies in it.

When I was on maternity leave, I made the bed around 9 a.m. when the baby had gone down for his first nap. This is also the time to open the window and let some air in. If you get up and rush out of the house for work, consider leaving the bed unmade (I can hear my mother groan at this advice) and make it when you get home. And if you go away for the weekend, strip the bed before you leave to let the mattress breathe. A friend strips her bed every Sunday morning and leaves it to air all day. She then remakes it in the evening with lovely fresh sheets ready for the week ahead.

* Change your sheets once a week (although you may wish to do this more often, especially in the summer when they can absorb a lot of sweat).

* One of the best ways to freshen linen and bedding is to lay it out on a sunny day. The sun's ultraviolet light acts as a germ killer, attacking dust mites and any other little gremlins that have set up home in your pillows and quilts. Wet fabrics fade more easily than dry, so hang out your linen and bedding for its sunbath when it is dry.

How to make: the bed

1. Start with a fitted bottom sheet. Make sure it's generous so that it covers the whole mattress; there's nothing worse than an exposed mattress choked by a too-tight fitted sheet. The easiest way to get this sheet on smoothly is to have two of you do it, starting from opposite corners. If that's not possible, start at the top right corner, tucking the elastic a little deeper than it needs to go. Smooth the sheet down to the bottom left corner and tuck that under. Do the top left next and then the bottom right.

2. I like the top sheet to have hospital corners at the bottom but to be left loose at the top. I don't like that tight tucked-in feeling, but I also don't want the sheet slipping away in the middle of the night. To make a hospital corner, drape the sheet across the mattress, leaving just enough at the bottom to tuck in neatly. Tuck in the bottom of the sheet. Then stand facing the bottom corner.

Take the drape about one foot from the bottom corner of the bed
and pull away from you and up over the mattress (if you've done
it correctly you'll have a triangle of sheet lying on the top of the
mattress). Take the piece of sheet left hanging and tuck it under
the mattress. Then tuck the draped piece in, creating a neat corner. Repeat on the other bottom corner.

3. If you like blankets on your bed, now is the time to add them.
   Repeat the process for the top sheet. Then fold the top of the
   top sheet down over the top of the blanket. This protects the
   blanket and makes sure you come into contact with cotton and
   nothing itchy. If you wish, tuck in the sides.

4. Plump pillows and lay down your quilt or comforter. My mother
   puts a bedspread on first, turns down the top of the bedspread,
   and then lays the pillows down so they cover the fold a few
   inches. She then folds up the bedspread to cover the pillows,
   leaving a satisfying little fold under the pillows and a nice plump
   top to the bed. This protects the pillows from dust during the
   day and looks neat. I put the pillows down and then put the
   quilt over the top without any tucking, simply because the quilt
   doesn't cover the pillows completely.

I used to forgo the top sheet and just use the comforter, as it
seemed easier to make the bed. But I missed the top sheet (a comforter can get too hot). So I've reintroduced it and the extra seconds
it takes to make the bed are well worth the comfort.

After you've made the bed, give the room a good tidying. Put
away clothes or throw them in the dirty-clothes' basket, recycle old
newspapers, and give your bedside table a wipe with a tissue.

How to wash: sheets

Don't buy sheets that need to be dry-cleaned. It's expensive and you run the risk of breathing in fumes from the fluid used that certainly can't be good for you. You need sheets that will stand up to a weekly laundering.

Wash sheets in hot water and a strong detergent. Use bleach periodically to get out stains and to sanitize. If your sheets are preshrunk – and most are – you should have no problem with shrinkage. If they aren't preshrunk, don't buy them. For more details on sheets, see pages 187–91.

How to clean: a mattress

Twice a year, flip the mattress and rotate it (some suggest you do this monthly – it's up to you). This way the same person isn't sleeping on (and flattening) the same spot. Give the mattress a sunbath twice a year if you have a garden. If not, try to leave it in a sunny spot in your home. You can leave it all day. Vacuum the mattress protector once a month when you change the sheet, and the mattress when you change the protector. This will help keep dust at bay.

To clean a fresh **stain** on a mattress, try covering it with talc and leaving as long as you can – at least a few hours. Vacuum off the talc and dab the spot with a cloth dipped in 10 parts warm water to 1 part household ammonia. This should remove the stain. Dry the spot with a hairdryer. For **bloodstains**, try a solution of 2 tablespoons of salt to 1 pint of cold water. Apply to the spot with a sponge. Work from the outside edges in and make sure you don't get the mattress too wet. Dry with a hairdryer when done.

How to iron: sheets

You can do this if you like, and have the time, because ironed sheets do feel lovely to sleep on. But there is no other real benefit. A good friend of mine irons just her pillowcases – a very simple procedure that leaves her bed looking neat.

Another friend swears by using lavender water when ironing her sheets. There are a few ways to do this. Either buy a prepared spray, or use a few drops of lavender oil in a spray bottle filled with clear water and spritz before you iron. Alternatively, add a few drops of lavender water (not oil) directly to your iron. Make sure it's only a small amount as I'm not sure what effect it will have on the iron long-term. Experiment with different smells. I love sage and it works wonderfully on sheets.

Watch out for wrinkle-resistant cotton sheets – they have been treated with an agent to stop the cotton wrinkling and (in my experience) don't feel as nice against the skin. Flannel and normal sheets resist wrinkles naturally. And any sheeting with polyester will resist wrinkles. However, if you have cotton sheets and wrinkles really bother you, there are steps you can take to get a wrinkle-free sheet without ironing.

1. If you **line dry** – hang the sheets very neatly, smoothing the hem and making sure they can billow out in the breeze. Once dry, they will be smooth. If they feel a little stiff, try putting them in the dryer on cold for a few minutes.
2. If you dry in the **dryer** – remove the sheets as soon as they're dry and shake out. Fold tightly and smoothly while still warm and place them at the bottom of the stack of linen so they will be weighed down and smoothed by the other linen.

How to fold: a fitted sheet

My cousin Luisa does this beautifully.

1. Flip the sheet inside out (so the seams are showing).

2. Grab the middle so that it folds neatly in half (the corners will be furthest from your hands).

3. Lay it flat (good to lay it on the bed where there's lots of room) and tuck the top fitted corners into the bottom ones.

4. Fold in half lengthwise. The corners are now all stacked on top of each other and should be very neat.

5. Now fold as you please. It makes sense to fold it to match the size of your folded flat sheet.

7. The Children's Bedroom

There's a lot of joy in decking out a child's room – and a lot of stress. The joy comes from making a place in your home that is totally devoted to the much-anticipated baby. In preparing for Jack, memories came flooding back of the rooms I'd had as a child. In one, my parents had painted a mural of a park on two of the walls. I shared that room with my brother and, from the top bunk, it felt like I was sleeping in the trees. I also vividly remember the first bedroom I didn't have to share with my brother. My father built me a loft bed out of wood that had been used in an old pickling barrel. The bed was great, a perfect hideaway, and I could fit my desk underneath. But unfortunately the smell of pickles never really left the wood, so my room and bed were always lightly scented with vinegar.

Outfitting a bedroom for a newborn baby calls for careful planning – and involves a certain amount of pre-baby jitters. The stress comes from trying to figure out exactly what you need. I had a sense of pending doom – that if I didn't get everything organized before

the baby arrived, I'd be too exhausted once he got here to do any-thing and he'd end up sleeping in a box at the end of our bed. You'll find a lot to read on this topic, but I can tell you from experience that the most important things are a crib and a good mattress, a place to store clothes (there seem to be an awful lot of clothes for such a tiny person), and a place dedicated to changing diapers (not necessarily a changing table). Eventually you'll need to think about storing toys and books, too.

You should also think about the longevity of the room. Will your child be in there for many years? If so, you may want to keep the baby decorations to a minimum – or at the very least make sure whatever you do is easy to change. A coat of paint is always easier to deal with than wallpapering, so perhaps think about changing the style of the room with color rather than paper. We will outgrow this apartment before Jack outgrows his bedroom, so I have painted trees and birds, and stuck stickers of numbers and letters, on the walls. I know that when the time comes to move, the stickers will peel off easily and everything else can be painted over.

Baby bedding

A newborn can go straight into a crib. You can feel quite safe about this if you simply fold the sheets short at one end and pop them in. (See page 215 for information on SIDS.) They do look a little lost, but more to your eye than their own.

Jack slept in the bassinet attachment for the carriage for the first few weeks (although this isn't generally recommended). I had a visit from a nurse from the local hospital and she went over all our equipment, which made me feel much more at ease about everything I'd chosen. When Jack was a bit bigger, we moved him into a beautiful white wicker bassinet borrowed from a generous family friend. It had been passed down through the generations and was still in excellent condition. For a little baby who didn't roll around much, it was perfect. The open-weave sides let air circulate and it sat on high legs that kept me from having to bend too much to pick him up.

Although they aren't essential, the best thing about bassinets is that they are often on a stand and so easier to access for a sleepy parent trying to pat a baby off to sleep. But don't go to a lot of expense, as they'll only be in this bassinet for a few months. You can buy sheets made specifically for bassinets and cribs but, especially for bassinets, it's just as easy to cut down a soft old cotton sheet of your own.

A fitted sheet for a crib, however, is a good investment, as a child can be in the crib for at least two years. I put a flannel (in winter) or cotton (in summer) cloth on top of the fitted sheet to catch minor spills so I don't have to change the bottom sheet all the time. You will also need a mattress protector.

Mattresses for cribs or bassinets should be firm. Go for an inner-spring or a solid foam type. Make sure they are completely covered and that there is no way a baby can get its head stuck between the cover and the mattress. When you buy a crib, check that:

1. the mattress position is adjustable. Then, when the baby is small and not sitting up (or trying to climb out) you can have the mattress at the highest position, making it easier on your back when putting them down.

2. there is at least two feet from the base of the mattress to the top of the crib side when it is on its lowest mattress setting.

3. there isn't a gap between the mattress edge and the side of the crib of less than one inch.

4. the area between the bars is 2–3⅓ inches wide.

5. there are no sharp edges anywhere on the cot and that the catches that control the drop-side won't jam or cut little fingers.

6. there are no decorations a baby could eat or lick or get tangled in.

If you do get a second-hand crib, it might be best to get it stripped and repainted with an appropriate paint, as some paint-work – especially old paint – can contain lead. Don't purchase a crib with wheels. If your crib does have wheels, remove them. Be careful with hand-me-downs – it's easy to get swept away by people's generosity but often it is better and safer to buy new. Unless the hand-me-down crib is in excellent condition, it's better to buy a new one, as the baby will be sleeping in it for some time.

A lot of cribs can be transformed into beds when the child is old enough to leave the confines of the crib. I think the best thing to be guided by is what you can afford. Cribs with a long life will be more expensive and it may not be a time in your life when you want to be spending a lot of money. Also, the crib you buy in the first flush of parenthood may not be something you will want to look at for the next five or six years.

SIDS

The major safety concern for babies in their first few months is Sudden Infant Death Syndrome (SIDS). The Sudden Infant Death Association has excellent recommendations on children's bedding. Call the association branch in your area (check the *White Pages*) or go to www.sidsandkids.org According to the SIDS guidelines, you shouldn't have anything in the bed but the baby and minimal bedding.

Place furniture carefully to give yourself a clear path in and out of the room at night. Night-lights might seem like a good idea but, in my experience, they keep the baby up – which is the last thing you want!

Necessities

✱✱

✱ **6 bassinet or crib sheets** – the more the merrier! Jack managed to vomit on them almost every night so there was a lot of sheet changing in the beginning. Then a friend suggested we line the bed with a soft diaper (I'd bought a pack of six flannel diapers to use as wraps). When a spill happened I could just whip off the nappy and replace it with a fresh one – much easier than changing the whole bed in the middle of the night.

✱ **1 mattress protector** – that you can wash easily. You don't want one that attaches with strings or elastic, as your baby can get its head stuck between the protector and the mattress.

✱ **Blankets** – 2 at least. Make sure there's no fringing or any kind of a design that could find its way into the baby's mouth or around its neck.

✱ **1 quilt or knitted/crocheted blanket** – again, you want to be careful the baby won't get caught up in the bedding, so it may be best to keep the lovely crocheted blanket your grandmother made until the baby is a bit older. We tended to use these blankets when the baby was in the carriage and it was chilly out. The bedroom was usually warm enough that we didn't need blankets.

The changing table

Here's an expensive item that you can do without. We have a pad that sits on top of a chest of drawers or bench where Jack gets his diaper changed. The disadvantage is that if you move it around, you don't always have all the stuff you need at hand. The great advantage of a proper changing table is that it holds everything – from diapers to jars of Vaseline. But don't be bamboozled into buying one. You can get a basket or even a bucket and fill it with all the necessities you'll need to have on hand by your changing pad. Be extra careful with changing tables once the baby starts to roll; at this stage, consider changing your child on the floor or in the crib if possible.

Diapers

Up until about six weeks, your baby could need a diaper change up to sixteen times a day with cloth diapers, and up to twelve with disposable ones. I had intended to use cloth diapers for Jack. I liked the idea of being able to use a diaper again and again. It just seemed so sensible. Plus I'd read that one baby uses about 6,000 disposable diapers in the first few years of its life. I had flashes of Jack's diapers packing landfills from here to Uluru. But in the end, the only cloth diapers I had I used as wraps and now have as rags (the flannel ones make excellent dusters).

Disposing of disposables

In one book I read, they insisted you scrape out the contents of a disposable diaper into the toilet before throwing it away. In a perfect world this may happen, but I don't know anyone who does it.

A friend in London sourced recycled, biodegradable diapers but I am yet to find anything like that in Sydney. Instead, if the diaper has solids in it, I wrap it in a plastic bag and throw it into the trash in the kitchen (which gets emptied daily). If it's just urine, I fold the diaper back up on itself and then put it in the trash bin.

How to clean: cloth diapers

The only person I know who opted for cloth diapers has a cleaning service that takes the dirty ones away and replaces them with fresh ones. If you are washing the diapers yourself, you need to scrape off solids, rinse in warm water, and soak in a diaper pail (simply a bucket with a lid) with baking soda or a enzyme presoak powder. Use 4–5 tablespoons of baking soda or follow the directions for the diaper powder. Then wash in your washing machine – either using pure soap or normal laundry powder. You can add a little white vinegar to the rinse cycle to make sure any soap residue is removed. Dry in the sun, as sunlight is a great antibacterial.

Chairs

Baby chairs are big and bulky items. We opted for a sleek Swedish chair made from wood that Jack will be able to use for years (it eventually transforms into a desk chair). But because it has such a long life, it was expensive. Just make sure that whatever chair you buy can be cleaned really easily, because you will be doing that constantly. And, of course, make sure it is safe. Check www.bestbabyproducts.com (see page 229) for the most reliable, up-to-date information.

Storage

At first, there shouldn't be too much "stuff." You'll probably find there are more clothes than anything else, but you don't want them lying around (although a few key pieces on hangers suspended from nails on the wall or behind the door can be lovely). My brother, a cabinet-maker, made us a tall narrow chest of drawers in American walnut. The drawers at the top are shallow and perfect for socks and onesies. They get progressively deeper so that the bottom two drawers hold bedding, wraps, blankets, and Jack's little bath towels. Initially I could fit everything in there. It has now spilled out into a lot of boxes and bags full of clothes Jack's too big for, which I am waiting to pass on. One of those cloth hanging pockets has taken a lot of the overflow. Plus it's perfect for all those cute little shoes. There's also a bar suspended high in the wardrobe to hang his shirts and jackets. As these things aren't very long, it's easy to fit a chest of drawers under them.

Toys have a dedicated cupboard in the living room where Jack does most of his playing. We've also got excellent (and cheap) plastic boxes with lids and wheels for toys and miscellaneous odds and ends. These boxes slide under his crib. I am a great believer in purging the toy box regularly. Children fast grow bored of certain toys that can be given away or stored, to be rediscovered later. Don't be lured into buying expensive storage boxes. I got mine at the local discount store and they work perfectly well.

Books have become a problem. Initially, I made room on one shelf of my bookshelves but it was soon overflowing with Jack's books. As with toys, he seems to become sick of books he looks at all the time, so I've taken to rotating them. The books that fit on one shelf stay out and the others end up in a box under the bed, to be pulled out when he's forgotten about them and they seem new again.

It helps to have a tidying-up routine with children's toys. Before each nap we read a book together, and before we sit down to read we tidy up. Or rather, I tidy up and Jack fools around. It means when he's gone down for a nap I'm not scurrying around cleaning, and he also gets to see that all his toys don't live scattered on the floor. It also means when he wakes up he gets to unpack all his toys again, which he loves doing.

Older children

My cousin has three girls, the oldest just 13. Her bedroom has grown with her – from a pale pink fairy-princess haven where stuffed animals and dolls seemed to line every surface, to a rather grown-up hideaway that befits a sophisticated 13-year-old with definite musical tastes. The dolls have made way for posters of her favorite musicians, a stereo, and a computer. A desk now holds pride of place where there used to be a chest full of toys.

Children's needs are similar to your own – a desk to write at, a place to store clothes and books (and toys), art for the walls, and pleasant lighting (see pages 183–200 for tips on arranging and lighting). It is also a room where children get to express themselves without your benevolent hand. So let them choose paint colors and furniture. It seems a shame to stifle a child's choices. Having said that, a bit of commonsense must prevail. A good friend's daughter insisted on dark pink walls for her bedroom. Without too much trouble, my friend steered her towards a much gentler lilac, with the bright pink kept for the bedding. She soon got sick of pink and wanted blue sheets – which were much easier to change than the color of the walls. Compromise is another good lesson for children to learn.

Bunks are an excellent option for children sharing a room. They provide a private corner away from siblings and are very space-efficient. Most major furniture stores sell bunks. The key here is that they are securely constructed. I shared a bunk with my brother and ours was made of pine. The frame was pretty indestructible, but after one rather boisterous jumping session the top bunk collapsed onto the bottom one. (Luckily, my brother was with me jumping on the top bunk at the time, and not underneath!) Consider having one custom-built by a reputable cabinet-maker if you can't find one that fits your space or seems sturdy enough.

Single or double beds for children fall into the same category as for adults (see pages 185–6).

How to child-proof: the house

Safety is so important and often it's the little things that you miss that can cause harm to your child. One tip is to get down on your hands and knees and crawl around the whole house. You'll be amazed at what you see. There are many traps for inquisitive little hands. Visit www.checklistmaker.com/home/childproof.html for a detailed list of tips. If you've covered the following points you are well on the way to making your home child-safe.

In general . . .

Blinds or shades – avoid those with pull-strings that babies can either chew on and choke, or get caught up in and strangle.

Child-proof gates – use these to block stairs at the top and bottom. You can buy them at hardware and most major toy stores.

Cords and wires – tie all blind cords up high and get wires out of reach any way you can. Cover electrical outlets – supermarkets and hardware stores sell plugs for this purpose.

Driveway – have a fence that restricts access to the driveway and the street. This is so important, especially around driveways where it's easy to pull out without paying attention to what's directly behind you. They may not look lovely but they are essential.

Fireplace – always use a screen that completely covers the fireplace.

Flame-retardant curtains – use these in a child's bedroom. Check with the retailer to see if the fabric is flame-retardant.

Furniture – keep it away from windows. You don't want to be making a set of steps to a dangerous area. Screens are not enough to keep a child from falling out of a window. You can get child-safety bars that are easy to remove if there's a fire. Check with your local fire department for the best source.

Garage – store all dangerous chemicals, and other products and tools, in locked cabinets. Never let children play in a garage.

Garage door – test by placing a cardboard box underneath the door and then closing it. If it crushes the box, it can crush a child.

Heavy objects – place these out of reach and consider anchoring standard lamps, either with something heavy at the base or by attaching to the wall. Are large objects like TVs, entertainment units, or wall units secure (i.e., so they can't fall down on children)? Not a lot of us think about pulling a television down on top of ourselves, but toddlers are fascinated by televisions and are surprisingly strong. Make sure all the elements of your entertainment system are either placed out of reach or securely latched down.

Indoor plants – place these out of a child's reach; they can choke on their leaves, and some plants are poisonous.

Lead – check the content in paint on old fences and furniture. If it exceeds an acceptable amount, you will have to remove as much of the paint as possible and cover what's left with at least two coats of lead-free paint.

Play equipment – make sure all nuts and bolts are tight and don't protrude. Cover any chain with rubber to prevent pinching. Line outdoor play areas with mulch, bark chips, or some other material that will cushion falls.

Safety plugs – are these placed in spare electrical outlets? You can buy them at your local supermarket or hardware store. They make it impossible for a child to stick anything into an outlet.

Sharp corners – it may be your favorite coffee table or the edge of a wooden chair. Consider getting plastic corners (available from hardware stores) to soften hard corners.

Shatterproof safety glass – if you have the option, consider installing this in windows and glass doors. Our French doors out to the balcony don't have safety glass and I am paranoid about Jack smashing them, especially since he's taken to banging toys against the glass. Call your local glass supplier for a quote on safety glass. Colored stickers and safety film really don't mean anything to a stubborn toddler.

Smoke alarms – make sure these work and are installed on each level of the house. And be sure to change the batteries regularly. Another handy trick is to put a sticker on your child's bedroom window. If there's a fire, the fire department will then be able to identify which room the child is in.

Stairs – make sure the rails are closely spaced so a child can't fit his/her head through.

Swimming pools and play areas – fence these in. Don't take your baby in the pool until he/she has good head control. Have a poster that explains CPR (cardiopulmonary resuscitation) somewhere close to the pool.

Windows – make sure they all have a lockable safety catch, and that they are locked even when you are home.

In the kitchen . . .

Jack has just learned how to pull himself up to standing position and he's doing it on absolutely everything, including the kitchen cupboards. He reaches up to the counter and pulls down anything that might be interesting. Any cords that dangle over the countertop are an invitation to him. I've wound up the toaster cord and fastened it with a rubber band so that it sits on the countertop behind the toaster. It no longer attracts the toddler, and I must admit the kitchen looks a lot neater with all that stuff hidden.

Cleaning products, chemicals, and medications – keep these all properly labeled and stored in a locked cupboard at least 5 feet above the ground. Many laundries are equipped with high shelves. If you only have storage under a counter, make sure the cabinet doors lock well. Restrict access to the kitchen and laundry if you can. Many laundries these days are secreted away in a closet or room. Make sure the door to that space is always closed.

Eating area – be extra careful around the area where your child eats. They inevitably toss food around and the floor can become very slippery – for you as well as your child. Jack has taken a few spills on the odd squashed grape. It's always best to clean up before you get them out of their chair.

Knives – store these and other sharp objects out of reach. Check with your local children's hospital about safety devices for the home. They actually aren't as easy to find as you might think. There are special locks you can get for drawers and cabinet doors that make them impossible for kids to open.

Stove – use the back burners and turn pot handles around to prevent pots being pulled from the burners. This is a good habit to get into whether you've got children or not.

Other large appliances – check to see if these can be locked. Our dishwasher has a childproof lock on it.

In the bathroom . . .

✱ You can turn down the water temperature at the source. Just check the controls on your hot water heater. Most water heaters have a thermostat that will let you control the hot water temperature. Set it to 125°F to prevent serious burns.

✱ I find nonslip mats in the bath rather disgusting. They inevitably get slimy and they look horrible, but when you've got a toddler who likes to stand up in the bath and throw toys around, a nonslip mat is a blessing. To avoid the sliminess, make sure you peel it off the bottom of the bath every time you use it and hang it over the side of the bath to dry. Soak it once a week in a sink with a little white vinegar or bleach to keep it squeaky clean.

✱ Keep any electricals (hairdryers, electric shavers, etc.) stored safely out of reach and, when in use, away from water. A child should never have a chance to play with anything electrical in the bathroom.

In the living room . . .

* We moved our alcohol into a high cupboard to make way for Jack's toys – which are stored in a floor-level cupboard in the living room. It was one of those moments when you know your priorities have seriously shifted.

* Keeps toys away from the main walkways. This is not easy to do. One way is to have good storage for toys and to limit the number that are actually out at one time.

* Are rugs and mats secure to prevent a fall? A pad under the rug or mat will keep it in place. You can also try double-sided tape for those annoying corners that seem to have a mind of their own. Your local hardware store will have strong double-sided tape you can use for this.

* Are there any low-level tables that dangerous items could be placed on (e.g., watch batteries, tea and coffee, peanuts)? The answer is yes for about 99 percent of us! The trick here is to remove those things from the table, not to get rid of the table.

Essential reading

✳ *Baby Love* (M. Evans & Co., 2002) by Robin Barker is an excellent guide through the first year. Her chapter on choosing baby products helped us navigate the stores with confidence.

✳ An online source of baby product reviews can be found at www.bestbabyproducts.com. The site includes manufacturers' information and is updated every 3 months. Best of all, its editors are all mothers who know their subject firsthand.

✳ *Bun in the Oven* (Ten Speed Press, 2003) and *Kidwrangling* (Ten Speed Press, 2004) by Kaz Cooke are wonderful books that give you the information you want, with a good dose of humor.

✳ *What to Expect When You're Expecting* (HarperCollins, 1987) by Arlene Eisenberg, Heidi Murkoff, and Sandee Hathaway is an excellent, if sometimes overly earnest, companion to Kaz Cooke's *Bun in the Oven*.

Armed with the books above, you'll have all the information you need to make informed choices on everything from wallpaper to breastfeeding.

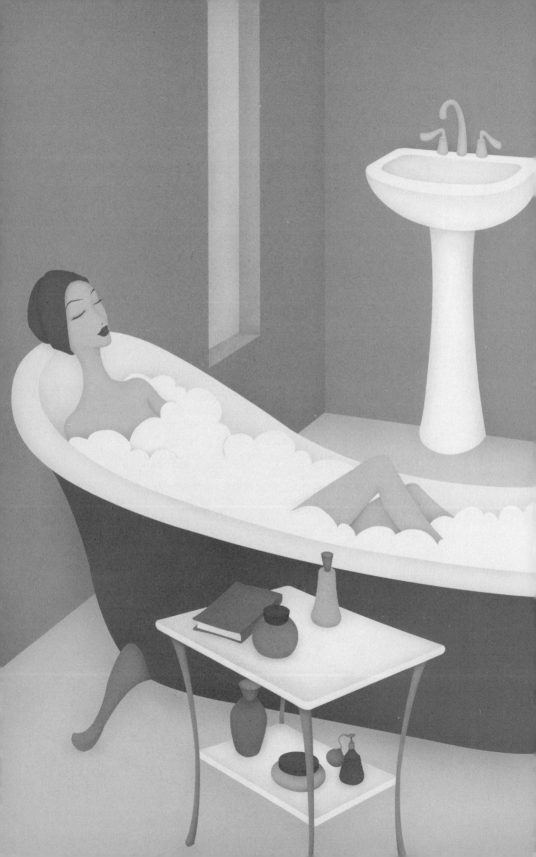

8. The Bathroom

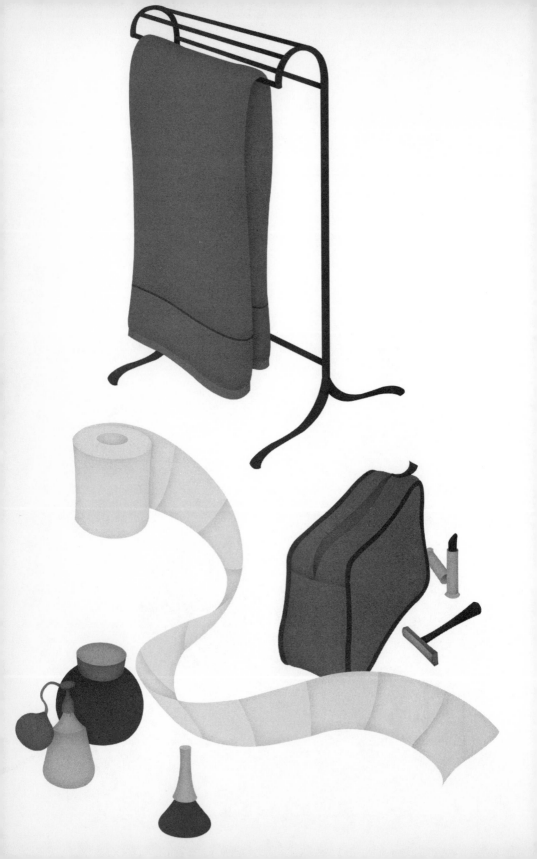

$\mathcal{Our}$ bathroom has three distinct personalities. For our son, it's a place to play. It's the one room he gets to strip out of all his clothes, shed his diaper and splash around. It's all about freedom for him. For my husband, it's a utility room – a place to shower and shave. For me, it's a room I can escape to. I run a bath and, as long as the water stays warm and the door is shut, I'm very happy. Whatever the bathroom is to you, it needs to be cleaned regularly and thoroughly. I find it one of the easiest rooms to clean (and usually start my cleaning here) because all the surfaces can take lots of water. There's nothing precious involved in the bathroom, and I like that.

Revamping your bathroom

If you've inherited a bathroom and aren't able or inclined to redo it from scratch, here are a few things you can do that will make it feel like a luxurious new room.

1. **New towels** – don't keep your towels forever. New towels will give your bathroom a new lease of life. Get the best you can afford (see page 242 for advice) and use old ones for dust rags.

2. **Decant** – if you dislike looking at all that packaging, you can decant just about everything in your bathroom into pump bottles or pretty jars. Just be careful that you don't forget what's in the jar; a labeling system is good here.

3. **Plants** – I love indoor plants and they love the steaminess of the bathroom. I've had maidenhair ferns and orchids in the bathroom, and both have thrived.

4. **Paint** – it's a quick fix. Choose a paint that is easy to wipe down – the shinier the surface, the easier this is. Enamel isn't as easy to apply as other paints, but it does give you a surface that's easy to clean. If you want to experiment with color, this is a good room to do it in. Most bathrooms are not too huge so if you hate the hot pink or bright green you've chosen, you can always paint over it.

5. **Regrout** – it's amazing how this spruces up a bathroom. A tip here is once you've regrouted, don't use bleach to clean as it kills the mold inhibitors in grout. (Check the *Yellow Pages* for local regrouting services.)

6. **Mirrored wall cabinet** – these aren't expensive and are worth the investment. You can buy them from places like Ikea or Home Depot, but you can also have one custom made. A local cabinet-maker can do this for you and it will mean the cabinet fits your bathroom exactly. We got rid of our nasty little plastic job and replaced it with a three-panel mirror; the narrow middle panel opens to reveal all our stuff.

Bathrooms are notoriously expensive to redo – there's a huge amount of plumbing and heaven knows what else involved. However, if you are embarking on a bit of DIY, here are some things to keep in mind. (Don't forget, though, that a good tradesman/architect will be able to help you on all these points.)

Lighting

Bathrooms should have good overhead light. You can now get a combination light/fan/heater, which needs to be installed by an electrician. You'll also have to make sure there's enough room in the bathroom ceiling to take the whole unit. I find that mirror lights or some other task lighting are also essential – in fact, absolutely necessary – for applying makeup, for safe shaving, etc.

Ventilation

Without good ventilation you get mold growing – in fact, you know instantly if a bathroom is well ventilated by checking the tops of the walls and ceiling (where steam gathers) for signs of mold. You can ventilate a bathroom simply by opening the window a crack. Or you can go to greater lengths and install a fan. As mentioned above, there are now fans that come with heat lights – my parents have one and it instantly heats the otherwise chilly bathroom in the winter. Some people feel that enamel paint is a good thing to have on the walls in the bathroom, as a mold deterrent, but actually it's no better at keeping mold at bay than other paints. It's just easier to wipe down, which is practical in the bathroom.

The basin

Pedestal sinks are a good option if your bathroom is small, although you lose precious storage underneath. This can often be made up in a mirrored wall cabinet. Make sure the sink has a bit of an edge so you have somewhere to place a water glass and toothbrush. If you're choosing a basin, think cleaning. You want as few seams as possible. With this in mind, inset sinks (this means the lip of the sink sits below, rather than above the counter) are best for bathrooms. Or sinks that are molded out of the counter material. Basins that sit above the counter are not easy to clean behind and around.

Ideally, the basin should be 8 inches from the end of the countertop. Twin sinks should be 1 foot apart. An ideal height for a bathroom counter is somewhere between 30–35 inches, depending on how tall you are.

The bathroom cabinet

So many bathrooms skimp on counter space. If you have the space, make sure you put in a generous sink base unit or wall cabinets, with good storage in the form of drawers or cupboards. You really need somewhere to place the hairdryer while you reach for the brush.

Our bathroom cabinet has turned into a home for all sorts of odds and ends, including some clove-scented massage oil from Kuala Lumpur and a rather sticky bottle of hair gel. In an attempt to inflict some order on that unruly cupboard, I try to make sure I go through it once every month or so and throw out anything past its use-by date, and anything I haven't used recently. The cabinet has two shelves: the bottom shelf is devoted to everything that's not medicinal and the top to all things medicinal. So, when you stumble into the bathroom with an awful hangover, you always know where the headache tablets are.

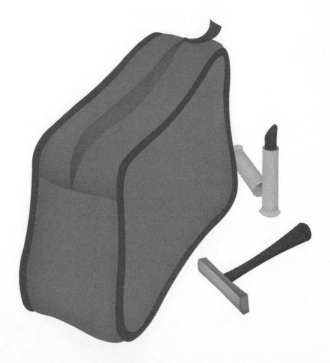

Most houses would have at least something resembling a medicine cabinet. The absolute basic contents of this should be: Mercurochrome or Betadyne, Band-Aids, scissors, tea-tree oil (as an antiseptic), sterile gauze for treating wounds, tweezers, an over-the-counter analgesic like aspirin or Tylenol, cotton balls, nonmercury thermometer. (Drugstores and office supply stores sell excellent first-aid kits containing all the basics in a specially marked box.)

There's a bit of a trend towards "decanting" everything in the bathroom. I remember researching a story for *Martha Stewart Living* where they scoured junk shops for quaint little containers for everything from cotton swabs to shampoo. The result was pretty but I'm not convinced you need to take everything out of its original packaging and put it in an old jar. The cupboard door is usually shut so you don't see all your hard work and the container my cotton swabs come in is perfectly adequate for storing them. I also think it gets a bit dangerous when you start decanting things that need their labels. So perhaps decant the stuff that sits on your bathroom counter – that way you'll get to look at the pretty jar and enjoy your work, while the stuff hidden away in your cupboard can stay in its own packaging.

How to choose: a hairbrush

I have far too many hairbrushes and all they do is take up precious room in the bathroom. I use only one – a cheapie I bought on vacation. I like it because the bristles are tipped (so they don't scratch your scalp) and they are well-spaced (so it doubles as a comb as well as a brush and I can use it to detangle wet hair). A tip on tips – look for a brush that has the tips as part of the bristle. Separate tips will eventually drop off, leaving some very sharp bristles. Of course, my hairdresser says you must never use a hairbrush on wet hair. You should use a wide-toothed comb, and once the tangles are gone and the hair is partially dry, then you can use the brush.

One way to keep static to a minimum is to use a brush with natural bristles. Don't be sucked in by the hype surrounding boar-bristle brushes. Any natural bristle will do.

There are basically three types of brush. The **paddle brush** has a wide flat head and is best for making long hair straight. It will flatten out layers so if you are looking for volume, you don't want this brush. Then there's the **cushion style** that is good for hair that's already smooth and straight. These brushes are easy to spot because the brushhead has a flat back. And lastly there's **round-** or **barrel-headed** brushes. These are used for adding volume and curls. The ones with the metal heads heat up as you blow-dry and act as curlers.

How to clean: a hairbrush

* First remove any hair. My mother uses a comb and rakes it through the bristles to do this – it works beautifully!
* If the brush doesn't have a pad that the bristles sit in, you can immerse the whole thing in warm soapy water and swish around to clean. Repeat the process in clear warm water to remove soap. Leave the brush bristle-side down on a towel to dry.
* If the bristles do sit in a pad, you can dip just the bristles in warm soapy water and then clear water. Avoid getting the pad too wet. If the pad looks like it needs a cleaning, go over it with a scrubbing brush (nail brushes are perfect here) dipped in soapy water and then again with clear water.

The bath and shower

I love taking a bath and have spent ridiculous amounts of money on bubble bath that comes in nice-looking bottles. I like to see these bottles arranged around the edge of the bath, as opposed to plastic bottles of shampoo or face cleansers. Luckily, our bath is a perfect length for me – it's one of those items that are expensive to replace if it's not right. If you are choosing a bath, a comfortable size (for most people) is 5 feet long and 28 inches wide.

Cast-iron – these baths are coated in porcelain. Most often they are freestanding and they hold the heat well for long baths.

Enameled steel – these baths are not as durable as cast iron and don't hold the heat as well.

Fiberglass or acrylic – both lightweight and cheap bath materials. Many baths these days are fiberglass, which is cheaper than cast iron or steel. However, they do scratch quite easily and don't hold the heat well.

Shower stall – these should be a minimum of 3 feet square, but better to go up to 4 feet square. For a shower/bath combo, which is a great solution for the compact bathroom, bath taps should be 28–33 inches from the bottom of the tub. Shower taps should be 48–52 inches from the bottom. A shower head should be 69–72 inches high. Water-saving shower heads are definitely the way to go. The new ones are excellent and inexpensive.

Whirlpool – these baths are usually made out of lightweight fiberglass or acrylic. The large amount of water needed to fill these tubs adds a considerable weight to the bath. Make sure you have the right supports.

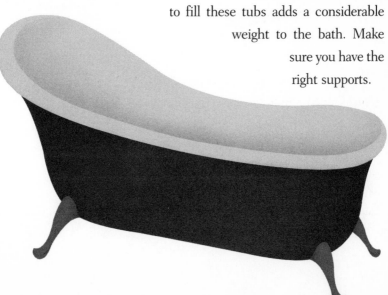

Towels

Weight, rather than softness, is actually a better indicator of a quality towel – the heavier the feel of the towel, the better. Soft towels have often been washed in a fabric softener that coats the fibers in a waxy substance and cuts back on their absorbency. Look for all-cotton towels. Combed cotton is the best cotton for towels as only the highest quality cotton (with longer fibers) can be combed.

Textured towels are woven on a different loom than smooth towels, and velour-feel towels have had the loops cut. These towels are very absorbent but they can take a long time to dry. And the looped variety brush water off you as well as absorb it. All that's hard to test in a store so, when buying, look at weight and, if possible, loops per square centimeter – you want a high number.

Standard sizes for towels are:

* Regular bath towel   24 × 46 inches
* Face cloth   12 × 12 inches
* Hand towel   18 × 30 inches
* Bath mat   19 × 27 inches
* Bath sheet   38 × 72 inches
* Guest towel   12 × 18 inches

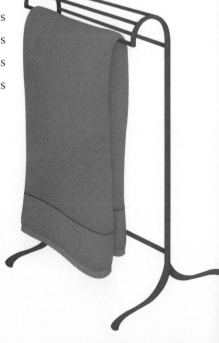

One further note on towels – heated towel rails are wonderful things. If you have a choice, do choose one.

How to wash: towels

Wash new towels before you use them so there are no nasty surprises from the dye. Some people recommend washing towels separately for sanitary reasons. I don't do this. Darks go with darks, lights with lights. The key to washing a towel is to make sure it's balanced in the machine. Wash two at a time and place evenly in the bottom of the machine so there's no chance of unbalancing (if you have a front loader you won't have to worry about balancing the towels – just chuck them in). Don't use hot water or overdry in the dryer as it weakens the cotton and shortens the life of the towel. It's much better to line dry if you can. Shake the towel when it's wet and again when it's dry to fluff it up and counter some of that scratchiness it gets from line drying (although I know a lot of people who like their towels a little scratchy). Ironing towels can reduce their absorbency by flattening the nap. To increase towels' absorbency, you can soak them overnight in borax: 1 tablespoon of borax per quart of water. Then wash them normally in the machine. For a guest bathroom, make sure there's fresh soap and towels to make your guests feel welcome.

Bath mats

I've had them all: the slatted wooden one that seemed to grow mold the second you turned the shower on; the lovely fluffy one that felt great underfoot but collected every speck of dust and refused to release it; and the cheapie terry toweling mat that turns up in every linen shop around the country. The terry toweling mat has proved to be the stayer. It doesn't feel very luxurious, but it does its job protecting your feet from the cold tiles very well. And it dries easily – just hang it over the edge of the bath or, better still, pop it on a heated towel rail.

How to wash: the bath mat

If the mat is wooden, use a mixture of salt and vinegar to remove stains. You can also try rubbing it over with a small amount of wood oil to stop it cracking. Teak oil is a good choice here. A fluffy mat needs to be washed regularly. Put in the washing machine as per instructions for the material.

The toilet

Believe it or not, there are serious trends in toilet design. The big debate is whether to have a two-piece toilet with the bowl on a pedestal base on the floor, or a floating bowl (no pedestal, easy to clean underneath, the toilet seat is usually fourteen inches off the floor). The next question is whether to bury the cistern in the wall behind the toilet (looks good but hard to get at for repairs) or have it suspended on the wall behind the bowl (doesn't look as streamlined but much easier to get at). Whichever you choose, make sure it is installed by a professional and that you are very clear about exactly how your model works. Toilets aren't difficult to fix when things go wrong, but each cistern is a little different and you need to know the quirks of your particular model.

Smells in the bathroom

Combating smells in the bathroom is like combating them in the kitchen – once they are there, they're hard to mask. In my experience, an open window combats most smells very efficiently and fills the room with fresh air. A friend lights a match after using the toilet and that also seems to work. You can try room fresheners – they do hide smells, but only by blanketing the room in a manufactured scent. Do indulge in nice soap and your favorite body wash, though.

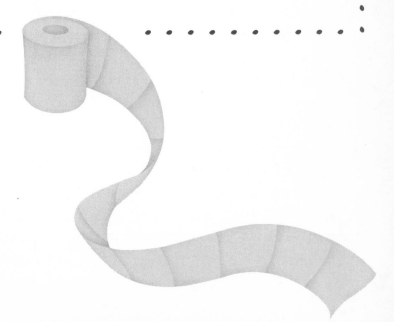

How to clean: the bathroom

necessities

****

* ✱ **Clean rags, cloths, or sponges** – rags and cloths are easier to clean than sponges (throw them in the washing machine after you've used them, and wash on hot with detergent and a splash of bleach). Sponges are trickier – they'll need to be soaked in bleach and water overnight, and then washed normally.

* ✱ **Disposable rubber gloves** – you can buy these from the supermarket. Or, use normal rubber gloves (have a pair set aside just for the bathroom) and give them a good washing with a mild bleach solution when you're done.

* ✱ **Toilet brush**

* ✱ **Paper towels**

There's a method to the madness in my bathroom-cleaning. While most rooms can be cleaned in whatever order you find convenient (although there are a few basic rules that makes things easier), the bathroom really benefits from a stricter routine. If you follow this guide, you are cleaning from the least to the most dirty part of the bathroom, and spreading fewer germs as you go. If you don't have time for a thorough cleaning, grab a bucket of very hot water, a splash of bleach *or* household ammonia (never mix the two, as mentioned on page 32), put on your rubber gloves and wipe down all hard surfaces with a cloth (best to use a cloth you can then throw in the washing machine). Start with the sink, the counter around the sink, cupboard doors, bath and area around the bath, and end with the toilet. Follow with a dry cloth in the same order – this will buff everything up to a nice shine and help remove any bleach or ammonia residue.

When you have time to give the bathroom a more thorough clean (once a week), follow the procedure below. Cleaning products vary and are detailed where necessary.

1. **Toilet** – give it a once-over with a toilet brush every day. This will stop any buildup and rings forming around the water level. Don't use a cleaner, but rinse the brush with a few flushes.

    For a proper clean, pour cleaner into the toilet bowl to let it stand while you clean the rest of the bathroom (you'll tackle the toilet last). You can use ¼ cup of bleach or ¼ cup of vinegar. Or try a commercial cleaner. Gel or liquid ones should be sprayed high on the bowl and allowed to dribble down to the water. Dry cleaners work best when you flush the toilet, wetting the sides of the bowl so the grains of powder will stick.

2. **Bathtub** – if the tub is **porcelain**, undiluted bleach can eventually eat away at the surface. Abrasives will also scratch it. Rinse the bath before cleaning to remove any debris including hair. I use warm water just because it's nicer to swish around in. Then, for an environmentally friendly cleaning, wipe with a solution of 1 part vinegar to 3 parts water. For hard-to-remove spots and rings around the plug hole, try a baking soda paste or a small amount of borax made into a paste with lemon juice. You may need to resort to a gentle abrasive cleaner like Bon Ami. I prefer using commercial cleaner, simply because I think it works more easily, but baking soda paste will also do the job. Rinse the bath well with clean water.

Check the drain and remove any hair. Lastly, dry the bath with a clean cloth or old towel. If the tub is plastic or fiberglass, follow the manufacturer's instructions. If you don't have these, try a nonabrasive cleaner or the water and vinegar solution. It's important not to let these baths scratch.

Baths that have been **reenamelled** need special care, as the new coating is often just a heavy-duty paint. Clean with a nonabrasive all-purpose cleaner, or vinegar and water. For stains in all types of baths, try 1 part vinegar to 1 part water. To remove stains or bad scratches from an **acrylic** or **fiberglass** bath, try sanding with very fine sandpaper and then buffing with silver polish. Rinse well with clear water.

3. **Shower head and walls** – tiles are the most common material used in lining showers. Tiles in the bathroom are often made dull by the buildup of scum. This is a thick film made up of body oils and soap residue. It attracts dirt and is a breeding ground for mold. I know some people who wipe down the shower walls and floors every time they have a shower to remove any lingering moisture. It's a good idea, but I'm not that kind of person. I think a good clean once a week suffices and the bathrooms I've used over the years have been none the worse for a weekly rather than a daily cleaning. You will need to use a low-abrasive cleaner. Follow the instructions for that particular product, making sure you rinse it off well. Or you can try wiping down the tiles with white vinegar (1 part vinegar to 6 parts hot water).

To get rid of mold if it does develop, try wiping over with neat white vinegar, leaving for an hour, and then scrubbing with a soft brush. If that doesn't work, try a solution of 1 part bleach to 2 parts water. Apply this with a brush so that you can scrub away at it. A toothbrush will probably be needed for the grout. If you've already used bleach, you'll have to continue using it. If the grouting is colored, use Epsom salts instead of bleach.

If your shower head gets clogged, you will have to take it off and boil it in a saucepan with 1 part white vinegar to 8 parts water. You can also try wrapping it in situ in a plastic bag filled with white vinegar. If the shower head is plastic, don't boil it, just soak it in equal parts vinegar and hot water for an hour.

4. **Shower curtain** – this often gets moldy. If you wipe it down with a little white vinegar and hot water, you'll help retard the mold. Scrubbing with a paste of salt and lemon juice will help remove soap scum from the bottom of the curtain. You can also gather the curtain while still hanging and place the bottom in a bucket full of warm water and diaper presoak detergent. Rinse using the shower. Eventually it will need a more thorough washing to really get it clean. Take it down and remove any metal rings (if you can). The care instructions on our 100 percent nylon white curtain say not to use bleach, so I dissolve powder diaper detergent in hot water in the washing machine. I then add the shower curtain and let the cycle run just long enough to get the curtain thoroughly soaked (I use the delicates cycle, because it doesn't need a violent washing). Pause the machine – ours has a button to do this but often you can stop the cycle just by opening the lid. You want the curtain to soak completely submerged. Inevitably there are air pockets. I poke the curtain down with plastic chopsticks kept in the laundry for this purpose. Follow

the soaking instructions for that powder. Because there's metal sewn into the bottom of our curtain (to weigh it down and stop it flapping against your legs when you're in the shower), I'm only supposed to soak it for an hour. But that doesn't work, so I soak it for three and the metal is fine and the curtain is white as new. When you are done soaking, close the lid and let the curtain go through the rest of the cycle. I have read of much more complicated soaking methods that involve using lemon juice and salt at different stages of the wash. If the method above works, why complicate it? If it doesn't work for you, I'd repeat it until it does rather than adding strange things to your washing machine.

For glass enclosures, wipe down regularly with a little white vinegar to inhibit mold. For a thorough clean, add a dash of household ammonia to hot soapy water and scrub the glass using a plastic scourer. Buff with a dry cloth.

5. **Basin** – clean this as you do the bath. Don't use anything abrasive here. Try all-purpose spray cleaners, vinegar and water, or a paste made from baking soda (good for grime). For **taps**, refer to kitchen taps on page 113.

6. **Mirror** – clean with a little white vinegar or household ammonia and water. Polish off with newspaper for a streak-free finish. I've read that one way to keep steam off the mirror is to wipe it down with 1 part glycerine to 1 part rubbing alcohol. I tried it and my mirror still steamed up!

7. **Toilet** – using the toilet brush, scrub the bowl clean, making sure you get up under the lip and down as far as you can into the drain. If there's caked-on dirt, use disposable gloves and a paper towel with either a thick paste of powdered cleaner or

a strong liquid cleaner. The idea is to throw away the gloves and the paper towel rather than using something you'll need to disinfect.

For the exterior, treat in the same way as the sink. The toilet brush also needs a cleaning – shake it around in the clean toilet bowl to get it free of any bits. Soak in the toilet bowl with a good splash of bleach, and leave for a good 10 minutes. While the brush is soaking, clean the holder with a disinfectant. Rinse the brush by flushing the toilet a few times and replace the brush in the stand. The seat and lid should not be treated in the same way as the bowl. They are generally made from softer material like wood or plastic, so you'll need to use a nonabrasive disinfectant cleaner.

* Hard water can leave a ring of calcium at water level in a toilet. You can try dousing with white vinegar, leaving for a few hours, and then scrubbing with a stiff brush.

* Rust stains are caused by a leak in the toilet. First have a plumber fix the leak then, to remove the stain, try making a paste with cream of tartar or baking soda and a little peroxide, and pack the paste directly onto the stain. Leave overnight if you can and scrub off the next morning with a stiff brush.

* If there are stubborn stains, you can try making a paste of borax and lemon juice and spreading it over the spot. Leave it for at least half an hour before flushing.

8. **Floor** – lastly, mop the floor. Use a sponge mop dipped in hot water with a dash of household ammonia, followed by a dry rag. Our bathroom floor is so small I get down on my hands and knees and wash it with a rag. You get into all those nooks and crannies around the toilet a lot more easily if you do it this way.

How to wash: the bathroom ceiling

This is not a fun job and won't need to be done too often. Do it once a year, or more if you notice mold growing. Bathroom ceilings are prone to mold no matter how well the room is ventilated. A painted ceiling will need to be scrubbed with a medium bleach solution. Try 1 cup of bleach to a bucket of water, or you can use sugar soap (available from supermarkets and hardware stores). Painters use this soap to clean the walls before they paint. You can also try a commercial mold remover – just make sure it can be used on paint. You'll need to get up on a ladder or footstool and scrub with the solution, following with a wet cloth dipped in clear water to rinse any bleach residue, before drying with an old towel. To avoid drips running down your arm, try turning up the cuffs of your rubber gloves. See pages 248–9 for how to remove mold from tiles.

How to clear: clogs

You'll need a plunger to clear these. For sinks and baths, first remove the bulk of the water by scooping it out with a cup or mug. Leave about an inch of water in the sink or tub. Place the plunger over the hole, making sure you have a perfectly airtight seal, and work it up and down. The idea is to force water into the hole and back out again, sucking up any blockage (or pushing it down) as you go. A plunger will fix most clogs but if it doesn't, try a commercial drain-cleaner (like Drāno) and lots of hot water – this will cut any grease that may have built up. (Be careful using large quantities of strong cleaners as they can damage pipes.) Leave the cleaner overnight and, if the clog is still there, you'll have to call in a plumber.

Toilets are unclogged in much the same way. First, make sure you don't make the problem worse – stop flushing and turn the water off. The tap is usually at the base of the toilet, at the back. It's a good idea now to just wait and see if the water goes down. If it doesn't, or only goes down a little, then you will have to use a plunger. If the toilet is full to the brim, this can be a messy job. I suggest you scoop out some water with a container that you can throw away. The water should be poured down a drain and then that area will need to be disinfected. With the plunger securely over the drain in the toilet, press down and release a few times. If there's no water in the bowl, pour in a little as it will make plunging easier. Don't flush! You could cause it to overflow. Once the clog is cleared, flush the plunger in the toilet with a splash of bleach to disinfect it. Shake it off, dry with paper towels, and store it again. If you find the plunger doesn't do the trick, you should call in a plumber.

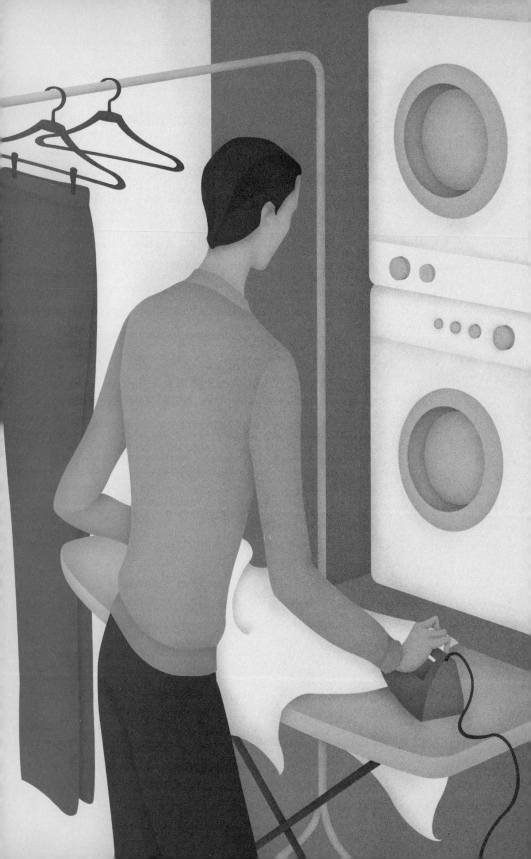

9 . The Laundry

A friend

of mine is convinced people fall into two camps – those who love to do laundry and those who simply do laundry. She loves it and does it beautifully. I love it less and do it adequately. I'm convinced I'd do a better job if we had a better laundry – ours is in a closet outside the bathroom. The dryer sits above the washer and there's a narrow shelf to the left that holds all our cleaning aids. To the right is a slim space where we've managed to fit the ironing board and an array of mops and brooms. It is not an ideal laundry but it is functional. I do yearn for a room with twin tubs, an easily accessible washer and dryer, and counter space for folding. A place where I can bleach, scrub, and even dry my sweaters flat would be lovely.

Laundry DIY

If you're rearranging items in your laundry, take into consideration the plumbing that's already there – the closer the washer, dryer, and tubs are to existing plumbing, the cheaper they will be to install. Also consider access. You don't want to be lugging baskets of laundry up and down stairs if you can help it. For an ideal set-up, you'll have to be clever about space. You'll need about 3 feet in front of a washing machine (24–30 inches wide) to make it easy to load and unload. The same goes for the dryer. Consider the size of the drum when deciding which dryer to buy. If you have a family and are washing large loads, go for a bigger drum. Install a high shelf near the washing machine that will hold powders and other things that you use regularly. This should be as high as you can comfortably reach, to make it hard for children to access. Everything else should be in a lockable cabinet under or over a counter.

Buy in bulk (it's cheaper) and decant into smaller, easier-to-pour containers. Make sure you label everything carefully. Keep a supply of smaller see-through containers (plastic takeout food containers are excellent) – put stain removal products in one container, buttons that have fallen off in the wash in another, mesh bags for washing delicates in another . . .

Good lighting is important for spotting stains, so make sure there's a strong overhead light to work by. Natural light is a plus but most laundries aren't placed to capture the best light, so make do with excellent overhead light. Try to have the light positioned in such a way that it doesn't cast a shadow onto your work area.

How to machine-wash

There's a lot of information on what order to put things into the washing machine. With the detergent I use, the instructions recommend dissolving the detergent in water first, then adding the clothes. (If you've got a front-loader you will probably be asked to place the detergent in a drawer at the front of the machine, from where it will be released into the wash. There's no reason why you can't dissolve the powder before you put it in this drawer, although I'm not convinced this is necessary.) I don't find that very practical, as I'd have to return when the machine was full of water and put the clothes in. I like to limit my visits to the washing machine if possible. Anyway, with my machine you put the detergent down the central stem so there's no chance of powder settling on the clothes and damaging them. One great laundering friend swears by putting the powder in first, then the clothes on top, and then turning the machine on.

She says that way there's no risk of oversudsing and less risk of more delicate clothes being damaged by contact with full-strength detergent. However you decide to approach the finer points of machine washing, there are a few basic rules that will ensure the best care for your clothes.

1. **Sort** light from dark. You can take sorting to great lengths – sorting heavy from light, extra dirty from lightly soiled. But I find if you separate dark stuff from light stuff, put heavy clothes at the bottom of the machine and give heavily soiled items a good soaking first, you really don't need to do more sorting.

2. **Check** pockets. There's nothing more annoying than little shreds of paper stuck to everything. And coins can crash around and damage the lining of the machine.

3. Get to **stains** before you wash. Give the item a good soaking (see page 265).

4. Make sure you use the prescribed amount of **detergent**. If you wash in cold water, dissolve the powder first or use a detergent formulated for cold water.

5. Read the **labels** on your garments. Don't put hand-wash-only items in the machine.

6. Check for **color fastness** on new clothes. Wet an inconspicuous patch, leave for a minute or two, and then dab with a white rag. If color comes off on the rag, the piece will run in the wash. Wash it with darker colors for the first few washes. Then repeat the dab test to check that the color has stopped running.

7. Wash **delicates** in a special bag (or pillowcase) on a gentle cycle using a mild detergent. A gentle cycle will agitate and spin at a much slower (and kinder) rate.

8. Don't **overload** the machine – it means there's less room for water to swish around and do its job, and clothes can rub against each other and cause damage. You can also permanently damage the drum's balance, which can cause your machine to shake and wobble no matter how much is in it.

Generally, hot water is good for whites and very dirty clothes. (Blood is an exception here – hot water sets the stain so only use cold.) Warm water is good for the average wash. Cold water is best for anything that is likely to fade. Hot water can shrink a garment (as can hot air in the dryer). Short cycles are just as efficient in cleaning your clothes unless they are very dirty. Fabric softeners give a waxlike coat to fabric making it easier to iron, reducing static and making it feel smoother. They aren't essential and if anyone in the family has allergies, fabric softeners might cause a bad reaction.

Spot-cleaning before you wash a garment works miracles with certain stains. One friend always scrubs his shirt collars and cuffs with a laundry soap before washing. This is not a bad practice as these areas do become grimy. But you need to weigh up the wear and tear this kind of cleaning will cause. Perhaps scrubbing every few washes would be just as effective. A gentler alternative is to spray the offending areas with a laundry spray (like Shout) before you put the garment in the washing machine.

Front-loaders

My cousin Julia swears by her front-loader and her laundry does always look impeccable. There are a lot of positives to this kind of washing machine, but when it has come to actually buying one I've always been put off by the high price.

Front-loaders are thought to be gentler on clothes. They rotate around a horizontal axis instead of around a central vertical column like a top-loader. The clothes are rolled in and out of a small amount of water at the bottom of the drum (the water fills to just below the level of the door). The direction of the drum alternates to stop the load tangling and clumping.

Because front-loaders open from the front, they are easier to load. They use less water (up to 50 percent less than a top-loader, depending on which model you buy). Less water means less heat (electricity) is needed, and heat makes up 90 percent of the energy used in washing machines. The spin cycle goes to a higher speed and therefore takes out more water and reduces drying time.

Disadvantages include having to bend down to get a load of laundry from the machine. Washing times are also longer than a top-loader. Front-loaders are also, almost always, more expensive than top-loaders.

Powders and softeners

My mother's washing always smells good and it's the brand
of washing powder she buys. It's highly scented and I now
connect that smell with clean clothes. Fabric softeners are
often scented and, if you like the smell, feel free to use one.
In New York I used little paper towels that I threw into the
dryer. Supposedly they stopped static, but I think their
main purpose was to scent the clothes – they were heavily
perfumed. Try lots of different brands of washing detergent
before you settle on one that does the job and smells good.

How to hand-wash

1. Fill a bucket or sink with water (usually warm but read the directions on the garment) and a mild detergent. Completely dissolve the detergent.
2. Immerse the garment. Try not to twist or rub. Simply lift the garment in and out of the water, making sure it is thoroughly soaked. Only leave very soiled items to soak, and never leave wool to soak (see next page for wool).
3. Rinse in clear water and gently squeeze dry. You will have to repeat this several times to get rid of all the soap. Adding a dash of white vinegar to the last rinse will help get rid of soap.
4. Roll the garment in a clean towel to remove extra water.
5. Most hand-washed items will need to be dried flat. Follow the drying instructions on the label.

Wool

Hand-washing wool is the best way to care for it, although I have been known to put some of my less precious sweaters in the washing machine on a delicate cycle. For pieces that seem to take forever to dry, try rolling them in a towel and placing in the washing machine on the slowest, gentlest spin cycle. (But don't do this with cashmere or anything precious.) This will rid them of most of the water. Dry garments inside out and never in direct sun.

Martha Gardener's wool-mix, first published in *Everyone's Household Help*, has been a stalwart for generations of Australians. Combine 4 cups of soap flakes, 1 cup of rubbing alcohol and 1.5 ounces of eucalyptus oil. Mix all this together in a plastic container and it will become the consistency of mashed potato. Then spoon out 2 tablespoons to 1 quart of warm water to use for washing.

Wash wool garments by hand in a sink full of warm water and wool-mix. Immerse the garment and gently squeeze it until it is completely wet. Empty the water and rinse with lots of cold clear water until all the soap has gone. Or use a commercial detergent specially made for woolens, such as Woolite.

How to soak

Soaking in normal laundry detergent is often all a dirty piece of clothing needs. It's important for the environment and the life of your clothes to limit your use of bleach, and it's surprising how well normal detergent works. Before you reach for the bleach or presoak, try soaking overnight in your regular detergent. If that doesn't work then try something stronger. I soak whites (T-shirts, shirts, and napkins) overnight in detergent and they almost always come clean – especially if I've treated stains before the soak.

1. Read the label to make sure the item can be left to soak. (You may need to leave it overnight if the stain is a stubborn one.)
2. Fill a bucket or tub generously. You don't want the item to be squashed and it must be fully immersed. (Your washing machine may have a prewash soak option which makes things rather easy.)
3. Use just the amount of detergent suggested and dissolve thoroughly in the water.
4. If there's a bad stain, you can rub a small amount of neat detergent directly on the spot, then leave to soak. Leave in the water for at least two hours, or overnight if necessary.
5. Rinse thoroughly and wash as you normally would.

How to dry: on the line

This is a great luxury for me. I love the way my clothes smell after they've been line-dried (although I still prefer to put my towels in the dryer so they don't end up stiff and scratchy). My small balcony faces south so drying on the line is never a quick or sunny proposition. Whenever I get the chance, I hang things in the sun. The trick is to hang items so they can be easily folded. A drying rack is handy for items that won't go in the dryer but are too delicate to whip around on the line outside. Those inexpensive white plastic-coated metal ones are excellent. You can't always pick a day to hang out your laundry, but obviously the sunnier and windier the better. In fact, keep drying times in mind here – you won't have to leave the laundry out as long on a hot sunny day (the sooner you get it in, the less chance it has of getting messed up by a passing pigeon!).

Store a few extra plastic clothes hangers in the laundry for drying shirts that can't go in the dryer. Don't use metal ones, as they can rust.

1. **Clip** trousers and shorts by the waistband, after giving them a good flick and smoothing them well.
2. **Hang** T-shirts, skirts and dresses upside down from their bottom hem.
3. Hang shirts on **plastic hangers** on the line.
4. **Spread** sheets out if there is room and hang from an edge. The same goes for towels and tablecloths.

How to dry: in the machine

1. **Check** the label to see if the item can be put in the machine and what temperature it will tolerate.
2. **Wring out** as much water from the item as possible. If still wet, give an extra spin in the washing machine.
3. Note that if you **overload** the machine, the items will take more time to dry and can come out wrinkled.
4. **Synthetics** shouldn't be dried in a hot dryer. And don't dry anything with rubber or elastic, even on a cool setting. Pleated items should be hung on a line. Wool items should be dried flat.
5. Don't **overdry** items as they can wrinkle. If this does happen, consider putting them back in the dryer with a damp towel and running it for a few minutes.

How to fold and hang

I remember what a revelation it was to see Janeane Garofalo in *Reality Bites* folding T-shirts at Gap. She plays the manager and in one scene she is folding T-shirts perfectly with the aid of an letter paper–size board. I always wondered how they got those perfect stacks of clothes.

I'm not suggesting you rush out and buy a board to fold your clothes around (although you can use a clean chopping board). But systematic folding is a great way to keep clothes neat between the wash and wear.

Give yourself lots of room. A clean kitchen table is a good place to fold clothes.

✱ Lay **sweaters** and **T-shirts** flat on the table with the back facing up. Fold the arms across the back, taking a narrow part of the body with it. Then fold the body in half and flip over.

✱ To save the elastic in your **socks**, think about folding them together rather than balling them up.

✱ I am not a great one for folding **underwear** (hence my rather messy top drawer) but I know people who do. It does help keep that top drawer tidy if you neatly fold your underpants (at least in half), and the same goes for bras, boxer shorts, and anything else you might store with your underwear. If this all seems too fiddly, invest in some neat little boxes that sit inside your drawer (I notice that Ikea now sells perfect little white canvas ones). Then you don't need to fold – just make sure you put like with like!

✱ Don't fold **trousers**. They need to be hung in your wardrobe – either by their hems so the center fold on each leg faces out, or by the waistband (also with the center fold on each leg facing out).

✱ **Skirts** benefit from a hanger with clips. I've got a wonderful tiered hanger that holds six skirts. Suspended from clips, they keep their shape. You can hang them off a normal hanger if they have hanging strings attached.

How to iron

The key to easy ironing is to iron clothes (or anything else) when they're still slightly damp. A steam iron or a spray bottle to dampen clothes will also make things easier. The ironing board should be at hip-level so you don't have to bend. Choose an adjustable board so that you can set it to your desired height. Make sure the board is well padded. A silver cover will disperse the heat well, or slip a piece of foil under a normal cloth cover for the same effect. We stopped using a commercial starch spray because it was clogging up the iron and our clothes seem to be fine without it, but I know a lot of people who use a spray and love the crispness that it gives.

For the best results, follow the ironing procedure below.

1. Before you start, get the items to be ironed ready by stretching and smoothing them.

2. Sort the clothes according to temperature (check the care label on each item). Iron from coolest to hottest. If temperature is really important, you may need to let the iron sit for a few minutes to adjust to the new level.

3. Cotton and rayon should be ironed right side up. Polyester can be ironed either way. Iron all other items inside out. To prevent shine on dark fabrics, always iron inside out. Fragile fabric such as silk won't tolerate a hot iron, so make sure it has properly cooled to the appropriate setting before you use it. Always test it on an inconspicuous bit of the garment first.

4. To iron out sharp creases, use the burst of steam feature – if your iron has it. If not, use a spray bottle to dampen the area.

5. For all flat items (linen, tablecloths, napkins, etc.) iron damp and on the back first.

6. When ironing large tablecloths, place the board next to a table. As you iron, drape finished pieces of the cloth over the table to prevent creasing. To iron a round tablecloth, break it down into segments the size of your board. Iron each segment until you reach the beginning. (When storing linen tablecloths, consider rolling them around a tube or hanging them to prevent creases.)

7. To protect dark or sensitive fabrics, use a pressing cloth between the fabric and the iron. Any thin white cotton cloth will do. Try an old pillowcase.

8. To iron flat items with monograms or embroidery, place a thick towel on the ironing board. Place the dampened item embroidery-side down and iron over. Turn over and iron around (not over) the embroidery.

How to iron: a shirt and trousers

Once you've mastered a shirt and trousers, you can tackle pretty much anything. It's easier to iron a shirt on an old towel. The fabric will grip better to the terry toweling and will give the buttons a cushioned surface to sink into when you pass the iron over them.

Shirt . . .

Begin with a well-washed and damp shirt. Spray each section with sizing or starch as needed when you come to it. For example, a cuff or collar may benefit from a little stiffening, as may the area at the front of the shirt around the buttons. Also, have a spray bottle of water ready in case you need to dampen an area (this is a must if you iron a crease into the garment – a good spray of water will dampen it enough to allow you to properly remove that crease). Don't use too much starch as it can make the garment stiff.

1. Do the cuffs first. Lay one sleeve along the length of the board. The bulk of the shirt will be hanging off the square end of the board. Iron the inside of the cuffs and up the split in the sleeves.

2. Smooth the sleeve with your hands, flattening out any wrinkles as you go. Then iron up the sleeve, moving the iron back and forth (never move in a circle as this can damage the fabric). Repeat with the other cuff and sleeve.

3. Slide the tops of the sleeves over the pointy end of the board and iron them smooth.

4. Now do the collar. (The idea is to do all the fiddly bits where you need to handle the shirt a lot before you do the larger sections. If you don't do it this way, you might crease the body of the shirt

when you're ironing a cuff or collar.) Lay the shirt open on its back so you can iron the inside of the collar first. Iron from the middle of the collar out to avoid any creasing. Flip the shirt over and repeat on the outside of the collar.

5. Turn the shirt around and pull one of the front panels over the square end of the board. Carefully slip the iron around the buttons. Do the right front first, then the right side seam, then the back and left side seam, and finally the left front panel.

6. Hang the shirt on a hanger and button it up to keep it in place.

Starch

Commercial starch sprays usually contain modified cornstarch for body, silicone that prevents the iron from sticking, borax that keeps the starch from breaking down, and fragrance. Sizing is gentler than starch and won't leave the garment feeling so stiff. It usually contains cellulose gum for light body, borax, and fragrances. Both are available at the supermarket.

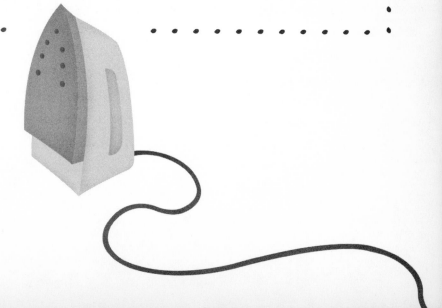

Trousers . . .

Zip or button the trousers closed before you begin.

1. Start at the waistband. Pull the trousers over the pointy end of the board. Press rather than move the iron back and forth over the waistband. Rotate the trousers until the whole band has been pressed flat and smooth.

2. Now iron the pockets flat. It may be easier to pull them inside out to do this.

3. Iron the rest of the top of the trousers around the pointy end of the board.

4. The legs are next. Lie the trousers flat on the board and align the seams. Peel back the top leg and iron the inside of the bottom leg. Flip the trousers and repeat.

5. If you are ironing in a crease, start it midway down the zipper and right in the center of each leg. If the trousers are pleated, start the crease where the pleats end. For a firm crease, give a good spurt of steam from the iron (or dampen with water from a spray bottle).

6. Once ironed, hang as mentioned in how to fold and hang on pages 268–9.

How to clean: the iron

To clean the scum off the bottom of a nonstick iron, turn it on, let it heat up, then turn it off. While still quite warm, rub it with a clean cloth and a little vinegar and water, or try warm soapy water. You can also rub it over with a damp cloth and a little toothpaste (not the gel type). For irons that are not nonstick, either try the same method, or wipe the plate with a damp cloth dipped in baking soda and then heat the iron. Iron over an old cloth to remove any built-up grime and cleaning residue. A pipe cleaner will get into the steam holes.

To clean the inside of the iron, flush it out with vinegar. First, half-fill the iron with plain water. Then fill to the top with white vinegar. Turn the iron on to its hottest setting and leave for 15 minutes. Turn it off and let it cool completely, then empty it out. Repeat the procedure without the vinegar. Once cooled and emptied the second time, it's ready to use.

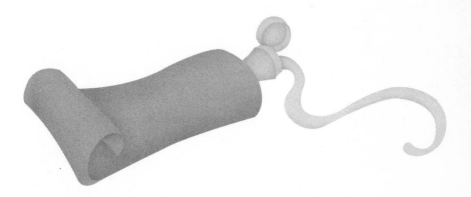

How to care: for fabrics

Acetate – you'll often find this fabric as a lining. It drapes well and doesn't wrinkle easily. Usually you'll have to dry-clean it. If the label says washable, make sure you check for colorfastness before you wash it with anything else, and always wash in cold water (because it can shrink) on a delicate cycle.

Acrylic – mimics wool and is often blended with wool. Wrinkle-resistant and dries quickly. Wash as for wool – either by hand or machine-wash on a delicate cycle. It may pill, so turn inside out before washing.

Cashmere – wash in a mild shampoo (try Johnson's Baby Shampoo), wring out and dry as for wool.

Cotton – can be machine-washed but read care instructions and check for colorfastness. White cotton can be bleached and washed in very hot water. It wrinkles, but is easily ironed.

Linen – less strong than cotton. Some linens can be machine washed – check the care instructions. Wrinkles easily and should be ironed damp.

Lycra, spandex, elastic – used where a piece of clothing needs to hold its shape. Think swimwear and bike shorts. Wash as for wool.

Nylon – strong, lightweight, wrinkle-resistant. Hand-wash or machine-wash on a delicate cycle.

Polyester – strong, wrinkle- and shrink-resistant. Hand-wash or gentle machine-wash. Like acrylic, it dries quickly.

Rayon – made to mimic silk. Lightweight and strong when dry. Hand-wash or machine-wash on a delicate cycle. Has a tendency to shrink as it is a rather delicate fabric when wet. If the piece is precious, it's probably better to dry-clean.

Silk – the strongest natural fiber and the most wrinkle-resistant. Raw silk still has the natural gum present. Gentle machine-wash using a detergent formulated for delicate fabric or wool. Or, if the piece is fine, hand-wash in cold water, adding 1 tablespoon of vinegar for every gallon of water to the final rinse. Dry flat. As for linen, iron while damp using a pressing cloth to stop shiny seams. I have hand-washed silk pieces that said dry-clean only. They are none the worse for it. But if the piece is precious, don't risk washing it yourself – get it dry-cleaned.

Wool – a strong fiber that resists staining and wrinkling. Hand-wash items labeled washable and dry-clean the rest. A few wool items can handle the washing machine (check the label). Wash them on the gentlest setting. Always use a detergent formulated for woolens and, if washing by hand, roll in a towel to get rid of excess water. No matter how you wash, dry on a flat surface.

How to wash: feathers

Most feathers can be washed in a laundry detergent formulated for delicate items. Fill the bath with about half an inch of warm water mixed with a small amount of detergent. Gently wash the water over the feathers. Let it drain and add fresh warm water to rinse. You may need to rinse a few times to get rid of all the soap. Let the feathers dry thoroughly, out of direct light – this will take at least a day.

Washing pillows or feather-filled quilts

Use a laundry detergent for woolens (see page 264 for Martha Gardener's recipe) to wash pillows or quilts filled with **feathers**. Set the washing machine to a warm gentle cycle. For pillows, it helps to balance the machine if you wash two at once. Dry them in the shade on a flat surface. The top of a drying rack is perfect. I've read that you can put them in the dryer (on low/cool) with a few tennis balls to plump them up, but in my experience there's no need, and I also think the tennis balls could damage the pillow's shell. If your quilt is large, consider having it dry-cleaned or take it to a laundromat where you can do it yourself in a large washing machine.

My **polyurethane** foam pillow came with a cotton case that zips off and can be machine-washed in warm water and tumble-dried. The foam can be sponged clean with a mild detergent and warm water, and then dried in the sun. If you need to wash the whole pillow, you can place it in a bathtub of warm water and mild detergent (a wool detergent is good here). Squeeze the soapy water through and rinse well. Finish the drying process by squeezing between towels. Don't lift a wet foam pillow as it can tear. Dry away from direct heat or sun. It will take at least 72 hours for the pillow to dry completely.

Pillows filled with **polyester** can be washed in a machine on a warm gentle cycle, and they can be warm tumble-dried. If you don't want to tumble-dry, they can also be dried on a rack like a feather pillow.

How to remove: fabric stains

For really stubborn stains on strong natural fibers (cotton, linen) you can use a tiny bit of stain remover – rub it on the spot, rinse immediately, and then machine-wash. But don't do this often, and only as a last resort on a really stubborn stain, as it will weaken the fabric. Otherwise, follow the appropriate directions below.

Baby formula – pretreat with a commercial stain-remover (or make your own paste from water and powdered laundry detergent). Soak for at least an hour. Wash as usual.

Berries – rub the spot with lemon juice, leave for 1–2 hours, and then wash as usual.

Blood – the trick here is cold water. If the blood is wet, rinse immediately with lots of cold water. If it's dry, soak the stain first in a paste of salt and cold water (or treat with a commercial stain-remover). Run water over the paste after an hour. You can also try soaking in bleach for about an hour. Wash as usual.

Brown stains – these often form on linen or baby-clothes that have been stored for a while. Rub the mark with a paste made from baking soda and lemon juice, then wash as usual.

Chocolate – wet the stain and rub over with stain-remover (or your own paste, as above). Wash as for that fabric. If the stain hasn't budged, try soaking in bleach for about an hour.

Fruit juice – rinse in lots of cold water (hot can set the stain). Wash as usual. If the stain remains, try soaking in bleach or treating with a commercial stain-remover.

Grass – soak natural fibers in 2 parts rubbing alcohol to 1 part household ammonia and 3 parts hot water. Wash as usual. For non-natural fibers, try a strong laundry soap and stiff brush.

Ink – try treating with a commercial stain-remover and washing as usual. If the stain remains, don't dry; instead, try dabbing with household ammonia mixed with a little water. Rinse thoroughly and rewash.

Jam – mix 1 pint of water with 1 ounce of borax and sponge onto the spot.

Lipstick, makeup – rub the spot with a cloth that's been dipped in water and a little household ammonia.

Mercurochrome – try calamine lotion on the spot. Leave overnight and then remove with a damp cloth. Rubbing alcohol can also be used on Mercurochrome.

Mildew – sunlight is mildew's worst enemy because it kills the fungus. Hang the fabric on the line on a sunny day. Cold frosty nights will also kill mildew, as will sponging with a mild bleach solution (before washing as usual).

Perfume – this can discolor fabric, often leaving a brown stain. Treat with glycerine – leave for a few hours and then wash in warm soapy water. Make sure you rinse well.

Red dust – if you've ever lived in or traveled through places like the desert, you'll know about this fine red dust that seems to get into everything. To wash, try soaking fabric overnight in cold water and borax (2 tablespoons of borax to 1 quart of water). Wash the next day in hot soapy water with 2 tablespoons of rubbing alcohol. Make sure colored garments can handle the alcohol.

Rust – soak the stain in 1 teaspoon of cream of tartar mixed with 1 pint of water. For really stubborn stains, make a paste of lemon juice and baking soda and leave on the stain for 20 minutes, then wash as usual.

Seawater – you need to dissolve the salt in the stain, by sponging with warm clear water. Follow this with a dab of rubbing alcohol, then wash as usual.

Seaweed – dab the spot with rubbing alcohol, then wash the fabric thoroughly.

Semen – soak in 2 tablespoons of borax and cold water, then wash as usual.

Sweat – Martha Gardener suggests damping the spot with white vinegar. Then crush 3 aspirins and mix with cream of tartar and a little water to make a paste. Leave on the stain for an hour, then wash as usual. Alternatively, dab the stain with household ammonia, then wash as usual.

Tea – shake borax directly onto the stain and then soak the fabric in warm water. Wash as usual.

Tomato – these stains are UV-sensitive, so dry the item in the sun for a few hours and watch the mark fade.

Vegetable – remove with a solution made from 2 tablespoons of borax to 1 quart of water. Wash as usual.

Wax – run a block of ice over the wax to harden it and scrape off with a blunt knife. There will be a small amount left that should come up with a cloth dipped in a little eucalyptus oil, nail-polish remover, or rubbing alcohol. You can also lay brown paper over the wax and then iron with a warm iron (just warm enough to melt the wax). Keep ironing over fresh patches of paper until the wax has disappeared.

Wine – on clothes, use soda water immediately to mop up. Repeat until the mark has disappeared, and then wash the garment as usual.

Laundry emergencies

Bleach – once something has been splashed with bleach, there's nothing you can do to save it. You could try getting it dyed professionally but more often than not the process won't be successful. Best to retire the item.

Color – you pull your favorite white T-shirt from the wash and find it's turned a pale pink. It's been washed with new red socks. In my experience, you can kiss the T-shirt good-bye (they make excellent rags). You can try immersing it immediately in a bucket of water with 3 tablespoons of bleach. I haven't had any luck with that option but I know people who swear by it. Make sure the fabric isn't too delicate or you could be doing more damage than good. (See how to care for fabrics on pages 276–7). If you can't bear to part with it, consider having the piece of clothing professionally dyed a darker color.

Shrinkage – I had the most amazing black dress made from beautiful Italian crepe. When my husband and I first moved in together, he did a load of wash and chucked every-thing from the machine straight into the dryer. The dress ended up looking like a child's T-shirt. There's nothing you can do about shrinkage – if something shrinks you simply can't reverse it. I still miss that little black dress.

Dry-cleaning

Water can't always be used to clean a garment – some fabric doesn't handle it well. Wool, for example, repels water. In dry-cleaning, a solvent is used in the place of water. The only dry thing about this method is that it doesn't use water. Originally, the solvent used was kerosene or gasoline. Today the majority of dry-cleaners use perchloroethylene. The clothes are washed in this solvent, and then the solvent is removed in an extractor. (If your clothes smell when they come back from the dry cleaner, they haven't extracted the solvent properly.) The clothes are pressed once they are clean (it's this pressing that can leave them shiny – not the actual washing). There is quite a bit written about the health effects of perchloroethylene. I must admit that I don't like to get anything dry-cleaned unless it's really necessary. A lot of dry-clean-only garments can actually be hand-washed. If you do get clothes dry-cleaned, don't stuff them in the wardrobe in their bags; hang them out to air first.

Bleach

There are two types of bleach. Chlorine bleach (active ingredient is sodium hypochlorite) is sold in a liquid form and often referred to as household bleach. It's used in the laundry for washing/soaking, and around the house for cleaning. Nonchlorine (oxygen) bleach has hydrogen peroxide as its active ingredient in liquid form, and sodium percarbonate or sodium perborate as its active ingredient in powder form. Diaper presoaks or nonchlorine bleach in powder form can be used on colored fabrics when ordinary household bleach is not recommended.

A mild bleach solution is 1 part bleach to 10 parts water. Don't soak anything in bleach for too long – 10 minutes might be all that's needed. A long soak can weaken the fabric and permanently damage it. With that in mind, always make sure you thoroughly rinse bleach out before you wash. Soak in warm rather than cold water.

WARNING – never use bleach with ammonia as together they can produce toxic fumes.

Bleach alternatives

Hydrogen peroxide – use a solution of 1 part hydrogen peroxide to 6 parts water. It's a milder bleach and can be used where normal bleach can't (wool, silks, and other delicate fabrics). Always check the care label and test a patch of clothing before using.

Lemon juice – a mild natural bleach and well worth trying before you use stronger chemicals.

Sunlight – a natural bleach. You can try hanging sheets and towels out on a hot sunny day to see if the stains break down.

How to arrange: the linen cupboard

A stylish work colleague admitted to me when I was starting this book that she is obsessed with linen. She has all the bed linen for her house folded neatly in sets, tied carefully with ribbons and scented with fresh lavender from her garden. I had a pang of inadequacy thinking about the state of my own linen. While it is all neatly folded, it sits on a high shelf in my son's closet and has never rubbed shoulders with a ribbon, much less a sprig of lavender.

I do love the idea of a beautifully presented linen cupboard and, when it comes to changing sheets, a well-organized one is a great help (no digging around for a matching bottom and top sheet). But I think this is one of those times when you really need to do what works for you. Scented bags of lavender, or any other herb you like the smell of, can be slipped between the folded sheets. Perhaps use the bags to separate sheet sets so they are easier to find.

One thing you really should do is put sheets away in sets – top and bottom sheets and pillowcases for each bed in the one spot will make your life so much easier. My mother is one of ten children, and when they were growing up they were assigned their own color. The yellow sheets, towels, face cloths, etc., were hers (she now has a sharp dislike for yellow). Or you can do what I do and buy all white – everything goes with everything else.

How to clean: the laundry

You'll find that cleaning this room is much like cleaning the bathroom, although if you have a dryer there will be more fluff and dust. It's basically a dust and then a mop. I wipe over the washing machine and dryer every few days, as I use them.

For a thorough clean, follow the directions below.

1. First **dust** and **vacuum** (starting as high as you can reach) the room to remove as much dust as you can. You want to get dust off any shelves (empty them first and wipe off everything as you move it with a barely damp cloth), the walls behind and around your washer and dryer, counters, and the appliances themselves (this includes vacuuming the filter on the dryer). It might help to use the vacuum's soft-brush attachment for tricky, narrow spots. Finally, vacuum the floor.

2. Now **wipe** down the shelves with a cloth wrung out in hot soapy water with a little eucalyptus or tea-tree oil added. This will help cut any grease spots and leave the surfaces smelling fresh. Wipe dry with a clean cloth. Do the same for the benches and also

wipe down the walls and appliances. When cleaning the outside of the washer and dryer, make sure you don't damage the control panels – wipe gently and carefully. Dry with a clean cloth. Replace all items on the shelf.

3. The inside of the dryer shouldn't need to be cleaned but **check** to make sure there's no debris lying in there. Make sure you check the dryer's filter every time you use it.

4. **Wash** the inside of the washing machine only if it needs it. It can become dull if you use a lot of fabric softener. Do a short cycle with two cups of white vinegar or Epsom salts poured into the section that usually takes laundry detergent. Clean out the soap dispenser and the lint collector.

5. Lastly, give the floor a good **mopping** with hot soapy water. Rinse with clear water and buff dry with a clean cloth.

10. The Study

This is where the business of the house goes on. Bills get paid, files stored, writing is done, accounts balanced. For some, this area is distilled to a drawer and a patch of kitchen table; for others, it's a bookshelf-lined den with an antique desk and a favorite easy chair. For me it's a corner of the bedroom. This is where my lovely walnut desk sits. It is where my computer lives. Where my files are. Where I can surf the Net, and download pictures of my baby to send to friends. It's where I can gaze out the window through branches of a gum tree to a bustling city road . . . when I really should be writing.

This is the modern study, home office, library. Call it what you will, the challenge is to turn a corner of your home into a spot where you can get done what you need to. This space is all about productivity.

At a minimum you'll need a desk, a chair, and some kind of storage. This is hard for us because space is so limited in our place. We invested in a laptop because it takes up less room, but the printer is still a bulky ugly object (I hate poorly designed technology – it's so intrusive). I refused to get a fax machine as people can e-mail documents or mail them if need be, and that saved considerable space. I replaced the filing cabinet with accordion files that sit on the bottom shelf of a coffee table. The coffee table also houses the printer and paper and a few books perfectly.

The home office

Desk – 28 inches (same height as a dining table). If you type at the table then make it 2 inches lower. It shouldn't be more than 35 inches deep. If you have shelves above the desk, make them no higher than 18 inches above the surface of the desk. Any higher than that and they can't be easily reached.

Computer – consider size. You want the best computer you can afford, but you also want it to take up the least amount of room on your desk. A laptop may be the answer here. Ideally, the top of the computer screen should be level with your forehead and about an arm's length away. The height of the **keyboard** should leave your shoulders relaxed, your hands and wrists straight, and your lower arms forming an open 100° with your upper arms. Ergonomic keyboards are now widely available and are often recommended if you suffer from carpal tunnel syndrome (CTS) – as are wrist pads that sit in front of the computer and support your forearms. The computer's **mouse** can also lead to problems with wrists, fingers, shoulders, and arms. There are many designs on the market that claim to mini-mize these problems. One easy way to ward off CTS is to learn keystrokes that do what the mouse does, thus reducing your use of the mouse.

Wires – the bane of my office. I can't stand looking at that messy tangle. Try labeling the wires – you can write directly onto them with a permanent marker, or use stickers. Then hide them. There are a few clever wire-hiders on the market; check your local compu-ter store. Or you can simply use ribbon or a twist tie to bundle them up neatly behind the desk.

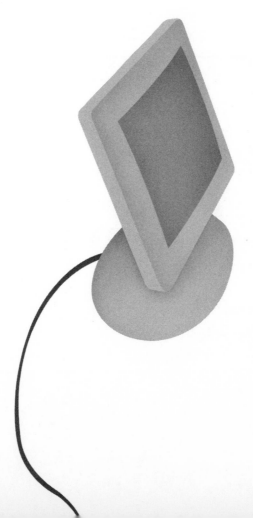

Lighting

The perfect work area will be evenly lit with no shadows near your hand. Consider concealed fluorescent lighting (perhaps built in under an overhead shelf). Their cool white light is ideal to work by, but the trick is to use this light sparingly – don't light the whole room with fluorescent light, just the work area. Make sure any light source is well-covered – you don't want any distracting glare.

The best position for your desk is at right angles to the window. This will cut down on glare to the computer screen and light your keyboard effectively. Initially, my desk faced the window. I had romantic notions of writing and gazing out onto the tree outside. As it happens the window, even though it is south-facing, was too bright and the computer screen was hard to see. The strain as my eyes constantly had to readjust from the brightness of the window to the dark screen and back again meant it was uncomfortable sitting at my desk – not very handy when you've got a book to write. My desk is now to the left of the window. There's a desk lamp on the left side of the desk. I'm right-handed so the light falls well and doesn't cause shadows on my work.

Chairs

Not all expensive chairs are well designed and not all chairs that claim to be ergonomic really are. Use the checklist below, not the price, as a guide when buying.

A good work chair:

* is adjustable in height with a separate adjustable backrest that moves backward and forward as well as up and down
* has a seat shallow enough to allow you good back support without cutting the circulation off at the back of your legs
* has a strong "five star" base (i.e., five prongs spanning out from a central shaft, for stability)
* has sufficient padding so you don't feel the seat base cutting into your legs.

Your chair should be adjusted so that your feet sit flat on the floor when your hips are pushed back in the chair as far as they will go. (I have a phone book to put my feet on as the desk is a little too high.) Your knees should be level or very slightly lower than your hips. You want your lower back to be supported, so use inflatable cushions if necessary. If you've got armrests, make sure they are adjusted so that your shoulders are relaxed (not hunched). For more information on setting up an office go to www.ergonomics.com.au.

Storage

No matter how big your office, the rules for setting up your workspace are the same. But if you have more room to work with, be sure to set up the space so that the things you use often are within easy reach.

According to one storage expert, home offices hidden in a storage unit is what most clients want. Figure out exactly what you need to go into the unit, measure it all and design shelf space accordingly. Shelves that slide out are perfect; just make sure you get strong hardware for the sliding mechanism. It's very important to read the manufacturer's instructions and leave the correct amount of space for ventilation of all electronics. This is often not considered in home offices, and can result in overheating problems that jeopardize the electronics.

There's no great secret to storing things. Just make sure you know where everything is.

How to store: documents

* Keep them dry. That means cool. Warmth can lead to humidity, which will greatly damage paper.
* Store paper in acid-free boxes, plastic, or a safe metal.
* Try not to fold, as documents will deteriorate and tear along the fold line.
* Keep away from light as much as possible. Store in the dark.
* Don't laminate – the materials in the laminate and some other plastics such as polyvinyl chloride will encourage deterioration.
* Store precious papers in a safe-deposit box and keep copies for your reference at home.

How to file

I hate doing it. It's not in my nature to put things away. But I do get a certain satisfaction out of our file drawers with their neatly labeled manila folders. And, come tax time, it's so much easier to sort everything out if you know where to find it. (According to the tax department, we have to keep records for five years.)

I have a drawer that holds hanging files – a much nicer storage solution than a filing cabinet, which all seem to be very ugly. The files are organized by utility, bank, and insurance – all the usual categories. (Be guided here by the bills that you get. When we bought our apartment, our filing system expanded enormously. We added files for the mortgage, taxes, home insurance, etc. For each bill that comes in, there is now a manila folder waiting.) When a bill comes in, it gets put with the other bills in a tray on one of the bookshelves and, when the pile gets too unsightly, it gets filed. We pay almost everything electronically so the bills function more as records than anything else. I also have boxes in the drawer of my desk where I put receipts that I'll use for tax deduction. Occasionally I transfer these to the hanging file.

Another (lazier) option, if you don't like dividing all your bills into separate folders, is to simply have two files: one for long-term stuff like birth certificates and warranty cards, the other for bills. For the bills, you will need 13 hanging files – one for each month and one for papers pertaining to tax (receipts, invoices, etc.). As bills come in, file them away in that month. Choose a day in the month and pay everything that needs to be paid, then put the paid bill back in that file. At the end of the year, remove all items from the hanging file, clip them together, and store them in one large file.

How to organize: manuals

Manuals always come in handy. I've recently filed all our manuals by room. So, instructions for kitchen appliances (small electronics, fridge, dishwasher, etc.) are in a manila folder marked "kitchen." This also contains things like brochures on pots and pans, knives, and any other interesting kitcheny snippets. Household appliances like the vacuum cleaner and electronics like the stereo and television are in a file marked "living room." With this system, I find it much easier to find what I'm looking for. (Although my husband liked the old system – his system – which was to lump all the manuals together in a box. It meant you had to wade through 20 manuals until you found what you were looking for. However, you did know that it would be there somewhere, in that one spot. He complains that we now have to look through a bunch of manila folders to find anything. I think he just needs to get used to the new system.)

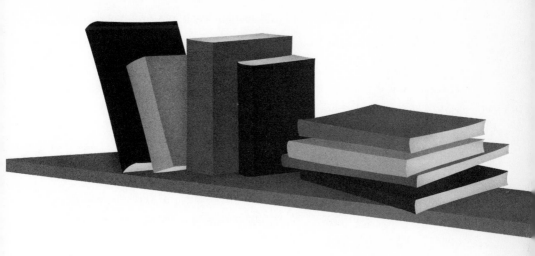

How to store: books

When the boxes were unpacked for the apartment we live in now, I was in hospital having just given birth to Jack. I had no say in where my books went – and there are a lot of them. In the past, I had always separated fiction and nonfiction, and roughly put fiction in alphabetical order. Now they are all over the place and I still haven't got around to the enormous job of pulling them all off the shelves and reordering them.

Do take time to give your book collection some sort of order (I once did it by color – you couldn't find a thing but it looked great) because it gives you a chance to cull. And cull you must. There are books that are precious. Some remind me of where I was when I was reading them (Crete for John Fowles' *The Collector*, Alice Walker is New York, and Malcolm Knox's *Summerland* is a rainy weekend at my parents' beach house). Some are first editions and too precious to give up. Others are just great books and I want Jack to be able to read them when he's old enough. I love all my books and have a very hard time culling, but the few that don't fall into any of these categories get packed away and given to my mother, who sells them at the local community center where she works. Consider offering your old books to local schools or charities. The local community center is often happy to take them off your hands.

It's best to store books on shelves where the temperature is as even as possible. If you have a choice, don't put shelves on outside walls where temperature extremes between night and day will be felt most. Go for interior walls away from heat sources like fireplaces. Adjustable shelves are the best option, so that you can fit large picture books if you need. I found that, for most of our books, 11 inches between each shelf is perfect. Most paperbacks are about 7–8 inches high and hardbacks around 9 inches, so 11 inches gives you a good amount of room to fit your hand in and slide a book out. It also gives you enough room to clean easily. Make sure the shelves aren't too long as they will sag in the middle. Anything longer than 3 feet will need bracing. Our shelves are a generous 13 inches deep; 9 inches is the bare minimum. A little deeper is better so that air can circulate around the books, keeping them cool and dry.

Your collection, rare or not so rare, also needs to be protected from sunlight, humidity, dust, and insects. The best way to do this is to **dust** the tops of them once every few weeks. I find this hard to do because the books must be kept perfectly dry, and yet a dry duster just spreads the dust around. Vacuuming with the soft-brush attachment would make more sense. But, according to the head preserver at the New South Wales State Library, vacuuming can damage books by sucking too hard and perhaps taking up brittle paper or bindings. She recommends taking precious books outside in the sun and dusting with a soft brush like a shaving brush. Hold the book's spine and brush along the top of the book away from the spine.

Insects like silverfish will eat the glue that holds a book together and some will eat the paper. Best to have a professional come in to deal with them if you find insects in any quantity. (See pages 372–89 for advice on dealing with pests.)

Sunlight will fade books, so keep them out of direct sun (unless cleaning). The best temperature to store books at is 68°F.

Humidity or **damp** can do a lot of damage to a book. Humidity will cause books to grow mildew and mold (dust creates the right environment for mildew, so dust well) and generally shorten their life. The highest moisture level books are happy at is 50 percent relative humidity. For detailed instructions on drying a book that's got wet, ask at your local library. This is no small task and can take a lot of patience.

If a favorite or precious book is deteriorating, there are complex and expensive ways to save it – none of which you can easily do at home. Book **repairs** should really be done by a specialist. Try contacting your public library or local university to find binders in your area. Or, refer to the Web site of the Library of Congress (www.loc.gov/ preserv/presfaq.html).

Lending books

Don't do it if the book is precious to you. There's something strange about lending books – they seem to disappear into a black hole, never to be seen again. Only give what you are happy not to get back. Or do what my mother does – write your name in everything and keep a list of who has what. She also does a regular browse through my bookshelves and always comes up with books she's lent me that I haven't got around to returning.

How to clean: the study

If you work in the study every day, do a tidying at the end of the day. As with your bedroom, it is important that this room is dust-free and neat. Sort through the papers on your desk and file what is necessary. Put away books you've used and turn off the computer. Collect any newspapers or magazines and put them away or recycle them. I find there's always an empty mug or two floating around that needs to be taken to the kitchen. The more tidying you do now, the nicer the room will be to return to the next day. Make sure the desk surface is clean and the computer is dust-free – see below for cleaning the computer.

Once a week, give the whole room a thorough cleaning: dust, vacuum, and wipe down surfaces. If you suffer from allergies, you may want to dust and vacuum more regularly.

Computer – first turn off the computer, then dust with a slightly damp lint-free cloth. Wipe fingerprints off the screen and the body of the monitor. You can use a mild detergent if you think it's warranted. Clean the keyboard regularly with a can of compressed air (photographic and computer stores stock these) or try sucking up dust and grit with the soft-brush attachment on your vacuum. You can clean dirty keys with a slightly damp cloth or a very small amount of rubbing alcohol on a lint-free cloth. Again, make sure the computer is turned off when you do this. Never let the computer get wet. If you are likely to spill anything on the keyboard, purchase a plastic cover that you can type through (available at computer stores). Our printer is used rarely and gets very dusty. We cover it with a cloth to help keep dust at bay. Clean and dust the printer as for a telephone (see below). As with the fax, check regularly that paper is well stocked.

Telephone and answering machine – dust these well, then put a few drops of rubbing alcohol on a cloth and wipe down the machine. A good way to remove dust from around keys and in crevices is to use a small brush or a can of compressed air. If you use the air, make sure you aren't just blowing the dust around. You'll need to follow with a good vacuuming and then wipe down with a rag dampened with a few drops of rubbing alcohol. You can also use the soft-brush attachment on your vacuum.

Fax – again, rubbing alcohol will remove any marks on the machine's casing. Dust as for the telephone (above). Now is a good time to check the paper and replace if necessary. You can also wipe out the inside if it needs it, with a cloth dampened with alcohol.

Photocopier – clean and dust the outside as for the telephone. The glass will need to be cleaned of fingerprints and any grime. Do this with a cloth dampened with rubbing alcohol. You can also use a commercial glass-cleaner but spray onto the cloth and then wipe rather than spraying the machine (otherwise you risk getting it too wet).

Typewriter – these usually come with a case or cover and you should make sure you use it when the machine is not in use. The outside of the machine can be wiped with a damp cloth. Try a pipe-cleaner or small paintbrush for those hard-to-reach bits inside. You can clean the keys of an old-fashioned typewriter with a cotton swab dipped in rubbing alcohol. Follow the manufacturer's instructions for cleaning the inside of the machine, replacing the ribbon, and maintaining the daisy wheel or font ball.

Supplies

It's important to have a good supply of stationery to keep your office running smoothly. I think the key here is to not overstock. I have a tendency to buy too much paper and then I find there's nowhere to store it. Depending on your workload, buy what you need to keep equipment tided over – for example, have a spare printer cartridge. I always seem to be running out of ink and it's incredibly annoying when the cartridge dies halfway through a document. But have one spare cartridge – not four.

11. The Entrance Hall

Transitional

spaces such as the entrance hall tend to be overlooked, but it's these places that people first notice when they come to your home. They set the style and tone for the rest of the house. Is there art on the walls, books on the shelves, a rug or bare floorboards? Unfortunately the entrance hall is also the first room you stop seeing. Because you pass through this space and don't actually spend time sitting in it, this is an easy area to neglect. The main function of an entrance, no matter how big or small, is to welcome you into the home. It's a passageway, so having to navigate obstacles like bulky furniture or overstuffed shelves is not a good thing. You want minimum clutter here.

The entrance hall is also a place for storing things. Get it right and you'll save yourself a lot of mess in the rest of the house. A narrow hall table with a drawer can work well for keys and mail. A friend has a long Chinese black lacquered bench in her entry hall. She's placed a small inconspicuous waste bin underneath. When she gets home from work, the keys go on the bench, all the junk mail goes straight into the bin, and the letters she wants to look at go next to the keys.

My aunt is a real stickler for avoiding the double-handling of paper. She's an extremely organized woman who seems to have lists for everything. Her entry hall has a beautiful art deco table where there is always a vase of fresh flowers. When she gets home in the evening her keys go right back into her handbag and her mail goes onto her desk (which she passes on the way to her bedroom to get changed from her work clothes). That way the bills are already in the spot where they will be dealt with and her entrance hall stays clear of clutter.

We are a little less organized. We've got a book-shelf at the end of the entrance hall and one shelf is devoted to keys, loose change, cell phones, and mail. It functions well in that all those day-to-day effects are in the one spot, but it can get messy and I'd pre-fer a drawer so that all the stuff was hidden.

A good friend has a few simple hooks along the wall in the hallway that take her keys and handbag. She always knows where they are and is one of the few people I know who doesn't have that last-minute panic as they leave the house, wondering if they've forgotten some-thing. She also has the luxury of a hall closet. I covet a hall closet! It's the per-fect home for all the stuff in your house that has a life beyond the home – not just jackets and coats but also sports equipment, umbrellas, beach and picnic paraphernalia, etc.

Lighting

Consider light for the entrance hall carefully. An entry should be well lit but not bright. You don't want to feel like you are being interrogated every time you enter the house. This is one of those spots that benefits from spending a bit of money on an appropriate light fitting. Our high-ceilinged entrance hall had two spotlights when we moved in. The previous owner had them trained on a mirror and a painting. The hall is too narrow to really show off artwork to its best effect so we painted it white and put in a bookshelf at the end. And we installed a hanging light fitting that casts a gentle welcoming glow. Your eye now travels down the hall to the shelves and up to the lampshade.

It's a good idea to install dimmers on hall lights. The brightest setting on the dimmer is great to use when you are vacuuming.

How to clean: the entrance hall

Keep this area tidy with adequate storage. A thorough vacuuming once a week (more often if you have time) is all that's necessary for the floor. Every few months, take out any floor coverings and air in the sun (or drape over a balcony or out a window). This will kill off dust mites and give the rug a chance to breathe. It will also allow you to wash the floor underneath. (See pages 152–5 for more on rugs and cleaning.) Keep furniture and artwork well dusted. Once a week should be sufficient for a thorough dusting. Pay special attention to any framed pieces, which tend to collect dust easily (see pages 167–9 for cleaning artwork).

How to care: for plants

Many an indoor plant finds its home in a hallway or entrance. There's something lovely about being greeted by a beautiful bit of nature when you come home. Indoor plants seem to go in and out of fashion. I've always had plants in the homes I've lived

in and I think they are a must, especially in apartments where green space is at a premium. The University of Technology Sydney conducted a study in 2003. It showed that indoor air quality is poor and that the air in our houses is sometimes more polluted than the air outside. This is the result of new building methods that lock air into the house, and the use of building materials that emit pollutants. The study found that leafy indoor plants like the kentia palm, peace lilies, and dracaena remove harmful compounds from the air. But, they don't start removing these compounds until they've been in the house for a while and adapted to their new surroundings. So, you need to maintain the plants you have and keep them healthy and happy.

How to choose: the right plant

Your local nursery should be your first port of call. They will know what works well in your area and have good solid advice for you. It's best not to have very high expectations here. Don't expect a windowsill full of roses if that window is in shade most of the day.

Light

Light is needed for photosynthesis, which is how the plants manufacture their food. Flowering plants need more light than foliage plants, and variegated need more light than fully green plants. When choosing a plant for your home, remember that the darker the foliage, the more likely it is to survive in a dark spot (that's because the darker the leaf, the more chlorophyll it contains so it has a greater ability to make food with less light). Rooms on the south side of your home will be brighter and warmer than rooms on the north.

One way to test whether there is enough light for an indoor plant is to hold a white sheet of paper in front of the window. Hold your hand about 8 inches in front of the paper. If there's a clear shadow, you can leave a plant there. If there's no shadow, you can still leave a plant there but not for a long time; it will need to spend some time in a brighter spot (one week in the dark spot and two weeks in a brighter spot is recommended).

No matter where you place the plant, you will need to rotate it very slightly each day to let all the leaves get equal amounts of light. This will stop the plant bending toward the light and growing at an angle.

You also have to be wary of too much light. Most indoor plants are accustomed to growing in the shade of shrubs or trees. Direct sun dries them out and can burn the leaves. Consider using gauzy curtains to help filter the light from south-facing windows.

Not enough light – signs to look for are small pale leaves, lack of flowers, lower leaves turning yellow and falling off, spindly growth, and variegated leaves turning green.

Too much light – there are very few indoor plants that can stan ﹖ strong direct light. Cacti can and that's about it.

Water

I have a tendency to overwater plants and then underwater them because they look soggy. It's important to remember that you can't water on a schedule, as the same plant will use water at different rates depending on the climate and time of year. Generally, the plant will need more water in the summer than the winter. The best way to tell if the plant needs water is to use your fingers. Poke down about 2 inches and when it feels dry, water it. Don't be surprised if you are only watering once a month using this method. Trust your touch – if it feels moist, it is moist!

In cold weather, use lukewarm water and don't water if the soil feels damp. If you can get the plant outside to water, this is the best method. If not, spray it with a fine mist so that dust is washed off the leaves and branches. You can also try putting it in the shower and giving it a good gentle soaking. I also give my plants the occasional soaking in the sink. Leave them to drain for a few hours before replacing them in their saucers. Never let water stand in the pot's saucer. It soaks into the potting mix and can rot the plant's roots.

A good tip when watering hanging pots is to tie a shower cap or plastic bag to the base of the pot, to protect your floors. The cap or bag can be removed in a few hours, when the plant stops dripping.

Too much water – leaves will be limp and soft areas may appear. There will be poor growth and the edges of the leaves may curl. Leaves will yellow and wilt, and the tips may turn brown.

Not enough water – tips will turn brown and leaves will curl. The plant will droop and lose leaves.

Temperature

The ideal temperature for an indoor plant is 68°F with no great fluctuations. When temperatures fall below 60°F, your plants may begin to suffer. With this in mind, don't place a plant near a heater, fireplace, or directly in line with an air-conditioning unit. And don't put a plant on a windowsill and close the curtains over it; the space between the curtains and glass will get very cold at night.

Too cold – leaves will brown, curl, and fall off.

Too hot – there will be spindly growth even though there is enough light. Flowers won't last long; lower leaves will wilt and fall.

Humidity

Most indoor plants like a bit of humidity. You can achieve this by misting the leaves weekly. Try massing plants together. They will create their own microclimate, producing higher humidity in their vicinity. But you don't want too much humidity because it can cause fungal diseases.

Too dry – leaf tips will turn brown and shrivel, leaf edges will turn yellow, buds and flowers will fall.

Too humid – leaves will go yellow and fall, brown tips or edges will appear on leaves. Fungus or mold may grow on the plant or on the surface of the soil.

Fertilizer

New plants won't need to be fertilized. Remember if there's not a lot of light, there's not a lot of growth, which means the plant simply won't need much fertiliser. In winter when plants aren't growing, you won't need to fertilize at all. Once a month from spring to autumn, you can use a weak dose of liquid fertilizer, or once a year in mid-spring give plants a dose of slow-release fertilizer. Make sure you follow the directions to the letter. But to avoid overfertilizing with soluble fertilizer, mix it a little weaker than the directions suggest and always apply to wet soil. Feeder roots are away from the trunk of the plant so always put fertilizer around the edges of the pot.

Pests and other plant foes

Aphids – these tiny soft-bodied insects suck the life out of plants. Signs that aphids have made themselves at home include yellow, stunted, or curling leaves. Wipe them off with a damp cloth or paper towel and spray the plant with a very mild soapy-water solution, or with pyrethrum or malathion. You can also squash them by hand if there are just a few.

Botrytis – great for grapes that are going to be made into dessert wines but not so good for your plants. Leaves have brown spots or blotches. If it's humid, you can also get furry growth on the brown spots. Unfortunately you'll have to throw the plant away.

Dust – keep plants dust-free and they will thrive. Smaller plants can be placed in the shower and given a gentle spray with water. Larger plants that may be difficult to lift should have their leaves wiped. Try using a soft lint-free cloth (an old T-shirt is good) dipped in warm water. You can also polish leaves of a broad shiny-leafed plant (like a rubber plant) with a cloth dipped in a little milk (1 teaspoon of milk to 1 cup of water). Furry-leafed plants like African violets can be dusted with a soft brush.

It's a good idea to put plants outside when it rains. This will wash off dust and help clean the soil of any salts that have built up from tap water. Don't do this during winter or in direct sun, and never do it if the rain is heavy as it might damage the foliage.

Mealy bug – you will find these bugs on the underside of leaves. They are white cotton ball-like insects. If there's just a few, you can wipe them off with a damp cloth. Otherwise you could try swabbing the leaves with rubbing alcohol, or use a contact insecticide like pyrethrum. Repeat the process two weeks later to get any bugs that may have hatched after the first spray. Any spraying should be done outside.

Scale insects – these appear as flattened red or brown scaly bumps. If there are only a few, you can wipe them off or scrape them off with your fingernail. If the infestation is large, you'll need to spray with white oil (available from garden centers), which smothers them, or try using diazinon or malathion.

Spider mites – these tiny creatures leave telltale fine webs on the underside of leaves. You can spot them easily using a magnifying glass. Leaves can become mottled and fall. The mites are not easy to get rid of. They like dry conditions so remove the top layer of soil, wipe away any web, and spray the plant with a weak solution of horticultural oil (available from garden centers). Make sure you also spray under the leaves. You may have to do this two or three times, every two weeks, to completely eradicate the mite. Best to leave the plant outside while you are doing this. Certainly keep it away from other plants. You can also control small infestations by watering the plant well – getting the leaves wet.

How to go: on vacation

Ideally, have someone water your plants for you (leave detailed instructions as overwatering can be just as deadly for a plant as no watering at all). If you can't find someone to come in and water, you could take an old towel and soak it with water. Line the bathtub with plastic bags (garbage bags are good) and lay the wet towel out. Sit the well-watered pots on the towel and they will be able to absorb water while you are away. You can also try punching tiny holes in the bottom of a plastic container and filling the container with water. Sit it on the soil surface of your indoor plant and it will slowly water the plant.

Fresh flowers

In high school, my best friend and I used to fantasize about what our lives would be like as adults and she always included a house full of fresh flowers. It seemed so luxurious and special. We've now got our own homes and hers almost always has a giant bunch of lilies in the living room.

Keeping cut flowers fresh takes a minimum of care. Follow these simple steps and your arrangements will give you pleasure for much longer.

1. If they come from your garden, keep them in water until you are ready to put them in a vase.
2. Make sure the vase they are going into is spotless.
3. Before you put the flowers into water, trim their stems so they can take up water more easily. Cut them with sharp scissors at an angle.

4. Florists often include a packet to add to the water to lengthen the life of the flowers. If they haven't, you can add 1 tablespoon of sugar or white vinegar, or an aspirin.

5. Change the water often. Fresh water daily will lengthen the life of the flowers.

How to choose: a vase

I've got lots of vases. My most coveted is the Alvar Aalto white glass Savoy vase. It was a wedding present from a dear friend and I love its sinuous form, like a tiny body of water. I also have a wonderful French designer *tse tse* vase that is a series of glass test tubes linked by zinc clasps into a long snake. Each tube takes a flower and you arrange it into whatever shape you like. While these vases are my favorites, the one I use most often is an inexpensive one I received with a bunch of flowers about six years ago. It has a round bulbous bottom and a narrow neck that flares out. On its own it's not a particularly beautiful thing, but it holds flowers like a hand – tight around the middle but loose at the top and bottom. It works especially well for big bunches of flowers.

There are no hard and fast rules when it comes to matching vases and flowers. Some of the most beautiful displays I've seen break the obvious conventions. Before it became trendy, a friend would fill a glass vase with limes or lemons rather than flowers. Another trick of hers was to use either huge amounts of cheap flowers all in the same color, or a small number of expensive flowers (always in odd numbers as they look better that way). Feel free to experiment. Perhaps try submerging flowers completely in the water of a generous glass vase, or don't include flowers at all – go for a bouquet of elephant-ear leaves or a branch from a eucalyptus tree with their lovely drooping tear-shaped leaves.

Here are a few things to keep in mind when choosing a vase for your arrangement.

* Large stiff-stemmed flowers – think lilies, roses, etc. – often look best in a wide-necked vase where they have a bit of room to move. You don't want to be jamming them into a narrow-necked vase, especially with lilies that need room for all the flowers to open.

* Floppy or soft-stemmed flowers – like poppies – may need a bit of help from the vase. You'll find these do better in a narrow-necked vase that can keep them upright. Remember to singe the bottoms of poppies with a match or a gas flame; this will prolong their life.

* Small blooms can look beautiful in their own little vases. Try massing those vases together in odd numbers.

* Single large blooms like camellias can look beautiful floating in a shallow saucer or bowl. This can also work well for a mass of frangipanis. You can also try popping flowers into old teacups or shot glasses and lining them along the middle of the table for a centerpiece.

Artificial or dried flowers

Forget those dusty tired arrangements – artificial flowers are now hard to distinguish from the real thing. A great tip passed on by a friend of my mother's is to mix them with real flowers. She takes lovely blowsy silk roses and mixes them with fresh ones to great effect. We live above a florist who does something similar with cloth orchids. It's almost impossible to tell the difference between the real and the fake. I think the key is not to ever let them get dusty, and to make sure you retire them every now and again so they don't become too much of a fixture.

Plastic flowers – wash in a sink full of hot soapy water. Rinse in warm water and hang to dry.

Cloth flowers – the best way to clean these is to put a cup of salt in a plastic bag, put in the flowers head-down, and shake. Dust and dirt should dislodge into the salt. You may be able to wash gently in warm soapy water but check for colorfastness first. Rinse in clear water and hang to dry.

Dried flowers – dust with a feather duster, outside if you can. Or try blowing the dust off with a hairdryer or fan – again best to do this outside. Clean as for cloth flowers – upside down in a plastic bag with salt. You can spray them with hairspray for protection.

12. The Outdoors

The outdoor room is very much an extension of a home. In fact the further south you travel, the more the line between inside and out blurs. Your patch of outdoors might be a tiny balcony with a few potted plants and a single chair to enjoy the sun, or a large sprawling lawn with a generous outdoor setting for eight. We've managed to fit a barbecue on our small balcony and, during the summer, most of our dinners are cooked on it (no washing of pots and pans is a major plus).

It doesn't matter how big or small your outdoor space is, when it comes to cleaning and maintaining outdoor furniture, paths, and the outside of the house, the key is protection from the elements. In general, paint or seal surfaces wherever possible to protect them from rain and sun. If that's not an option, use materials that weather beautifully, like teak that turns a lovely silver with age. The major exception to the painting/sealing rule is brick – think very carefully before you glaze a brick wall. Brick is extremely low-maintenance but once you paint it, or cover it with any kind of glaze, it will need to be repainted/reglazed regularly.

Outdoor furniture

Keep two questions in mind when choosing outdoor furniture: how big is the space and what will you use the furniture for? I know in theory folding furniture is wise for a small space, but I've found in practice you rarely actually fold the thing up and the few times you do there's still the problem of where to store the folded piece.

There's a row house nearby where the owner regularly drags out an overstuffed armchair to read in the sun on the front balcony. I like the idea of utilizing your indoor furniture outside. There's no reason to sit on an uncomfortable folding plastic chair just because you're eating lunch in the garden or reading in the sun on your balcony. Take out your dining chairs for lunch – just remember to take them back in again. If you are putting them on the grass, protect their feet from dirt and dew by wrapping them in little plastic bags.

If you do buy furniture dedicated to the outdoors, you need to make sure it's not only hardy but also comfortable. Test chairs by sitting in them – it seems like such obvious advice but I know many people who don't do it. The following list of materials will help you choose furniture that meets your specific needs.

Aluminum – perfect for lightweight pieces that you may need to move around. Choose this material if you want a minimum of maintenance. While this metal doesn't rust, it can become pitted when left outdoors. Try cleaning with warm water and lemon juice or white vinegar and then polishing with a dry rag. You can protect it with a silicone-based car wax.

Bamboo, cane, wicker – these materials make for very comfortable seating because there's give in them. They do demand more care than metal. They will eventually break down with exposure to the sun and rain, and are really best kept undercover. They can be sealed with lacquer. If already sealed, clean by dusting well (you can use a vacuum, brush, or soft broom to get into the crevices) and wipe down with a slightly damp soapy cloth. If unsealed, clean with warm, slightly soapy water and let dry in the sun. (For more on caring for wicker, see page 166.)

Canvas – a very easy material for outdoor seating as it's light and comfortable to sit on. It will eventually rot and strong colors will fade if exposed to sun and rain. Spot-clean canvas as for any strong cotton fabric. First, remove as much of the matter as you can and then, using a white paper towel or cloth, dab the area with warm soapy water. Follow with a dry cloth to absorb as much of the water as possible. Leave to dry thoroughly in the sun.

Canvas (especially umbrellas) often gets moldy. To get rid of mold, try scrubbing both sides of the canvas with warm soapy water and a stiff brush. Rinse with clear warm water and sprinkle baking soda over the stained areas. Wait for a few minutes, hose off, and leave to dry thoroughly (umbrellas must be left open). You can also use a mild bleach instead of baking soda. First make sure the piece is colorfast, and ensure that you thoroughly rinse all the bleach out of the canvas.

Nylon or vinyl – often used in webbing for seating and, like canvas, is comfortable to sit on although it can get a little sweaty. It's long-lasting and holds color well. Clean with water and mild detergent. If really dirty, use a scrubbing brush to get into all fibers. Rinse with clear warm water and leave in the sun to dry.

Painted metal – this furniture is usually heavy and best kept in the one spot. It's long lasting and looks good but the seating will need some kind of cushion if you are to sit on it for long. To clean, use a soft cloth, warm water, and a mild detergent. Don't scrub with anything abrasive as you can easily scratch the surface. Try using a car wax to protect it.

Plastic – light and generally pretty comfortable, although most plastic seating benefits from a cushion of some kind. It is long lasting, and generally colorfast in sun and rain. Be careful cleaning as abrasives will scratch. Wash with detergent and hot water. You can try polishing with a car wax.

Wood – teak is popular for outdoor furniture because it is a dense hardwood that resists mildew, cracking, insects, acids, and metal stains. It will fade from a rich brown to a silvery gray. You can prolong any wood's life by oiling it. Unsealed wood of all kinds should be cleaned with a cloth wrung out in warm soapy water and oiled yearly to prevent cracking. Try oiling with 4 parts raw linseed oil to 1 part turpentine. Wash sealed wood in the same way and repaint or seal when the finish becomes dull.

Whatever material you choose, the kindest thing you can do for your outdoor furniture is to keep it sheltered. This might mean bringing it undercover when it rains or, during a particularly sunny stretch, dragging it into the shade to stop the sun fading and drying it. And no matter how hardy a piece is, it will benefit from a regular cleaning and polishing.

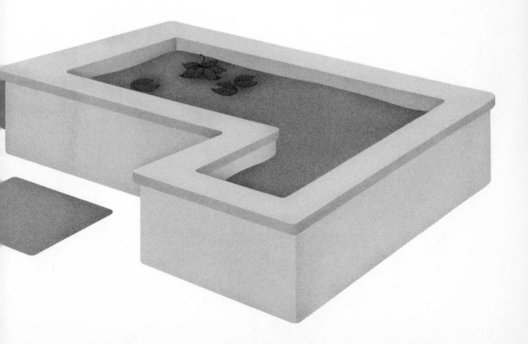

How to clean: the barbecue

It doesn't matter what kind of barbecue you own, they all need the same kind of care. The best thing about a barbecue is that it doesn't need a lot of cleaning. Grease and food scraps tend to get burnt up in the cooking process. Just ensure there's no food left lying around on the cooking plate or grill. To clean, let the grill cool down completely, and then go over it with a wire brush. Rub down with a few paper towels to finish. This will get up any scraps or bits of grease that may linger and attract animals.

Once a year, it makes sense to do a proper cleaning. I do it at the beginning of summer. If the cooking plate is removable, take it into the kitchen, soak in a sink half-filled with very hot soapy water and scrub with a wire brush. Our brush came with the barbecue and also has a handy dull-edged metal scraper to get off baked-on bits. Dry the grill or plate with an old cloth and return it to the barbecue. Wipe it down with a bit of olive oil and heat it up to reseason it.

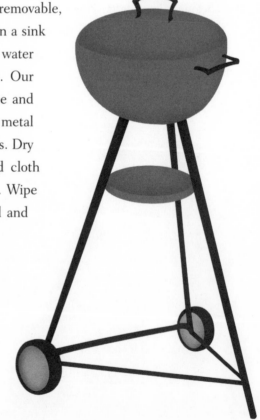

If the plate isn't removable, try sprinkling a little sand onto it (don't do this to a grill as it will fill the fire-pit with sand). The sand will help soak up the grease and can be removed with a wire brush and paper towels. Give it a good scrub with a wire brush dipped in hot soapy water and then wipe down with hot water and paper towels. Let the plate dry out by firing up the barbecue. Use a dustpan and broom to clean out any leftover sand once the plate has completely cooled.

Outdoor tableware

As with outdoor furniture, I'm a great believer in using what you've already got when setting the table outdoors. Just because I'm having lunch in the backyard doesn't mean I want to eat off a plastic plate with a plastic knife and fork. And drinking out of plastic is never good! Having said that, there are places where your indoor tableware just won't do – the poolside, for example, or anywhere there are children and hard surfaces. There are excellent plastic cups you can get from stores like Williams-Sonoma and Ikea. They don't cost the earth and are well designed. Camping stores are also a great place to find wonderful outdoor implements – enamelware is especially good for outdoor use.

How to control: insects

Insect zappers don't really help control the mosquito population, and the ultraviolet light may actually attract unwanted biting insects into the backyard. **Citronella oil** is known to have good mosquito-repelling qualities. But don't be duped into buying the candles. You'd have to stand in the smoke plume to actually get the benefit of the citronella. The same goes for **mosquito coils**. The best way to control mosquitoes is to make sure there's no standing water for them to breed in and to use an insect repellent on your skin. Try your local drugstore. (See pages 384–5 for more on dealing with mosquitoes.)

Trash bins

These can get very smelly. Give them a regular washing with hot soapy water and rinse out with the hose turned on high. Try wiping the inside of the bin with citronella or eucalyptus oil.

Depending on which state you live in, there are various laws governing recycling. I have specific bins for plastic, glass, and paper as well as regular trash. The super for our apartment building maintains these bins, but the same method for cleaning your normal bins goes for these. Make sure you follow your trash collector's directions when filling these sorts of bins. Often, paper needs to be tied in bundles, and cans and bottles need to be placed in a separate crate or bin. Cans, bottles, etc. should always be thoroughly rinsed before you throw them away.

How to clean:
the outside of the house

Wood, aluminum siding, stone, and brick walls can be cleaned with a hose (except during water restrictions) and a scrubbing brush dipped in hot soapy water. First, hose the surface thoroughly to loosen dirt and get rid of any debris, then follow with a gentle scrubbing – too strong a brush could take off paint. Finally, hose to get rid of any soap and dirt. Best to do this on a sunny day so that the surface can dry well.

Wash painted walls twice a year. You'll be amazed at the difference this can make to a house, especially if you live in a busy area where airborne pollutants can discolor paint. First, brush the house down to get rid of cobwebs and dirt deposits. Use a soft brush on a long handle. Wash with warm soapy water or try sugar soap (available in liquid or powder form from hardware stores – follow directions on the bottle and wear gloves). Use a large sponge to wipe the walls, and a hose to rinse. Be gentle as you don't want to shorten the life of the paint.

If the house is really dirty, consider getting a professional in to give it a thorough cleaning. They use high-pressure steam to remove dirt and it really is incredible how much better the paint looks after they've been through. You could also hire a steam gun yourself, but you risk removing paint with the dirt (and damaging soft stone like sandstone) – best leave this somewhat tricky job to a professional.

How to clean: gutters

If you have the right equipment, this unpleasant job can be made a lot easier. Arm yourself with a small trowel, gloves, and a stiff scrubbing brush. The trowel will dig out packed-in dirt and leaves from the gutter, and the gloves will allow you to get your hands in and pull out what the trowel can't reach. The scrubbing brush lets you get at the dirt that's often left behind by decaying leaf litter. Give the gutter a good hosing down once you're done. If you suspect a downpipe is blocked, try pouring hot water down the pipe and then flushing with the hose. If overhanging trees are a problem, consider investing in mesh to keep leaves at bay.

How to clean: the shed

Since I left home, I've never lived in a place with a shed. It's one of those things, like a hall closet and a bigger laundry, that I covet. I love the idea of having all your tools in the one place. Right now I store a hammer and nails in the bottom drawer in the kitchen, and cans of paint left over from renovating are kept at my parents' place (much to my mother's dismay).

A shed calls for a certain degree of organization. Tools need a home – my father has a wall covered in Peg Board (a type of Masonite with tiny holes all over it). Tools hang off hooks attached to the board. It means you can see everything and find it all easily. Old filing cabinets also come in handy for storing power tools and pieces that are too heavy to hang. Mark the drawers so you know what's in them. A high shelf or lockable cupboard is essential for paints and anything else that may be poisonous.

Cleaning a shed shouldn't be a huge chore. I don't think this space has to be pristine. Dust first and then give the floor a good sweeping and moping. If you do this regularly or after you've been working, it will keep the room looking good and mean the cleaning job will never get too out of hand.

Most tools – whether they are for the garden or the workshop – benefit from a good washing or wiping-down with warm soapy water. Make sure you wipe them dry thoroughly to prevent rusting. Oiling blades and mechanisms will also help prevent rust.

How to clean: garden paths

Brick and stone – for a general cleaning, simply sweep. To remove **moss**, pour undiluted white vinegar (or simply very hot water) onto the moss and leave for 10 minutes, then scrub off with a stiff brush. Rinse well. If the moss still remains, try rubbing alcohol and water (see page 32), or a solution of household bleach (1 part bleach to 6 parts water). To rinse, mop with 1 part vinegar to 6 parts warm water. (See more about brick floors on page 342 and see below for more on stone.)

Concrete – as for bricks, a good sweep is all that's needed for a general cleaning. To wash, scrub with a stiff brush and hot soapy water. To remove **grease** stains, try dampening, dousing with kitty litter, and scrubbing with a stiff brush. Sweep up kitty litter and hose clean. (See page 342 for more on concrete.)

Tiles – sweep regularly and wash as for bricks.

Stone floors

Stone falls into two broad categories, and cleaning and maintaining your stone depends on which category it falls into. **Hard (siliceous) stone** is made up of silica, the main ingredient in sand. Granite, slate, quartz, and sandstone are examples of hard stone. **Soft (calcareous) stone** is composed mostly of calcium carbonate. Think marble, travertine, and limestone. They are more porous and vulnerable to acids, even mild ones like lemon juice or vinegar. To check which kind of stone you have, use a small amount of vinegar on an inconspicuous area. If the vinegar etches the stone, the stone is calcareous.

Both types of stone are finished by polishing or honing. A polished surface will be shinier than a honed one and is most often found indoors. Honed finishes are best used on floors, as they are less slippery.

How to clean: stone floors

Vacuum or sweep often, at the very least once a week. You can vacuum porches or balconies. Make sure your vacuum cleaner hasn't got any worn bits (wheels or attachments) that may scratch the stone. Mop as often as needed using warm water and a mild dishwashing detergent. Rinse with clear warm water, ensuring you get rid of all soap residue, and dry with a clean cloth. Waxing stone floors can make them dangerously slippery so best avoid it.

How to remove: stains on stone

As with carpets, the best way to prevent a stain is to get the mark off the stone as quickly and efficiently as possible. Blot the spill with a paper towel (use only white paper towels as the dye in others may add to your problem). Wipe over the area with clean water and a bit of detergent. Repeat this process until the stain disappears. If it doesn't disappear, you need to take more serious action. There are a lot of products on the market for cleaning stone.

Etch marks – will happen in softer stone, especially marble, if an acid is left on the surface. Try buffing out with a marble-polishing powder. Sprinkle the powder on the area and then buff with a damp cloth. Keep rubbing until the etched area disappears. If this doesn't work, you'll need a professional.

Ink – includes permanent ink. On light-colored stone, try bleach or hydrogen peroxide. On dark stone, try a paint thinner or acetone (nail-polish remover). Or use the poultice method under metal, page 340.

Metal – these stains are green (copper), orange, or brown and need a poultice to remove them. They are difficult to get up and may be permanent. There are many ways to make a poultice but basically you are creating a sticky substance that will sit on the stain and draw it out. For **copper**, try using a poultice of ammonia and white cotton balls, paper towels, or muslin. For **iron**, try a commercially prepared rust remover on cotton or paper. Let the cotton or paper soak in the cleaning fluid but don't make it dripping wet. Use distilled water to wet the area you'll be treating. Lay the wet material on the stain, making sure it covers the area completely by about 1 inch. Cover the area with plastic and tape it down to seal. Check the poultice in 24 hours to see if it has dried. If it hasn't, remove the plastic and allow to dry completely. It can take up to 48 hours to dry. This process pulls the stain up into the cloth. Once the poultice is completely dry, remove, and wash the area with more distilled water. Buff it dry with a clean cloth. For really difficult stains, you might find you have to repeat this process up to five times.

Mold – includes algae, lichen, and moss. Try scrubbing with ammonia (½ cup in 2 quarts of water). If that doesn't work, you can try bleach diluted in the same way. If the stain is very stubborn, try the poultice method.

Oil – these stains can be caused by anything containing oil, including coconut milk and cosmetics. The trick is to dissolve the oil without damaging the stone. Try using straight laundry detergent. If this doesn't work, try ammonia. Mineral spirits or nail-polish remover can also be tried. Make sure you don't mix anything containing bleach with ammonia (see page 32).

Organic – includes coffee, tea, foods, leaves, and bird droppings. You will need to bleach out these stains. They are often brown in color, and will respond to a scrubbing with hydrogen peroxide or a few drops of ammonia. For really stubborn marks, use the poultice method.

Paint – if it's a small amount, let it dry and remove with a razor blade. Or try rubbing it off with a bit of paint thinner. For large amounts of paint, you'll have to use a commercially prepared paint remover. Try your local hardware store and follow the instructions on the can. Repolishing may be necessary as these removers can sometimes seep into the surface of the stone. Make sure you wash the area well after you've removed the paint so as not to leave any residue.

Water – will appear as spots or rings and can be buffed out using a very fine dry steel wool.

Brick and concrete floors

Brick and concrete are fantastic outdoor materials, although they can also appear indoors (in warmer climates), often in high-traffic areas like the living room. These hard surfaces are best sealed before dirt or stains get to them. A good sealant will add years to the floor. Check with your retailer for the best sealant for your floor. Concrete floors can be painted, but a more durable way of adding color is to add it to the concrete as it is mixed, or to the sealant. Paving paint tends to wear badly in high-traffic areas.

How to clean: brick and concrete floors

Use a damp mop with a small amount of detergent in warm water. Rinse well after mopping to avoid a film building up from the detergent. If you do get a film, mop with 1 part vinegar to 6 parts water. I find warm water works best. Make sure you avoid solvents (organic or chemical-based), powders, and oils as they will ruin the finish on the floor.

Terrazzo floors

You'll find terrazzo turning up in some older homes, especially in high-traffic areas like steps. Terrazzo is made by laying marble, quartz, or other stone chips in mortar, and polishing.

How to clean: terrazzo floors

For high-traffic areas, try washing the floor once a week using a damp mop and warm water with 1 tablespoon of detergent added. If the floor is really dirty, leave the warm water on for about five minutes before rinsing clear (don't let it dry on the floor). Rinse with clear cold water and dry completely using an old towel. Mop up spills immediately to help prevent any liquid seeping in and staining. Don't wax this floor as it can get dangerously slippery.

How to maintain: terrazzo floors

If the terrazzo becomes worn, you may need to get someone in to sand it back and reseal it. Worn areas can become porous and will absorb water.

Pets

I can't wait to get a dog or a cat. We've decided not to do it until we live in a bigger place. It seems unfair to have a dog in a two-bedroom apartment, and the chaos of kids and cats in a small space doesn't thrill me. So we wait, and in the meantime I satisfy my urge for a pet by playing with other people's animals.

When it comes to cleaning, houses with pets need special attention. If you suffer from allergies then you'll have to be extra vigilant with your housekeeping. If you don't, it's still worth being a little more thorough for the sake of visitors and friends who may be allergic. It's the dander and saliva from the animal that causes allergic reactions. Dander is flakes of skin shed by the animal. Saliva, which contains allergens, is passed onto fur and skin by licking. Urine can also carry allergens. To help control allergies, wash the animal when necessary (depends on the animal and where it has been). And don't let the pet into your bedroom.

Consider also the paraphernalia pets attract – balls, chew toys, collars and leashes. Make sure these toys have a home. Try a plastic lidded box and ensure you hose it out regularly. The best place for the animal's leash is on a hook by the door – or at least somewhere you can easily find it.

How to clean: a house with animals

1. **Vacuum** with a vacuum cleaner fitted with a HEPA filter (see page 40 for more information). This should stop the allergens getting back into the room. Vacuum carpets, upholstery, and curtains. Carpets hold a lot more allergens than hard floors. To remove hair, use the attachment appropriate for the surface you are vacuuming. (To remove hair from clothes, try those rolls of sticky tape on a stick). Vacuum twice a week unless you have serious allergies; if you do, it may be necessary to vacuum daily. Vacuuming will also rid your house of fleas (see page 386).

2. **Dust** with a damp cloth to stop dander and allergens spreading.

3. Good **ventilation** is important and will help keep the allergen levels down. Open windows whenever you can.

4. If possible, make sure you let the pet spend a good bit of the day **outdoors**. This may be hard with a cat in an apartment.

5. Keep the pet's area clean. **Wash** all hard surfaces with very hot soapy water and launder any towels or rugs it sleeps on in hot water.

6. If the animal goes outside, it will inevitably track dirt into the house. Make sure you have old rags or towels by the door to wipe it down before it comes into the house, and never let a wet pet sit on any uphol-stered furniture or rug.

Pet hygiene

A doctor and old family friend always told me that when I had
children I should keep them away from dogs and cats. He said
it was a myth that dog's saliva was clean – just think about
all the things they eat and lick! Now that I've got a child, I'm
careful to keep dog-licking to a minimum – although when their
little faces are at the same height as the dog's, it's not always
easy.

To protect you, your family, and friends from diseases and
bacteria that all pets can carry, follow these steps:

* Don't let dogs up on the couch or armchairs. They should
  be trained to sleep in their own beds.
* Don't let cats on counters, tabletops, or anywhere you
  prepare or eat food.
* Don't let any pet sleep on your or your child's bed.
* Avoid giving your pet food that is raw. You can give them a
  food-borne illness and that can be passed onto you.
* Don't let your children feed the pet from the table. Avoid
  having the animal around during mealtimes so there's no
  chance for it to beg.
* Don't let your pet eat off your plate and do wash their
  dishes separately from your own. Wash your pet's bowls
  as you would your own – after each use and in very hot
  soapy water.
* Wash your hands after you've patted a pet.

How to clean: litter boxes and cages

Cats – if possible, always change litter, and clean carriers and beds, outside. Cat's litter should be changed as soon as you can smell it, although this can be tough for an owner because you quickly get used to the smell. Cats won't use a dirty litter box and you definitely don't want them using anything else in the house. When I had a cat, I used a litter that had clay in it so that it clumped when wet and made removing pee easy. I changed the whole litter once a week and cleaned clumps out daily. You'll need to change the whole litter box more often if you use regular litter.

If you use a liner with the litter, you simply bag it up as you would your garbage and dispose of it in the trash outside. If not, scrape it all carefully into a plastic bag and then put it in the trash. Never pour it directly into the bin – think of the smell and mess your trash collector will have to deal with! Thoroughly wash the litter box with very hot soapy water and disinfect it by swilling a small amount of household bleach around and then rinsing in hot water. Don't keep the litter tray near any food areas. We had ours in the bathroom of the flat we were in at the time. Not ideal, but there wasn't a lot of room. If you can, keep it on a porch, balcony, other easily accessible outdoor area or a well-ventilated room in the house.

Mice and guinea pigs – clean cages as often as possible (daily if you can). They get very smelly and really benefit from a thorough cleaning. Check with your vet before you use any strong disinfectant like bleach.

Birds – cages need to be cleaned twice a week and all their toys washed thoroughly in hot soapy water. Wipe the outside of the cage with a damp cloth.

Fish – bowls need careful cleaning whenever they begin to look dirty. First, remove the fish along with some of the water. Empty their bowl and wash it in hot water. Don't use soap. To get rid of algae, try rubbing the glass with a soft scourer or a rough towel rather than using chemicals. Rinse the tank well in cool water. Replace the water and then the fish. Tropical fish are much more tricky so check with an aquarium before cleaning their tanks.

Pet smells

You can try store-bought remedies like Febreze – which works to stop the smell but is expensive. Your local pet store will also be able to help with suggestions. One easy remedy is to sprinkle baking soda over your carpet and let it stand for 30 minutes before vacuuming it up. The advantage here is that the baking soda won't damage the carpet and is nontoxic.

Cat pee is a real problem. Talk to any real-estate agent trying to sell a house that has been sprayed by a cat – it is one of the all-time put-offs. An unspayed male cat will spray everything in sight as a way of marking its territory, but any cat >

having a bad day can potentially spray anything in the house. The trick is to get rid of the smell as soon as possible so the cat won't return to that place and think it's OK to pee again.

Pet stores may sell odor-fighting cleaners and this should be your first stop. Just make sure the product you buy is appropriate for the item you want to treat. It's always best to test a small patch first and note whether the product cleans or just deodorizes (Febreze, for example, only deodorizes). If the problem is really bad, talk to your vet about solutions.

To clean up after a pet has used your house as a toilet:

1. Get up as much of the offending matter as possible before you treat the spot. Use paper towels that you can then throw away.

2. Avoid using ammonia products as these smell like cat pee and won't stop your cat revisiting that spot. A lot of books I've read suggest trying white vinegar, soda water, or even Windex. I've found vinegar too weak for this problem, but have had success with hot soapy water and a scrubbing brush or sponge.

How to protect: furniture from pets

Dogs – if your dog tends to chew furniture, your first port of call is your vet. They should be able to advise you on training methods and perhaps recommend a trainer if you feel the job is beyond you. You can also try the following:

* Make sure your dog has its own toys to chew on – things it's allowed to demolish, and that don't resemble your furniture in any way.
* Try a commercial dog repellent. Just make sure it doesn't stain.
* Try a bit of tea-tree oil. This smell often puts dogs off.

Cats – the problem here won't be chewing but scratching. De-clawing should never be an option. It's cruel and there are other ways of dealing with this problem. As with a dog, check first with your vet to see if there are steps you can take to train your cat. In my experience, cats are notoriously hard to train. But don't give up; there are steps you can take:

* I have found that scratching posts work well. Carpet-covered tubes on firm wooden bases were a favorite with my last cat. We attached wire with a catnip-filled felt mouse to the top of the pole and the cat loved it. Check your local pet store for scratching devices – there are a lot on the market.
* Keep the cat's claws clipped. Easier said than done, I know, but short claws do a lot less damage. If you get into the habit of trimming claws when the cat is a kitten, you might have less trouble later on.
* Consider covering furniture in fabric that doesn't pull so easily (though this is a rather expensive measure).
* As for dogs, try a commercial spray or tea-tree oil.

ASPCA

Check out the ASPCA (American Society for the Prevention of Cruelty to Animals) Web site at www.aspca.org., or visit your local ASPCA for more advice and useful pet products.

How to go: on vacation

Pets need to be looked after if left at home, and the best way is to have someone move into the house while you are gone. Then the pet gets to be looked after in familiar surroundings. The next best option is boarding, which can be expensive but is better for the pet than having someone drop in to feed them. Dogs especially get lonely and need humans around.

How to store: pet food

To keep dry food fresh, put it in a container that can be properly sealed. Wet food should be used up in one serving if possible. If not, cover well and store in the bottom of the fridge until the next meal.

Fences and signs

Check with your local government to see what kind of fences are mandatory for your pets. In some communities, ordinances require signs drawing attention to the fact you have a dog.

When thinking about fencing for your dog, consider the following:

1. The fence must be adequate to contain the dog on your property. You are responsible for any damage your dog does to other people's property.

2. Make sure the fence allows access for utility workers to read meters on your property and for mail to be delivered without the postal carrier being harassed by your dog.

3. You also want the fence to prevent people from being bitten or harassed as they walk past the property.

4. The fence must be too high for the dog to jump over, and have an adequate base to prevent the dog from digging out. Have a chat to your local pound, dog breeder, or vet. They will know what's appropriate for your breed of dog.

5. Consider planting low bushes along the fences that border the properties of neighbors who are dog-sensitive. This won't actually stop the noise of a dog barking, but it will help hide activity that may make the dog bark.

How to be responsible: for your pets

A certain responsibility comes with pet ownership. In New South Wales (Australia), for example, the 1988 Companion Animals Act requires that all dogs and cats over six months be microchipped and registered with the local council for life. The charges are minor, although if the animal is not neutered it can cost up to $100 to have it registered. Check with your veterinarian, regarding pet licensing, microchipping, and neutering.

13. Practicalities

You will need to bring people into your home to do odd jobs. Whether it is a cleaner, a plumber, or some other workman, there are simple steps you can take to ensure the jobs are well done. Not everyone has time to do all the housework and not everyone is cut out for DIY repairs. Sometimes it is better all round to get an expert.

How to find: a cleaner

The best way is through recommendations from friends and family. If that isn't an option, try the local classifieds and make sure you get written references. Do check these references and find out exactly what responsibilities the cleaner had in that home. Did they do heavy or light cleaning? How much were they paid? And how long did it take to complete the job?

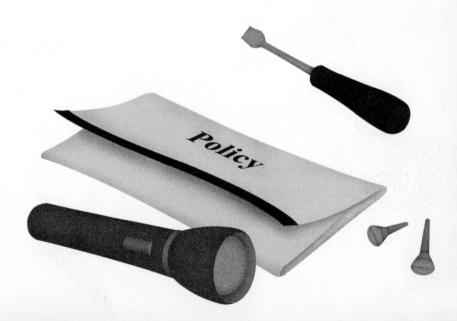

You can also go through an agency. Choose a reputable one that has been going for a number of years (you don't want a business that only operates from a cell phone number). In Australia, Dial-an-angel is an example of a national agency with a good reputation. I know people who use them once a year for a serious spring-cleaning. To do this kind of cleaning in an apartment will usually take a minimum of four hours, according to Dena Blackman, the agency's founder. A cottage will take about five hours.

Weekly or biweekly cleaners have a minimum of three hours per visit. If they bring their own equipment, it costs extra. They give minimum charges and hourly rates over the phone but a house that's been neglected may take a lot longer to clean, and it's not possible to take that into account over the phone. The cleaner will do high-priority areas first and leave a note if the client isn't there to authorize overtime to finish the job.

Making the cleaner's job easier

Good communication is the most important thing, whether the cleaner comes from an agency or through word of mouth. You need to spell out clearly what needs to be done. Make a list of jobs for the cleaner to do and don't take anything for granted. If you want the wastepaper basket emptied, then put that on the list. Besides helping the cleaner, this will also help you figure out how often you need someone and for how long. Make sure you discuss with the cleaners how long they think it will take to do the job properly. This is also the time to figure out how much to pay. If a friend recommended the person, use how much that person paid as a guide. Otherwise, ask around and you'll get a fair idea of going rates.

It is best to set a trial period for the first month (depending on how often the cleaner is coming). You can make sure the work is to your liking and the day chosen works for you both.

Make sure you declutter first. It's not the cleaners' job to tidy up before they start cleaning – besides, they won't know where anything goes and it takes up their precious cleaning time.

Don't expect cleaners to do extra work. If you need something special done, like cleaning out the fridge, drop another task (making the beds, for example) so they can fit the extra task into the time they allot for your house. On their first visit, make it clear how this kind of alternating of tasks will work.

If you are supplying cleaning products and equipment, make sure everything the cleaner needs is in the house. Check cleaning products regularly and replace as needed. If you aren't supplying cleaning products, make sure you are happy with the products the cleaner is using.

Check your household insurance to see what liability there is if someone is injured in your home. There may be a Domestic Workers Compensation attached to your policy (it's also available as a stand-alone policy). Also check the insurance that the cleaners hold. They may have their own personal accident and liability cover – although this is rare unless they are running their own business. Cleaning agencies should have their employees covered but it is important to check.

How to find: a repairman

As with a cleaner, it is always best to get a recommendation from someone who has used that person. If that's not possible, you can try the local paper, *Yellow Pages,* or even the local supermarket where people often advertise on community bulletin boards. You can also ask at your closest hardware store. They are working with local repairman all day and can often recommend people.

Before you make the call, know what needs to be done. Try to identify the problem clearly so you can let the repairman know over the phone what is wrong. This way they will be sure to arrive with the correct tools. For a big job, it is reasonable to ask for a quote.

Check that the repairman is insured and his company is licensed for the work you need done. If you don't feel confident about them, you can check with the Better Business Bureau to see if any complaints have been lodged there. Find out what kind of guarantees they have for their work. We recently had our apartment treated for cockroaches and the work was guaranteed for twelve months. This means if cockroaches return in that time they will come back and retreat the apartment for free.

When the repairman arrives, be sure to make it very clear what you think needs to be done. Discuss the problem and ensure he has everything he needs to get the job done. It is often handy to have the manufacturer's instructions if something like a water heater is being repaired.

When he leaves, it's important that he cleans up after himself. Make sure he has access to whatever he needs to clean up – a vacuum, dustpan and broom, etc.

How to choose: insurance

My husband says the only thing you need to know about home and property insurance is that you need it. True. But there is a bit more to consider when you are choosing an insurance provider. First, you can avoid all the fuss and research and go to a mortgage broker. They will put an insurance package together for you – the cost of which is normally borne by the insurance company. Use a reputable broker. It's always good to choose one that's been recommended by a friend.

If you want to do the legwork yourself, you'll need to consider the following.

* Do you want to insure your home (the building) and its contents? I think it makes sense to do both. And you will often get a discount if you buy home and contents insurance together.

* Some policies offer to cover "portables," which means if you lose your camera on a trip, it will be covered by your home and property insurance.

✱ Ask if you receive a discount if you also insure your car with that company.

✱ Get quotes from a few insurance companies so you know what you'll be in for. They will want to know how much the contents of your home are worth and what kind of building it is (wood, brick, weatherboard?). There are some excellent online calculators that take you through your home – room-by-room – and give estimates for absolutely everything.

✱ If you have special items that aren't included on the insurer's list, then make them aware of these items. In some instances they will cover things like paintings, photographs, certain jewelry or a Persian rug. There is usually a dollar limit on the amount you can insure these items for. But at least you will get something back if they are lost or damaged.

✱ Does your home insurance cover accidents like broken glass in windows as well as losing the whole house in a fire?

✱ Does the home insurance cover someone else injuring themselves or damaging their property in your home?

How to avoid: burglary

I have never been robbed. I've lived in nine homes since I left my parents' house, including a row house in Paddington and a loft in midtown New York, and have been incredibly lucky in all those places. I put it down to luck because we never took extraordinary security measures. My parents, however, have lived in the same house for 32 years and been robbed at least four times – once when I was eight years old and at home with the babysitter. The thieves came in the back of the house and we heard them but thought it was our pet rabbit crashing around in the kitchen. They made their way to the front room where we were watching television, threw open the door, grabbed the sitter's handbag, and ran back down the hall and out the back door. We ran out the front! I never saw that babysitter again and it was soon after that we got a dog; there were no more robberies after Andy appeared on the scene.

According to one Australian insurance company, 420,000 burglaries happened in that country in 2002. That is one every 1.25 minutes. They point out that it's only a matter of time before a thief breaks into your home. With that cheery knowledge, there are very definite things you can do to safeguard your home. And the safer it is, the cheaper your insurance will be. Most insurers offer discounts if you install security systems. Check each policy to find out what you can do.

In general . . .

* Don't leave signs around if you have just bought new appliances. Flatten cartons and bundle them into your recycling.
* Even when you are at home, don't leave bikes or your lawn-mower out on the lawn.
* External lights that are motion-sensitive are excellent deterrents. Make sure they are installed well out of reach.
* Consider investing in a timer that controls not only the lights but perhaps also the stereo.
* Make your home secure by replacing hollow-core doors with solid ones.
* Have deadlocks on all external doors and make sure everyone in the house knows where the keys are (see page 366 for more).

* The doorjambs need to be in good condition – there's no point in having an expensive deadlock if the doorjamb is easily jimmied.
* Hinge pins can be removed so make sure the hinges are on the inside, not the outside, of the door.
* Have window locks that are locked with keys (see page 367 for more).
* Make sure you don't hide a spare key in the mailbox or meter box, or under a pot plant, rock, or doormat. And don't attach any identification tag to your keys.
* Burglars like to remain hidden so keep trees and shrubs trimmed – especially trees close to your house that could be climbed.
* Consider engraving or marking your valuables with your driver's licence number. Make a comprehensive list of your contents with serial numbers for easy identification if recovered.

If you're going away . . .

* Stop your paper delivery and ask someone to collect your mail. If you'll be away for more than a few weeks, have your lawn mowed and garden tended. You could even have a neighbor park his car in your driveway every few days.
* Make sure a neighbor brings in your trashcan. A bin left on the lawn in front of your house for weeks on end tells people you are away.
* Leave your curtains slightly open. If they're fully closed for any length of time, it looks like you are away.
* Place a metal rod or piece of strong wood along the tracks of sliding doors and windows, as an extra security measure while you're away.

How to choose: an alarm system

If you go to the trouble of installing an alarm system, make sure that you put security stickers on your windows. In most states, a licensed security installer must install your alarm. Ask at your local hardware store or locksmith for a list of installers.

When choosing an alarm system, consider the following:

* You want to have intruder detection on or near the main entrances, i.e., the front and back doors and any windows a thief could access.

* Ask for a minimum of one internal siren. It's best if this is triggered close to a main entry.

* A strobe light and an external siren are also handy.

* Check with your insurer about what they require in terms of intruder detection devices (you can receive a discount on your insurance if it meets their standards). Some call for a minimum of four devices that can include motion detectors.

* Make sure the alarm is connected to your fuse box or circuit breaker and has a rechargeable battery – you don't want it failing if the electricity is cut off.
* Find out if the alarm has back-to-base monitoring. If so, is it 24-hours?
* Can you have the alarm on when you are at home? Can you disable some areas so you can still move around those parts of the house freely?
* What sort of maintenance and service does the alarm company offer? It is good to have the system serviced at least once a year.
* Can you get individual access codes for the alarm (so your cleaner, for example, has one code and you have another)? This allows you to monitor people's movements.
* Make sure the system complies with the local codes. Check with your local police precinct.

Locks

Deadlocks – these can be operated from inside and outside the house. If a thief gets in, the amount of things they can take is minimized as they won't be able to open the door. My parents have deadlocks and the last time they got robbed, the thief simply passed everything out one of the enormous kitchen windows . . . so deadlocks are good but not the complete answer. And don't lock them from the inside when you are at home, in case you need to get out quickly.

Key-operated window locks – I know these are a good idea (they stop the window from being prised open, and most insurance companies require or at least recommend them). But when there's all that glass that can be smashed, leaving a lovely big opening, it seems you should not be relying completely on key-operated window locks.

One good tip here is to have the windows keyed to the same key. This means it's easier to lock up when you're leaving home, and unlock when you return.

Security doors and bars

Bars on the windows certainly act as a deterrent to thieves, but they can make a house feel claustrophobic and prove to be a serious danger if you need to get out of the house fast. The best thing is to use them in conjunction with other security systems, such as an alarm and deadlocks on the doors, so that not every window in the house needs bars.

When choosing bars, make sure they comply with local fire and building codes. You'll find a lot of choices here: fixed, hinged, and key-locked bars. It's best to fit them on the inside of the window as this makes them harder to tamper with.

When installing a security door, check that it meets State housing and have it installed by a professional. As with window bars, you want to make sure you've bought the best and these often aren't cheap. But there's no point in getting a cheap security door that won't do its job.

Household safety

So many accidents can happen in the home and there's often very easy ways to prevent them.

Take the following steps to ensure you have a safe house:

1. Have an **emergency kit** prepared and stored out of reach of children. It should include: flashlight (and fresh batteries), battery-operated radio, candles and matches, canned food (for you and a child), can/bottle opener, water, spare eyeglasses and medicine, fire extinguisher, some kind of bedding (may be a sleeping bag or a blanket), first-aid kit, and an extra set of car keys. It's also a good idea to include a book with phone numbers for local emergency services and your family and neighbors, and any health information about family members (if the children suffer from asthma, etc.).

2. Avoid **electrical fires**, which have claimed many a house, by taking the following steps:
   * Don't overload an outlet or use cut, broken, or worn electric cords.
   * Call an electrician if your circuit breaker needs resetting often, your lights or television flicker, there are sparks, flashes of light or a buzzing noise when you plug into an outlet, or any part of the electrics in your house are warm to touch or discolored by heat.
   * If the lights in the house go off or an electric appliance you are using stops, you may have blown a fuse. You will need to find the fuse box and replace the fuse. It's always best to get an electrician to show you how to do this the first time.

3. Avoid **electric shock** by taking the following steps:
   * Always make sure the cord for any appliance is in good con-

dition. Unplug by pulling at the plug rather than the cord.
Get rid of a cord as soon as it looks frayed.

* Call an electrician if you need electrical wiring or repair, no
  matter how minor the job. This is not an area for DIYers!
* Be aware of where exposed powerlines are when working in
  the garden or on the roof.
* Know the location of any underground powerlines before
  digging in the garden. Your local department of public works
  can help you here.

See also pages 222–8 for information about safeguarding your
house for a child.

Gas

Natural gas is great for cooking and heating the house. It's a colour-
less and odorless gas that is lighter than air and predominantly made
up of methane. A smell is added to it so that if there is a leak you
can tell straight away.

If you smell gas . . .

* Put out all flames and don't operate any electrical appliances
  that could create a spark.
* Turn off all gas appliances and make sure their pilot lights are out.
* Ventilate the area by opening windows and doors.
* If you still smell gas, turn off the main gas knob at the meter and
  phone your gas company. The number will be on your bill.

Fire safety

* Make sure everyone in the house knows the best escape route in case of a fire. Agree on a meeting place outside the house.

* Close doors to bedrooms at night. This will slow down smoke and give you a chance to react to fire alarms.

* Have a small fire extinguisher in the kitchen and wherever you have an open fire.

* Be very careful with rags soaked in combustible liquid. These can self-combust. Let them dry before throwing them away. Your local garbage dump will have guidelines for getting rid of this kind of waste.

* If an outlet or switch is feeling warm, it needs to be replaced. And of course if sparks fly when you push in a plug, have an electrician attend to the outlet immediately.

* Make sure the lint is cleaned from your clothes dryer after each use.

* Test fire alarms regularly (once a month) to make sure the batteries are not lead. And make sure there's one on every floor of the house. The alarm itself will need to be replaced every ten years.

* Have baking soda on hand for grease fires.

* Make sure you don't let your Christmas tree dry out. It needs to be watered daily. A dry tree is highly combustible.

* Have a professional do a yearly inspection of your fireplace. Always use screens in front of an open fire.

Wildfires

As I'm writing this, fires are devouring great swathes of bush in New South Wales and Victoria. It seems to be an annual event. Summer comes and fires threaten our houses. Being prepared to leave your house in a hurry is one of the best things you can do.

To help prevent fires and protect your home:

1. Install **spark guards** in your chimney. Clean chimneys at least once a year.
2. **Clear** a 50–100-foot area around your home.
3. Install fire-resistant mesh **screens** in such areas as under the porch. This will stop sparks getting into the building.
4. Make sure you've got working **smoke detectors** on all levels of the house.
5. Don't store **flammable** liquid, propane gas bottles, or trash near the house.
6. Regularly **clean** the roof and gutters of leaves and bark, etc.
7. Have a **fire extinguisher** handy in the house and the garage.
8. Stack **firewood** at least 100 feet away from your home.
9. If there is a fire approaching, **block** downpipes with tennis balls and fill gutters with water.
10. **Mark** all water sources on your property and make sure access is clear for firefighters.
11. Make sure everyone in the house knows the **escape route** and the car is facing in the right direction. You may need to move fast. **>**

12. It's a good idea to round up your **pets** and have them in one room for easy evacuation.

13. It may be 100°F but make sure you have **long sleeves** and **long pants** plus **sturdy shoes** to protect yourself from sparks.

14. If you do have to leave the house and you have time, **close** all windows, doors, and vents, shut off the gas, remove gas cylinders, and pile any flammable furniture, curtains, and drapes into the center of the room.

15. Don't forget to **lock** your home if forced to evacuate and, if you can, **tell someone** where you are going.

Pests

If the problem is severe, it is always best to call in a professional. I had a terrible cockroach problem in an apartment I rented. It had been home to five backpackers before we moved in and their cleaning habits were not the best. A professional came in, used environmentally safe bait, and the cockroaches disappeared within the week.

No matter what is plaguing your home, here are a few tips for hiring a professional:

* Get a quote. Best to get them to come to your home and give an on-site quote. Phone or e-mail quotes are usually inaccurate.
* Ask to see a licence and insurance certificate.
* Ask about the chemicals they use. It was important to me that nothing of high toxicity was being brought into the home. Make sure they give you written information on the chemicals used.
* Get references and do call the referees.
* Make sure the pest controller has experience with whatever your problem is. No use getting a cockroach expert to rid your house of mice.

Mice and rats

Mice have between five and ten litters a year with about five or six babies per litter. So if you see one mouse, chances are that's just the tip of the iceberg! They come into the house looking for food, water, and shelter. So the first things to do are preventative.

Prevention

* Clean areas where food scraps might have gathered – under stoves, refrigerators, and dishwashers. Don't leave food or water out on counters overnight.
* Store food in metal, glass, or plastic containers – especially things like rice, pasta and grains, dry petfood, and birdseed.
* Clean and dry your pet's bowls at night – don't leave food out. Bird feeders need to be placed away from the house.

* Store firewood and compost away from the house. Firewood should also be raised off the ground.
* Remove any fallen fruit, vegetables, or nuts from the garden.
* Repair all small holes in the house. Use caulking, a concrete patch, coarse steel wool, copper mesh, or sheet metal. You could try impregnating the steel wool with borax and some peppermint oil (which mice and rats don't seem to like).
* Dispose of your trash properly.

Remedies

First try traps, then as a last resort use poison. The disadvantage with poison is that a mouse can die in some inaccessible spot and become very smelly. There is also a danger that other animals will eat the dead mouse and be poisoned.

There are three types of traps: the classic spring-loaded wooden mousetrap (best bait here is something sticky like peanut butter); the glue trap (made from a sheet of super-sticky cardboard); and the live trap (you release the mouse somewhere other than your own backyard). The choice is yours, but there are a few things to keep in mind. The spring-loaded trap is thought to be the most humane way to kill a rodent as it acts very quickly. The big disadvantage with glue traps is they don't kill the rodent – you will have to do that. We tried liberating a mouse from a glue trap and almost pulled its legs off. My boyfriend at the time ended up taking it onto the street, covering it in newspaper, and dropping a brick on it! Live traps, where the mouse crawls in and can't get out, will alleviate this problem but you will have to find a new home for the mouse. The local park is probably the best option.

Cockroaches

The key here is to deny the roaches what they most crave – food, water, and a place to hide. They like warm humid dark spots and you will most often find them under the sink, behind kitchen cabinets, under major appliances and countertops, and sometimes in laundry areas. They will eat paper, clothing, food, wood, books, and other small insects.

There are two types of cockroaches commonly found in homes – the American and the German. They are both nocturnal. The American is large and dark brown. They are the ones that really crunch when you step on them. The German cockroaches are smaller and lighter colored, and seem to move in packs. Once you see one or two cockroaches, be assured there are many more hidden away where you can't see them.

Remedies

* Sprinkle a small amount of boric acid where you've seen the roaches. You can buy this at the hardware store or supermarket. Cockroaches poison themselves by walking through the fine dust and then eating it during their grooming. WARNING – boric acid is also poisonous to humans so be very careful if you have children.

* Try making your own bait traps. Take a lid from a plastic container (takeout lids are perfect) and drop a tablespoon of equal parts baking soda and confectioner's sugar in the center. Leave the lid in a spot where you've seen roaches. The sugar and baking soda combo is lethal to them.

* Deny them water. (Cockroaches can go for months without food, but they need a daily source of water.) This means not leaving water in the sink or a kettle, never leaving dirty dishes or glasses of water out overnight, wiping out the bath, and checking for any leaky pipes that they may be visiting.
* Keep your home clean. A cockroach will gravitate toward spots that are littered with old cockroach droppings. Remove these with hot soapy water laced with a little disinfectant (bleach is fine).

If you have a bad infestation, you may need to resort to commercial traps. If you have children and pets, try the glue traps that the cockroach will stick to. Surface sprays, baits, and gels are all effective but be aware that you are introducing a poison into your home. If worst comes to worst, call in a professional.

Prevention

* Always clear food from countertops, tables, and any other areas of the house.
* Fix plumbing leaks and wipe up water spills immediately. Make a concerted effort to keep the house as moisture-free as possible.
* Declutter! Keep the area under the sink, and around washers and dryers and the fridge, as orderly as possible. Keep drawers tidy and avoid using paper to line shelves as cockroaches love to nest under paper.

Ants

There are hundreds of species of ants. Luckily for us, there are only about a half dozen that really seem to like it indoors. Pharoah ants, "crazy" ants, carpenter ants, black- and big-headed ants, and fire ants are the most common to plague houses. It is important to correctly identify the ant species before using a commercial bait or poison — see www.pestproducts.com/antindex.htm for the lowdown on identification.

Ants will feed on meat, grease, and anything sweet. They often nest where it is warm, especially around pipes or hot-water heaters.

Prevention

* In general, keep areas clean and uncluttered.

* Sweep, mop and clean floors, countertops, tabletops, and other surfaces where food crumbs and grease can accumulate. Keep your sink clean. Vacuum regularly, placing a narrow tube on the end of the vacuum hose to extract ants from crevices.

* As for cockroaches and mice, the best way to get rid of ants is to deny them a safe harbor. Like cockroaches, ants need water. Dry pots and dishes immediately after use. Repair leaky pipes and plumbing. Do not leave any leftover drinks in your cup or glass at the end of the day. Keep sinks and baths wiped down.

* Submerge infested pot plants in very slightly soapy water for 20–30 minutes.

* Smear petroleum jelly around electrical outlets and other places you can't fill to prevent access. Ants don't like to walk in the jelly.

* Store food appropriately, especially any sugary food. Consider keeping sugar and other sweet items like honey in the fridge.

* Rinse all recyclables and store them in a bin with a tight-fitting lid. Wash the inside and replace the liner each time the bin is emptied. Keep rubbish bins tightly covered. If possible, move all trash, especially food scraps, to an outside bin at the end of the day.

* Stop ants from getting into the house. Make sure that doors and windows are well sealed. Look for cracks in foundations, holes in walls, openings around plumbing or vents. Fill gaps in moldings, cupboards, sinks, toilets, pipe junctures, and hollow spaces where necessary.

Remedies

Once ants are in, clean the infested area with soapy or hot water and a dash of household ammonia.

If you can't fill the spot where they are getting in, try placing petroleum jelly in a thick smear around the entry point; they don't like to walk in it.

If worst comes to worst, try commercial baits or poisons. If the infestation is bad, place twice the recommended number for best results. Give them a couple of weeks to work and replace them as soon as you see even one more ant returning to your home.

There are lots of tips around for getting rid of ants. But the following is the only one that has really worked for me: mix borax with a little confectioner's sugar and place in a plastic lid in the ant's path. You can also try boiling 2 cups of sugar with 1 cup of water and 2 tablespoons of borax, and placing that sticky mess in their path. Or, try sprinkling diatomaceous earth in their path. It's available from hardware stores and seems to deter ants.

Flies

Houseflies, the most common type of fly, can develop from an egg to an adult in less than 14 days. Each female lays as many as 2,000 eggs, so fly problems can become serious quickly.

The best way to keep the number of flies down is to install screens on all your windows and doors, and then to eliminate their breeding grounds. Houseflies are attracted to decomposing vegetable matter that they use as food for themselves and their larvae (maggots). Blowflies, which are less common, prefer meat to vegetables.

Prevention and remedies

* Always cover trash cans and compost heaps with tight-fitting lids.
* Regularly remove pet droppings and any decaying plant and animal matter from around the home and garden.
* Wrap wet rubbish in an old newspaper and then put in a plastic rubbish bag.
* Don't feel you need to resort to chemicals to rid your house of these insects – they are easy to get with a swatter.

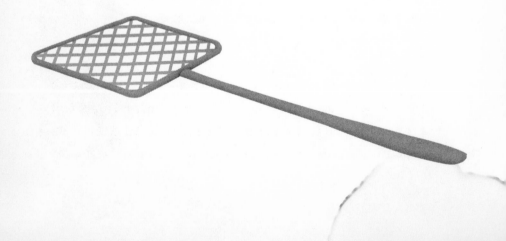

Moths

I've just pulled out my beloved turtleneck sweater from winter storage and there are holes in the neck and sleeves. It's not wearable, although I washed it in wool detergent before I put it away.

It's actually not the moth that eats clothes – it's the larvae. A moth will deposit her eggs (she lays up to 300 in her life) on or near to some material that's good for larval food. Unfortunately for us, they eat clothes, curtains, down, fluff in corners of cupboards, fur, hair, feathers, upholstery, and blankets.

The eggs may be laid on their own or in small groups and are attached by a sticky substance. They hatch in four to ten days and the larvae are smaller than a pinhead. At this stage they feed on soiled fabrics – without them they will die. Things like soup, gravy, beer, wine, and even urine or perspiration make the fabrics nutritious for the little larvae.

As they grow, they can survive on clean fabrics like wool, hair, or feathers but their development is delayed (not much good to you when a huge hole appears in your favorite sweater). Once they've eaten their way through your item of clothing, they'll look for a corner or crevice to build a cocoon.

Pretty much as soon they emerge from the cocoon, they mate and lay eggs, and the cycle starts all over again.

Remedies

While cedar wardrobes and chests smell lovely, they won't be effective in deterring hungry larvae. The seal won't be sufficient to keep the level of cedar oil high enough to be lethal or even act as a repellent. You can try hanging commercial moth strips, but be careful about excessive exposure to insecticides. The best remedy here is prevention. Make sure the garment is spotless and carefully stored.

Moths in food

Moths, along with beetles and weevils, can be brought home in dried food products. They can then spread to other foods stored in the same cupboard.

If you notice these:

1. Find the infested food. Throw it out. Don't try to remove the insects, and check carefully for any other food products in the same cabinet that may be infested. If moths have got into one item, you're likely to find them in others.

2. Check for eggs or cocoons in cabinet and drawer crevices. Thoroughly vacuum the area and wash down with a mild bleach and hot water solution.

3. Make sure you aren't bringing them home. Carefully inspect all dried food packages (cereals, beans, flour, dried fruits and spices, birdseed and pet food) for fine webbing, holes in the packaging, or the insects themselves. Don't buy broken or unsealed containers and always check the use-by date.

4. Once you've got the food home, store it properly. For dried food (including pet food), try using screw-top metal containers, glass jars with rubber seals, or plastic airtight containers.

5. Cold kills eggs and cocoons, so consider keeping dried foods in the fridge or even the freezer.

6. Buy dried food in small quantities so it will be finished more quickly.

Silverfish

These wingless insects are long and slender and grow to about ³⁄₈ inch. They'll eat animal and plant products but favor items containing starch or glue (paper, starched clothes, flour, photographs, books, and wallpaper).

They live for up to seven years, with adult females laying around 60 eggs a year. They are usually nocturnal and like to breed behind moldings and picture rails, in ceiling and wall cavities, and inside cupboards. If you have an infestation, you may find them in your bathtub or sink where they've become trapped looking for water.

Prevention

The best way to prevent silverfish from eating your books is to read them! Take the books off the shelves, open them, and expose them to sunlight, and you'll find that the silverfish flee. If you don't actually pull the books off the shelves, at least dust them regularly – this will disturb the silverfish and hopefully keep them at bay. For a serious silverfish infestation, you'll need to get a professional in, as there's no easy way to get rid of them yourself without damaging your books.

Mosquitoes

Mosquitoes drive me absolutely insane. I can't sleep if there's one in the bedroom. I've been known to pull down a corner of the sheet to expose my husband's shoulder in an attempt to lure one in so I can kill it. Not a particularly kind method, but desperate times call for desperate measures.

The hum of a mosquito is actually the sound of its wings beating. A mosquito's wings flap about 1,000 times a second. A female's wings make a higher tone than a male's, and the sound helps males find mates. It's only the female mosquito that bites. They sip their victim's blood, which they use for the development of the eggs inside their bodies.

When a mosquito bites you, it itches because the insect uses its saliva to stop your blood from clotting while it drinks. Most people are allergic to the saliva and that's what itches.

The main breeding time for mosquitoes is during spring and summer. The female lays 100–400 eggs, on the surface of water. If there's no water around, they will lay eggs in areas where water may accumulate. In these spots, the eggs may hatch in less than three days after a big rain. The larvae are around for 9–14 days and, towards the end of that period, they resemble the familiar wrigglers.

Prevention

* Have secure screens placed on windows and doors.
* Stop the mosquitoes from breeding. Don't let water accumulate around the house or garden. Check old tires, buckets, unused plastic swimming pools, the base of flowerpots, pet dishes, plastic covers, or any other container that may collect water. And

make sure you change the water in birdbaths, fountains, and wading pools at least once a week. Try stocking ornamental pools with goldfish – they eat mosquito larvae on the water surface.

✱ If you have a flat roof, check for puddles that the mosquito larvae might be swimming in.

✱ Check rain barrels for larvae. Obviously you don't want to be emptying these. Instead, use a tight cover to prevent egg-laying. A thin layer of oil (try vegetable oil) will kill larvae already present.

✱ Mow the lawn at least once a week. Mosquitoes like to hide in the shade of tall grass.

Remedies

Plug-in mosquito repellent (available from supermarkets) is effective. Before we had the baby, it's what we used. But it does emit a slight odor and, for safety around the baby, we use a mosquito net and screens on the window.

Fleas

Fleas live on mammals, including humans. They feed by sucking blood.

Remedies

Check to see if there is an infestation. Wear white socks and walk through the area. Fleas will get tangled in the socks' surface and show up easily against the white.

Vacuum carpets thoroughly, paying careful attention to the edges of the room. If possible, steam-clean the carpets, and also vacuum and steam-clean any upholstered furniture, cushions, and any bedding a pet may use. Place the vacuum bag in a tightly sealed plastic bag and either store in the freezer overnight to kill the fleas, or discard in the outside trash.

Wash pets (you can get anti-flea shampoos), and all of their bedding, frequently.

Spiders

I had no problems with spiders in the house until I had a baby. I'd read *Charlotte's Web* as a child and knew deep down that all spiders were good. Of course there are ones to avoid but, living in the city, I don't come across them very often. But then along came Jack and spiders were just another insect in a long line of them that were, at their worst, fatal and, at their best, pests.

I still don't believe in killing spiders. Pop on your rubber gloves (turn the cuffs down a little to stop spiders running up your arm) and get a jar and a piece of stiff cardboard. It's easy to scoop them up and release them outside.

Spiders live almost anywhere – inside the house and out. They eat living insects and small animals. Like wasps and bees, they won't normally bite unless provoked. Often a spider becomes aggressive when its nest is disturbed – a common occurrence when working in the garden or shed, or cleaning the house.

Prevention

Always check any shoes that have been sitting outside before you put them on. Don't do this by sticking your hand in! Tip the shoe upside down and shake vigorously, then step on the toes (at least then if there's a stubborn spider in there clinging to the inside of the shoe, it'll be squashed when you put your foot in).

Sweep or vacuum away webs, indoors and outdoors. This will remove eggs and the occasional spider. A favorite spot for funnel-webs is under pool filters. Check here weekly.

Spiders are generally beneficial to the environment so kill them only when absolutely necessary. There are commercial sprays available from supermarkets that do a good job if necessary.

Spider bite

If you think you've been bitten by a funnel-web or other dangerous spider, use an Ace bandage to wind around the area, starting just above the toes or fingers and continuing up the limb. The idea is to restrict movement. Call 911 for an ambulance and try to stay as calm as possible.

Dust mites

You can't see them but if you suffer from allergies, you know they are there. Hundreds of thousands of them live in your mattress, carpet, blankets, curtains, and even soft toys. They produce powerful allergens in their droppings, which can trigger asthma, eczema, and other skin irritations. They like warm humid conditions and their favorite food is skin scales – hence you'll find higher concentrations of mites in mattresses.

If you are allergic to dust mites:

* Try using cotton or polyester comforters or quilts.
* Avoid sheepskins for infant bedding.
* Use washable covers for pillows and mattresses. Air pillows and quilts in the sun weekly as sunlight kills the mites.
* Keep soft toys to a minimum and try to get ones that are washable.
* Try washing clothes, bedding, and soft toys in hot water (above 130° F if they can take it). Heat kills dust mites.
* Consider replacing soft upholstered furniture with leather. Alternatively, have loose covers fitted so you can wash them regularly. A cotton-linen mix is best here.

* Take mats, rugs, and curtains outside and let them have at least four hours of sun every two weeks.
* When using a vacuum cleaner, fit the cleaner with a two-ply (double wall) bag and a HEPA filter (see page 40).
* Use a damp cloth when dusting to avoid spreading dust around.

Wasps and bees

These generally sting only when they are disturbed or threatened. If you find a nest, call your local exterminator and they'll be able to recommend a professional to remove it.

Prevention

* In the unlikely event of bees swarming into your house in large numbers, try to remain calm (flapping about will antagonize them). Move out of the area very slowly, brushing bees off gently. Try to isolate the bees in one room and call 911 for assistance.
* In the more likely event that one bee or wasp is indoors, you can remove it as you would a spider – with a jar and cardboard to slip over it as a lid. Use a vacuum to suck up the insect, and either throw the bag away or open it and release the insect outdoors. If you want to kill it, you can't go past a rolled-up newspaper. Make sure you strike swiftly and don't touch it when you are cleaning up, as you may still be stung. As with spiders, there are commercial sprays available for bees and wasps but these other methods are less toxic and just as effective.

Index